Mencius
A Modern Translation and Contemporary Interpretation

孟子今譯時析

目錄

Table of Contents

治國方略

Governance Measures

Refinement of the Gentleman

性善及存養

The Nature and Cultivation of Human Goodness

Destiny

Teaching and Learning

聖人

The Sage

孟子其人

About Mencius

亞聖王政思想具時代意義

　　孟子是儒家思想的代表人物，通常「孔孟」並稱。孔子思想不乏繼承者，從其門徒七十子到子思、荀子、董仲舒，早期已大儒輩出，精彩紛呈。當中孟子在時間的浪濤中越發屹立，最終超出眾人，獲得「亞聖」的稱號。他被後世推舉到如此的程度，顯然跟他發揚並創新了孔子思想，使之與時代相適應，把握了人性的常情常理，說出了心靈固有的價值有關。

　　《孟子》一書被宋儒列入「四書」，與《論語》、《中庸》、《大學》並列，極大地塑造了宋代以來中國士子的心智；因此，瞭解孟子的思想，也就可以瞭解到中國傳統的一個重要面相。無論是朱熹、陸九淵還是王陽明，是理學派還是心學派，還是氣學派，都從孟子那裏獲益良多。當代港台和大陸的新儒家，從馮友蘭、熊十力到

Contemporary Significance of the "Second Sage's" Thought on Kingly Governance

As a representative figure of Confucian thought, Mencius is often placed alongside Confucius. While there have been numerous other successors to Confucius's way of thinking, from his seventy disciples to Zi Si and from Xunzi to Dong Zhongshu, it is Mencius who among the early renowned Confucian scholars made the most significant contributions to the school of thought; and, withstanding the test of the time, it is he who stands out and has acquired the honor of being known as the "second Sage." Such recognition by later generations results from his regenerative and innovative interpretation of Confucianism. It has resonated with the spirit of different times, captured the feelings and logic of humanity, and expressed the ultimate values cherished by the human mind. Confucian scholars in the Song dynasty grouped Mencius's writing together with the _Analects_, _Zhong Yung_ and _Da Xue_ as the "Four Books," classics which have helped shape the minds of scholars since the Song. Thus, knowing the thought of Mencius will help us understand an important aspect of the Chinese tradition. Zhu Xi, Lu Jiuyuan, as well as Wang Yangming, whether they were from the Li (principle) school, Xin (heart) school or Qi (vital energy) school, were all inspired by Mencius's thought.

唐君毅、牟宗三，都自覺地延續和更新着孔孟的傳統。

如果回到孟子的時代，回到他發聲說話的語境當中，就可以看到孟子並非一個坐在書齋裏打坐凝思的學者，而是一個針對時代困境向人們（尤其當權者）猛喝，讓他們良心醒悟的批判性的先知。孟子所處的戰國時代，列國紛爭，各國都要富國強兵，既怕被人兼併，又想侵佔他國人民土地；為此對內搜刮，對外動兵，摧城拔寨，殺人盈城；而統治者及時行樂，人民卻朝不保夕。

戰國的形勢比孔子時的春秋更為嚴峻、動盪。為了減少戰爭帶來的痛苦，孟子爭取君王實行仁政（王政），善待人民。他認識到對這些講求利益的君王，空泛的道德說教無用，必須曉之以「大利」，動之以「大情」。這個「利」就是「王天下」。孟子勸導他們說，只要實行了「王政」，

Contemporary neo-Confucian scholars like Feng Youlan, Xiong Shili, Tang Chuni and Mou Zongsan all dedicated themselves to continuing and reviving the Confucian tradition handed down by Confucius and Mencius.

If we were to go back to Mencius's time and consider the context of his dialogues, we would be able to see that he was not an armchair scholar contemplating in his study alone; instead, we would find a forceful prophet revealing unequivocally to people (in particular those in power) the predicament of the time, in the hope of awakening their consciences. Mencius lived in the Warring States period, a time that was marked by serious conflict between vassal states: every state sought to become rich and powerful so that it could annex other states, rather than be annexed itself. The states exploited their own people, waged wars against other states, destroyed cities and citadels, and in the process took the lives of countless numbers of citizens. The rulers cared only for their own pleasure while putting their people's lives in grave peril. The Warring State period was much more difficult and unstable than the earlier Spring and Autumn period during which Confucius lived. To reduce the suffering brought about by the wars, Mencius tried to convince the rulers to implement benevolent governance (also known as kingly governance)

就可以使人民心悅誠服，民富國強，順利地統一天下。對於「王政」的具體措施，孟子做了許多描述，從「與民同樂」到「百畝之田」，再說養雞養蠶之類，可謂不厭其煩。孟子喜歡以商湯代夏，周武代商作為榜樣，激勵君主實行仁政，取代暴政。

光是用「大利」來說理還不行，孟子還動之以「大情」。這個「大情」，就是人的同情心理。從齊王不忍看到牛被殺死，到鄰人不忍見到孺子在井裏溺死，孟子揭示了人性中有着內在的善良，人心中有着天然的同情共感，以及利他傾向。

這種善良是一種直接的本能，並不是事後的利益計算。如果我們將這種善性存養，將這種同情發揚光大，便可成就德性，成為一個道德君子。若能有本事惠及他人，以事功服務他人，便可成為聖人。如果一個國王能夠成為聖人，那就可以

and to treat people well. He realized that it was useless to try to persuade change in rulers who cared only about their own interests by using lofty moral principles, so he turned to talk about the "big interest" and sought to arouse their "big-hearted feelings." The "interest" he promoted to them was "to become the king of the world." Mencius persuaded the rulers to implement "kingly governance" so as to win the hearts of the people, explaining that if the people became rich, the state would become more powerful and unification of the world would seamlessly follow. Mencius also expounded in detail on specific measures of kingly governance, such as "sharing the joy with people," using the "field system of a hundred *mus*," as well as describing the skills needed in raising chickens and in silk production. In order to encourage the rulers to implement benevolent governance, Mencius liked to use historical examples to illustrate how benevolent rule could replace tyranny, such as how King Tang of Shang took over Xia and King Wu of Zhou took over Shang.

Since Mencius recognized that talking of "big interests" alone would not convince the rulers to change their ways, he also appealed to their "big-hearted feelings," that is, to our shared human compassion. In Mencius's writing we find several examples, like King Xuan of Qi who refused to witness the

成為跟堯舜禹湯周文武一個級別的聖王。孟子抓住一切機會，勸說齊王等掌權者實行仁政（王政），說只要他們能感受到自己的一絲「仁心」，就能夠施行「仁政」。

在孔子那裏，「仁」是最突出的德性，但是，到了孟子這裏，常常是「仁義」並舉。這或許是因為在戰國，「義」更為迫切（涉及對他人、鄰國的態度），或許孟子受到墨家的影響，因此將「義」附在「仁」之後，仁義並重。

在孟子看來，君王只要擴充四端之心，願意實行仁政，就可以實行仁政。他們之所以不行仁政，不是因為他們不能，而是因為他們不願。只要君王聽從內心之仁，就可以實行仁政，從而王天下。這是一個直接推論的過程。

孟子直接從君王一己的仁心推出仁政的實

killing of an ox, or the neighbor who wouldn't stand by and let someone else's child drown in a well, to show us that Mencius liked to demonstrate the intrinsic goodness of human nature, the shared compassion and empathy humans possess, and their altruistic disposition. This type of goodness is an intuitive response and does not involve any calculation of subsequent interests. If we nurture our goodness well and develop our compassion, we will be able to cultivate our virtues and become a moral gentleman. If we can extend our goodness to benefit others and are willing to serve others in our duties, then we will be able to become a sage. If a king can become a sage, then he will achieve the status of sage kings such as Yao, Shun, Yu, Tang, King Wen of Zhou and King Wu of Zhou. Mencius grasped every opportunity to persuade those in power, such as King Xuan of Qi, to implement benevolent governance, emphasizing that if only they could tap into even a little of their "benevolent heart," they would be able to put kingly governance into practice.

Confucius saw "benevolence" as the most outstanding virtue. Mencius, however, considered that "benevolence" and "righteousness" (or "justice," depending on the context) were commonly inseparable. This may have come about from the urgency of upholding "righteousness" (viz. in

行，具有古典道德政治哲學的特徵（西方亦有同樣的思想）。但是，政治有它自身的邏輯。在齊王伐燕的行動中，孟子「以仁伐不仁」的「正義戰爭」理想被扭曲，既沒有給燕國人民帶來好處，也沒有使齊王成為「王天下」的「聖王」，更沒有使齊軍成為「仁義之師」。孟子的「義戰」理論認為，對於殘暴的君王，有道的「王」可以以正義伐不義，解民於倒懸（類似於今天的「人道主義干預」）。

可是「義戰」的標準為何？孟子提出的幾條（比如使敵國安定，在佔領敵國後，扶立新王、不毀其宗廟、及時撤走等），並不能防止戰勝國的貪婪，客觀效果亦可能跟初衷恰恰相反。「義戰」所造成的損害常常不亞於不義之戰。「義戰」之突出道德，在後世常常被利用。打着「仁義之師」的旗號，實行無底線的戰爭，是歷史上的常態。

attitudes towards others and neighboring states) because of the dreadful tumult of the Warring States period, or it may reflect the influence of Mohism on Mencius, whereby he valued righteousness as much as benevolence, and linked the two. Mencius was confident that as long as the rulers sought to develop their four nascent, or budding, senses and were willing to put benevolent governance into practice, they would succeed and gain power. An inability to put benevolent governance into practice resulted not from incompetence, but rather from an unwillingness to try. Mencius claimed that once the ruler followed his own benevolent heart, he would be able to exercise benevolent governance and become the king of the world. This line of thinking shows an approach of direct inference.

Mencius's way of encouraging benevolent governance by appealing directly to the benevolent heart of a ruler is typical of classical moral political philosophy (the type of thought that existed in the West). However, politics functions with its own logic. As seen from the military action of King Qi against Yan, the "just war" ideal based on the "battle of benevolence against malevolence" as advocated by Mencius was distorted: the war did not bring any good to the people of Yan, neither did it make King Qi the "sage king" who would "manage the world"; nor did it make the troops of Qi become "an army of

　　為了說服君王實行仁政，孟子找到了惻隱之心、不忍之情，為了說明為甚麼會有惻隱和不忍，他解說這是出於人的天性。人的天性就是善。

　　在這裏，我們可以看出，孟子跟《中庸》的思路是一致的。《中庸》不是說過嗎？「天命之謂性，率性之謂道，修道之謂教」。我們的本性是天給予的，我們只要將天所給予的善發揚光大，便可替天行道，使世界美好。

　　這種觀點跟西方中世紀的自然法（本性法）異曲同工。後者認為，上帝在我們的本性中（心靈上）烙上了規則，我們天生便會按這些規則去生活，處理彼此的關係，比如為善避惡，自我保存，繁衍後代，不故意得罪他人，樂於學習等等。

　　那麼，如何解釋現實的人怎會如此醜惡呢？孟子認為，這是因為人們丟失了他們的本心，被

benevolence and righteousness."

According to the "just war" theory of Mencius, the king who follows the Way can fight against tyrannical rulers on the grounds of righteousness and save people from turmoil (similar to "humanitarian intervention" of today). But what are the criteria of a "just war"? The criteria that Mencius gave (such as to bring peace and order to a rival state, and after annexation, support the new ruler in establishing authority, prevent damage to ancestral temples and withdraw troops in a timely way, etc.) were not enough to stop the greed of victorious states. Furthermore, it was not uncommon for actual outcomes to be at odds with the initial good intentions. As a result, damage resulting from a "just war" was often no less than that of an unjust one. In later generations, wars were waged in the name of a "just war" so as to emphasize their moral clause. It has become a historical norm for countries to fight against others, regardless of the outcome, in the name of "an army of benevolence and righteousness."

In order to convince rulers to put benevolent governance into practice, Mencius called on their heart of compassion and the unbearable feeling caused by witnessing suffering. In order to give an account of this, Mencius turned to human nature:

後天的環境污染了，陷溺了，不純了。所以，「教」的任務就是「修道」，讓本心回到大路上來，「求其放心」，讓良心回家。這跟自然法認為現實的人性受到了「原罪」的污染，因此變得醜惡是一樣的。

有人說孟子是個樂觀主義者，其實，孟子瞭解他那個時代的慘烈。他只是為了仁政的理想而給君王打氣，「看，你們說自己無能為力搞仁政，人人都只能實行叢林法則，可是我跟你指出，你本性善良，本有惻隱之心，你只要將此心發揚光大，便可實行仁政，一統天下」。

關於孟子的性善說，後世有諸多爭論，我們在這裏不詳細列舉。我們只是要指出，孟子的性善說跟他所面對的時代問題緊密相關，不是一個學院派在書齋裏提出的抽象理論。可是這個學說在後世逐漸脫離了歷史情境，變成一個純理論問

human beings are by nature good. We can see that Mencius shared the same thinking with Zhong Yong, as in: "What heaven ordains is called 'intrinsic nature,' the actualization of the intrinsic nature is called 'the Way,' the embodiment of the Way through self-edification is called 'nurturance.' " Human nature is bestowed by heaven, and all we need to do is to develop the good bestowed to its fullest extent so that we can realize the Way of heaven and make the world a better one. This sort of perspective can be compared with natural law (law of human nature) put forward in the West in medieval times. This claimed that God has imprinted rules in our nature (mind) with which we can regulate our lives and our relationship with others, such as doing good and avoiding evil, managing self-preservation and procreation, not offending others without a reason, being willing to learn, etc. Yet if this is the case, how come human beings can still be so evil? Mencius contended that the cause lies in the loss of their heart; their initially pure heart has been tainted and spoiled by their environment. Therefore, it is the task of "self-edification" for "the embodiment of the Way" to put the heart back on the proper path; in other words, to "seek the missing heart" and bring conscience home. In the same manner, the ethics of natural law states that human nature has been corrupted by "original sin" and hence turned evil. Some people say

題。性善、性惡、性混、無善無惡論，各種理論紛紛出籠。在這些爭論中，對於「性」、「善」、「仁」如何定義，常常有着不同的尺寸，導致了說不清道不明的含混和矛盾。

在中國古代思想家中，孟子以其民本思想著稱。他將人民的生命財產放在首位，將社稷放在次位，將君主放在最後。他認清了君主的產生，原是為了保證人民的生命財產，他引《太誓》「天視自我民視，天聽自我民聽」，認為選取領導人要重視民意，要廣泛地聽取人民的意見，可以說，這是比較容易通向社會契約論、近代民主的思路。

歷史上，孟子引起了不少君主的痛恨，在明朝朱元璋時，他甚至成為皇帝的敵人，《孟子》書中的一些敏感章節被禁毀。但限於當時的條件，在如何保證君主真正為人民服務的方法上，

Mencius is an optimist. In fact, Mencius empathized with the terrible sufferings of his time. He only sounded optimistic in order to encourage the rulers to realize his ideal of benevolent governance. "Look, you say you are not able to put benevolent governance into practice and every man acts only according to law of the jungle. Now I tell you this: you are good by nature, your heart is capable of compassion; if only you would develop it to the fullest extent, you could put benevolent governance into practice and unify the whole world."

Mencius's doctrine of intrinsic goodness has been much debated, but we will not discuss this in detail here. It is enough to point out that his doctrine was highly relevant to the problems he faced in his time: it is not an abstract theory proposed by an armchair academic. However, the doctrine was later taken out of its historical context and discussed as a purely theoretical issue; many theories were put forward to claim that human nature is either good, bad, mixed, or neither good nor bad. Along with these debates, the concepts of "nature," "good" and "benevolence" were often defined with different criteria and as a result have caused much confusion and dispute. Among ancient Chinese thinkers, Mencius was well known for his people-oriented thought. He accorded primacy to the life and property of the people, put the gods of earth and grain

孟子並沒有找到有效的辦法。他找到的辦法主要還是君主個人的良心發現和道德本能。在西方古代,哲學家們也沒有找到有效的方法來防止君主對權力的濫用。

西方也只是到了近代才找到三權分立和投票選舉的辦法,避開了以暴力來更替政權的王朝循環。雖然投票也仍舊無法避免種種陰謀詭計,但總體上還是避免了革命導致的大規模死傷與動亂。當代新儒家嘗試以民本為基礎,從儒家的理想開出西方民主制度。現今執政的中國共產黨則稱遵從民本思想,用績優原則、分工制衡,達成良政,取得民心,以區別於西方式民主制度。

《孟子》有一些語焉不詳的段落,似乎有一種神秘主義。他說到「我善養吾浩然之氣」,但何為此「浩然之氣」,以及如何「養」,卻並沒有詳細說明。不過這個「浩然之氣」卻形成了儒

second, and the ruler the last. Mencius saw in the appointment of a ruler the responsibility of protecting the life and property of the people. Quoting from *Tai Shi*, "Heaven sees what my people see, heaven hears what my people hear," he claimed that the choice of a leader must follow the will of the people, and that people's opinions should be taken into good account. It can be seen that this stance is not dissimilar to social contract theory or the modern democratic way of thinking.

At times in history, Mencius was despised by certain rulers. One was Zhu Yuanzhang of the Ming dynasty who hated Mencius so much that some of the more sensitive passages in *Mencius* were removed from the work. But the restraints of the time meant that Mencius was not able to find an effective way of ensuring rulers would genuinely serve the people. The only solution he came up with was to prick their consciences and appeal to their moral instincts. This was also the case for ancient philosophers in the West: they, too, were unable to find effective solutions to curb the abuse of the "power of rule." It has only been in modern times that the separation of power and the electoral system has provided a way out of the dynastic cycle that previously saw regime change brought about only by violence. Setting aside fraud and conspiracy, which seem unavoidable in most elections, the modern system

家的一個「氣」的傳統，到了文天祥那裏，就成了「正氣」，正義之氣。它對應於基督教的「歷史中的聖靈」的傳統。「靈」的本義是風，是氣息。上帝通過聖靈掌控人類的歷史，先知就是受到聖靈澆注的人，而君王的作為受到聖靈的引導。黑格爾將這個聖靈（Holy Spirit）換了一個哲學的稱呼，「絕對精神」（Absolute Spirit），把神旨稱作「歷史規律」。實際上還是目的論。

在孟子那裏，「天將降大任於斯人」，就會讓氣在某些人身上得到存養和壯大，先讓他吃吃苦頭。這是孟子式的天命論和磨煉意志說，裏面不乏神秘主義的成份。

關於《孟子》的解讀，早已汗牛充棟。由於我們針對的是當今國際化的青少年，因此會從經典對讀和文化比較的角度，對能體現孟子思想特

avoids the heavy casualties and unrest that have resulted from revolutions. Contemporary neo-Confucian thinkers, based on the Confucian people-oriented idea, have tried to chart a route to the adoption of the Western democratic system. Today, the ruling Chinese Communist Party claims to follow the people-oriented thought in its own way, such as by a meritocratic principle and a division of labor to achieve balance of power and good governance, and in doing so implement an alternative system from the Western one and yet still win the hearts of the people.

In *Mencius* there are some passages that are obscure in meaning and suggestive of mysticism. Mencius wrote, "I nurture well my boundless vital energy [qi]." Exactly what this "boundless vital energy" is and how one can "nurture" qi, Mencius did not fully explain. Despite this, the coining of the term "boundless vital energy" gradually forged a Confucian tradition of qi. When it came into the hands of Wen Tianxiang, qi became "righteous vital energy" [zheng qi]. This can be compared with the Christian tradition of the "Holy Spirit in history." Etymologically speaking, "spirit" means "the wind," "breath." Through the Holy Spirit, God has guided humankind throughout history. Prophets are people who have been infused with the Holy Spirit; and the conduct of a good ruler is guided

點的一些重點段落，給以重新解釋。跟我們另外
的經典今譯時析一樣（本社已出版《論語》、《老
莊》），我們將孟子放在全球化多元文化的背景
下予以解釋，使讀者知道孟子的一些洞察即使在
今天的世界仍舊是重要的、有意義的。由於孟子
巨大的影響，瞭解孟子也就能瞭解到中國文化的
一些基本傾向和價值，甚至中國今後社會政治發
展的方向。

　　本書在內容的順序上，有一個大致的邏輯。
孟子針對時代的問題提出仁政主張，為仁政找到
人心的根據（惻隱、不忍、仁義禮智信），為惻
隱找到人性的基礎（性善說），個人道德的修養
（天爵），如何看待與道德無關的命，最後我們
對於孟子本人做一些瞭解（其抱負、性格與自
許）。

　　在體例上，我們依照前面出版的「今譯時

by the Holy Spirit. Hegel gave the Holy Spirit the philosophical term "Absolute Spirit," and he named the will of God as a "regularity of history." At heart, he was talking about teleology, the doctrine of purpose. Mencius considered that when "Heaven is about to confer an important mission to a man," it will allow his vital energy to be nurtured and strengthened through hardship. The distinctive Mencius-style doctrine of destiny and the theory of disciplining the will contain quite a few elements that share a similar spirituality with Hegel.

As regards the interpretation of *Mencius*, there exist already an immense number of works. As our target readership is the young generation who are growing up in a globalized world, our purpose is to cast fresh light on the key texts in *Mencius* that represent its salient thoughts and to compare them with both other Chinese classics and with other cultures. In the same way as with the other published titles in the Modern Translation and Contemporary Interpretation series (*The Analects* and *Laozi* and *Zhuangzi*), we have tried to interpret *Mencius* within the global context of a pluralistic culture so that readers can recognize the significance and importance of the work in today's world. Since Mencius has had an immense impact on Chinese culture, an understanding of *Mencius* can help readers comprehend more of the fundamental

析」，都先給出選定的原文，再進行白話文翻譯，然後予以分析和解釋。

原文一些難以理解之處，我們參考了楊伯峻和梁濤等學者的現代譯本，在此特意說明並表示感謝。

orientations and values of Chinese culture, and even grasp Chinese socio-political development.

The book's content has been designed in a logical sequence. Starting with Mencius's proposed fundamental measure of benevolent governance, aimed at solving the problems of his time, it moves on to explain the foundation of benevolent governance laid in the human heart (compassion, the unbearable feeling towards suffering, virtues of benevolence, righteousness, wisdom and trustworthiness); to offer an account of human nature in support of compassion (the doctrine of intrinsic goodness); to discuss the cultivation of personal virtues (heavenly honors) and the attitude towards destiny as extraneous to morality; and lastly, to look into the personality of Mencius (his aspirations, temperament and commitments). Like the other titles in the Modern Translation and Contemporary Interpretation series, this book first presents the selected text in its original classical form; this is followed by a translation in plain language; and the text is then finished with an analysis and interpretation.

We are indebted to scholars, including Yang Bojun and Liang Tao, whose works have helped us with the modern translation of _Mencius_.

仁政與
平天下

Winning over the World with Benevolent Governance

一

梁惠王曰：「晉國，天下莫強焉，叟之所知也。及寡人之身，東敗於齊，長子死焉；西喪地於秦七百里；南辱於楚。寡人恥之，願比死者壹洒之，如之何則可？」

孟子對曰：「地方百里而可以王。王如施仁政於民，省刑罰，薄稅斂，深耕易耨；壯者以暇日修其孝悌忠信，入以事其父兄，出以事其長上，可使制梃以撻秦楚之堅甲利兵矣。

「彼奪其民時，使不得耕耨以養其父母。父母凍餓，兄弟妻子離散。彼陷溺其民，王往而征之，夫誰與王敵？故曰：『仁者無敵。』王請勿疑！」（卷一 梁惠王章句上・五）

【今譯】

梁惠王說：「晉（魏）國，天下沒有比它更強大的了，這您老先生是知道的。可是到了我這時候，在東面敗給齊國，大兒子也戰死了；在西邊敗給秦國，把河西七百里地都丟掉了；在南方又

One

Translation:

King Hui of Liang said, "As you know, my good old man, there was no state as powerful as Jin. But now, under my reign, we have been defeated by Qi in the east, and my eldest son has been killed; we have lost seven hundred miles of land to Qin in the west; and we have been humiliated by Chu in the south. I am so ashamed of this and wish to wash away all this shame on behalf of those who have died. How can this be done?"

Mencius replied, "With even only a hundred miles of territory, one can rule as a king. If Your Majesty carries out benevolent governance, such as to reduce punishments, cut taxes, allow the people to plough deep and weed readily, and encourage the young to nurture their virtues of filial piety, fraternal respect, conscientiousness and trustworthiness, then they will serve their fathers and elder brothers well at home, and serve their elders and superiors well when they are away from home. These people could fight the fully armored troops of Qin and Chu with nothing but staves.

"The rulers of other states force people to fufill state duties during busy farming times so that their fields are left deserted

受到楚國的羞辱。我以這些為奇恥大辱，希望能替我國戰死者全部雪恥，我要怎麼辦才可以呢？」

孟子答道：「只要有方圓一百里的地盤，就可以憑仁政取得天下。國王您如果對百姓施行仁政，減輕刑罰，減少賦稅，讓百姓能夠深耕細作，早除雜草，使年輕人閒暇時學習孝悌忠信的道理，內以孝悌侍奉父兄，外以忠信侍奉上級，這樣，就是拿着棍棒也可以抗擊秦國和楚國披着鎧甲、拿着刀槍的軍隊了。這些國家在農忙時強行讓百姓服役，使百姓不能耕種來養活父母。他們的父母受凍挨餓，哥哥弟弟和妻子兒女東逃西散。這些國家使百姓陷入災難，您去討伐他們，那還有誰能和您作對呢？所以人們說『仁者無敵』，對此您不要懷疑。」

【時析】

孟子勸梁惠王以周文王、周武王期間周仍是小國時實行的仁政為榜樣，以獲得百姓擁護，達致富強，戰勝外敵。從孟子提出的具體的治國方案，如減輕刑罰，減少賦稅來說，跟當時別的學派（如法家）沒有多大區別。同時，在當時嚴峻的國際形勢下，魏國沒有多少喘息的時機去實行仁政，孟子所提的方案是否真能奏效，亦屬可疑；

and no food can be provided for their parents. As a result, their parents suffer cold and hunger while brothers, wives and children are separated and scattered. These rulers bring calamity to their people, so if Your Majesty wages war against them, who would be there to oppose you? Hence it is said, 'The benevolent man is matchless.' I beg Your Majesty not to doubt it!" (Chapter 1.5)

Contemporary interpretation:

Mencius advised King Hui of Liang to follow the examples of King Wen and King Wu in practicing benevolent governance when Zhou was still a small state, so that King Hui would gain the support of the people, attain prosperity and win wars against enemies. The governance measures that Mencius proposed, such as reducing punishments and cutting taxes, did not really stand out from other schools of thought (such as Legalism). Besides, in the midst of tense inter-state relations the state of Wei did not have much chance to implement benevolent measures; so whether or not they were effective solutions was never put to the test. No wonder it remains controversial as to whether Mencius's principles are realistic in the real world in complicated political contexts. Nevertheless, the most significant feature of his governance measures is a comprehensive elaboration of Confucius's benevolent

孟子這種理想的治國理念，是否真能在真實複雜的政治環境中落實，的確是充滿爭論空間的。但孟子的治國方案最難能可貴的，是他全面闡發了孔子的「仁政」思想，將「仁政」視為治國之本，提倡民本思想，強調君主施政必須把人民利益放在首位，這種充滿人道主義色彩的治國理念，對中國後世的政治觀念影響深遠，是當時別的學派所無可比擬的。

二

　　孟子見梁惠王。王曰：「叟！不遠千里而來，亦將有以利吾國乎？」

　　孟子對曰：「王！何必曰利？亦有仁義而已矣。王曰：『何以利吾國？』大夫曰：『何以利吾家？』士庶人曰：『何以利吾身？』上下交征利而國危矣。萬乘之國，弒其君者，必千乘之家；千乘之國，弒其君者，必百乘之家。萬取千焉，千取百焉，不為不多矣。苟為後義而先利，不奪不饜。未有仁而遺其親者也，未有義而後其君者也。王亦曰仁義而已矣，

governance principles, putting the people's interests as the top priority for any ruler's governance. Such a humanistic approach towards governance had a long-term impact on Chinese political thinking in subsequent years, and its influence cannot be matched by other schools of political thought of Mencius's time.

Two

Translation:

Mencius went to see King Hui of Liang. The king said, "My good old man, you have traveled such a long distance to visit us, your presence should be in the interest of my state, right?"

Mencius replied, "Your Majesty, why talk about interests when what really matters is that of benevolence and righteousness! When Your Majesty says, 'What can be advantageous to my state?' the ministers will say, 'What can be advantageous to my family?' and the junior officials and commoners will say, 'What can be advantageous to me?' When superiors and inferiors seek only their own interests, the state will be in jeopardy. Consider the following case: Who would murder the king of a state that possesses ten thousand chariots? It must be the one who already owns one thousand chariots. Who would murder

何必曰利？」（卷一 梁惠王章句上‧一）

【今譯】

孟子去見梁惠王。惠王說：「老人家，您不遠千里，到我們這兒，是為了對我國有利吧？」孟子回答說：「王啊！您何必說利呢？只要講仁義就可以了。倘若王說：『用甚麼法子才能有利於我國呢？』大夫也說：『用甚麼法子才能有利於我家呢？』士人和老百姓也說：『用甚麼法子才能有利於我自己呢？』那就會上上下下都去求利，國家就危險了。擁有一萬輛兵車的大國，殺害其國君的，一定是擁有一千輛兵車的大夫；擁有一千輛兵車的中等國家，殺害其國君的，一定是擁有一百輛兵車的大夫。一萬輛中擁有一千輛，一千輛中擁有一百輛，大夫的財產不能說不多。但是，假如他們利字當頭，輕視仁義，那就會不把國君的財富奪過來就不會甘休。不會有講『仁』卻遺棄其父母的，也不會有講『義』卻輕視其君主的。王啊，您講講仁義就好了，何必要說利呢？」

【時析】

梁惠王是想要稱霸天下的，因此所問之利是如何達到強國、稱霸的目的，而孟子則以仁和義來回答他。

the king of a state with one thousand chariots? It must be the one who owns one hundred chariots. To own one thousand chariots in ten thousand, or to own one hundred in one thousand, one must say these people are among the wealthiest people of the state already. Yet if they only retain an interest in their own wealth and belittle righteousness, they might resort to any means in order to seize the wealth from the king. Contrarily, any person who values benevolence will never abandon his parents, and anyone who values righteousness will never dishonor his ruler. Your Majesty, isn't it more important to talk about benevolence and righteousness instead of interests?" (Chapter 1.1)

Contemporary interpretation:

King Hui of Liang wished to seek hegemony over the whole world, so he was keen to learn of any advantages that would make a state strong and achieve supremacy. Mencius, however, replied by emphasizing the importance of benevolence and righteousness in governance. As stated in the *Analects*, "Acting only in one's own interests will result in resentment." If a family, a unit, a company, as well as a country acts only in its own interests, everyone will want to take advantage of others rather than being taken advantage of. People will become exhausted with calculations, yet in the end

《論語》說過:「放於利而行,則多怨。」如果一個家庭、一個單位、一個公司、一個國家,一切從利益出發,人人從利益出發,都要多佔,不要吃虧,就會天天算來算去,最終鬧得四分五裂,都有怨恨。比如,一個國家,如果富庶的地區完全從自己的利益來考慮,很容易會認為貧困的地區佔了自己便宜,就鬧分裂,那這個國家就沒有寧日了。

如果從整體出發,仁義才是大利,在整體內部建立公平、正義的秩序,讓成員都各就各位,做自己應當做的事,各得其所,整體得到發展。如果裏面的成員都利字當頭,那集體就危險了,集體一旦危險,個人的利益也會受損。可見,私利都是小利,仁義才是大利。在這裏表面看是義利相對,其實是說義才是大利。因此,義和利並不矛盾。

照梁惠王的想法,讓國家富強,稱霸才是利;但在孟子看來,在先講利的條件下去搞富強,方向和手段都有問題。真正能統一天下的只有仁政或王道,以仁義治國,才能天下歸心,這就免除了以戰爭、強權等霸道的做法。就國內秩序而言,也要以公義優先,而不是到處斂財練兵,否則,只會鬧得國家也四分五裂。

there will only be disintegration and resentment. For instance, if rich regions of a country were to only consider their own interests, they would advocate a separation on the grounds that they are taken advantage of by the poor regions.

As a result, the country would be in jeopardy because similar disputes between different parties would never end. If, however, the interests of the country as a whole are taken into consideration, the virtues of benevolence and righteousness as the "big interests" can easily be seen because they lay the foundation of a society with a fair and just order, so that every member does his bit in his position, fulfills his duties and gets what he deserves; at the same time, society as a whole will flourish. Contrarily, if individual members only care about their own interests, then the interests of the whole will be at risk, and the interests of individual members will thus be harmed. As the above shows, individual interests should be regarded as "small interests," and only benevolence and righteousness should be regarded as "big interests." At first, we might think that Mencius takes "righteousness" and "interests" as opposing values. Yet when we look deeper, we see "righteousness" is itself an interest, just a "bigger" one when compared with the others. In this way, righteousness and interests become complementary, and not two opposing ends.

　　義利表面看來是矛盾的，其實背後是統一的。比如，保護人權是義，但這個義是為了保護每個人的權利，每個人的權利得到保障，不就是保護每個人的利益嗎？可見，孟子講義，是有大利的考慮，這個大利就可以吸引諸侯去聽從。當時，墨子主張「兼相愛，交相利」，明確指出利的重要性，孟子表面看上去好像與墨子持相反意見，好像只講義不講利，但最後只要講到天下大治，就一定涉及大利，可見孟子反對的只是短時間、狹義的利。孟子從道德角度批評墨子「無君無父」，但他沒有批評墨子「交相利」的觀念。跟孔子相比，孔子只重仁，孟子則將仁發展為仁義並稱，而這個義正是墨子所強調的。所以，可以認為，孟子吸收了墨子重義的思想，並暗地裏將義作了大利的理解。

　　孟子只是先講仁義，並非不講利益，而是講仁義與大利有先後本末之別，只要先實行仁政，利益作為一個自然而然的結果會伴隨而來。因此是「德福一致」，有德就會有福。但反過來就不行了。所以，孟子的「何必曰利」實為「何必曰利先」。

　　在孟子的時代，各個國家在競爭中採納了諸

King Hui of Liang saw the acquisition of wealth, strength and hegemony as in the interests of his state. However, according to Mencius, prioritizing these interests as the goal of a state's development is wrong with regard both to the means and the end. The only proper way to unify the world is with benevolent governance, or the kingly way: to govern with benevolence and righteousness, so that the governed will gladly comply. This is also the way to avoid war or any kind of forcible measures. Also, when we talk about domestic order, justice should be prioritized before wealth seeking and troop building; otherwise the state will fall apart.

While righteousness and interest might seem to be in conflict with each other on the surface, they are unified in the deeper sense. For example, the protection of human rights is a righteous act, yet it is at the same time a protection of individual interests. When individual rights are protected, is it not that individual interests will also be protected? When Mencius talked about righteousness, he was actually thinking of the "big interests" to which vassal states could be convinced to conform. At around the same time, Mozi defended the importance of "altruism and mutual interest" and placed the emphasis on "interest." It might sound as if Mencius is putting forward an opposing point of view, only to talk about

子百家的一些學說，儒家的學說較少被採納。臨近齊、燕、趙的千乘之國中山國，對儒家學說很有興趣，這個國家採納了儒家學說，但是很不幸，在當時複雜的國際鬥爭中，因外交處置不當，趁燕齊戰爭吞併了大國的一些地盤，最終反被周圍幾個大國滅亡。

三

宋牼將之楚，孟子遇於石丘，曰：「先生將何之？」曰：「吾聞秦、楚構兵，我將見楚王，說而罷之；楚王不悅，我將見秦王，說而罷之。二王我將有所遇焉。」曰：「軻也請無問其詳，願聞其指。說之將何如？」曰：「我將言其不利也。」曰：「先生之志則大矣，先生之號則不可。先生以利說秦、楚之王，秦、楚之王悅於利，以罷三軍之師；是三軍之士樂罷而悅於利也。為人臣者，懷利以事其君，為人子者，懷利以事其父，為人弟者，懷利以事其兄，是君臣、父子、兄弟終去仁義，懷利以相接；然而不亡者，未之有也。先生以仁義說

righteousness but not interests; actually, any talk about good governance of the whole world must involve the discussion of big interests.

What Mencius opposed, instead, was short-term interests or interests in the narrow sense. He did criticize Mozi for his "disregarding the ruler and the father" from a moral perspective, but he never rejected Mozi's concept of "mutual interests." In comparison, Confucius put emphasis on "benevolence," while Mencius developed the concept of "benevolence" to become "benevolence and righteousness." "Righteousness" is a core concept in Mozi's doctrine. We may say that Mencius adopted the concept of "righteousness" from Mozi and quietly interpreted it as "big interests."

For Mencius, benevolence and righteousness should always be put above any talk of interests, but this does not mean that he rejects any such talk. Instead, Mencius claims that once benevolent governance is in place, interests of various kinds will be attained accordingly. This is the so-called "unity of virtue and fortune": good fortune will come to those who are virtuous. Yet it would never be the case the other way around. Therefore, when Mencius said, "Why talk about interests?" it actually means "Why talk about interests first?"

秦、楚之王，秦、楚之王悅於仁義，以罷三軍之師；是三軍之士樂罷而悅於仁義也。為人臣者，懷仁義以事其君，為人子者，懷仁義以事其父，為人弟者，懷仁義以事其兄，是君臣、父子、兄弟去利，懷仁義以相接也；然而不王者，未之有也。何必曰利？」（卷十二 告子章句上 · 四）

【今譯】

宋牼要到楚國去，孟子在石丘這個地方遇到了他，就問：「先生要去哪裏呢？」他回答說：「我聽說秦國和楚國要打仗，我要去見楚王，勸他罷兵。如果楚王不高興，我就去見秦王，勸他罷兵。兩個國王，我總能遇上一個。」孟子說：「我也不想問得太細，只願聽您說說大旨。您將怎樣勸說他們呢？」宋牼回答說：「我將說打仗的不利之處。」孟子說：「先生您的志向很大，您的理由卻不行。先生您用利來勸秦楚兩王，秦楚二王喜歡利，於是撤回大軍，這就會使大軍官兵樂於罷兵，以利為先。做臣子的，抱着利的觀念來侍奉君主，做兒子的，抱着利的觀念來侍奉父親，做弟弟的，抱着利的觀念來侍奉哥哥，這會使得君臣、父子、兄弟之間最終都摒棄仁義，

In Mencius's time, different vassal states adopted doctrines from various schools of thought. Confucian doctrines were seldom endorsed. As an example, a rising power close to Qi, Yan and Zhao — Zhongshan — was interested in Confucianism and adopted Confucian doctrines in its governance. Unfortunately, being involved in intricate inter-state politics at the time, Zhongshan attempted to seize some territory from other powerful states during the Yan-Qi War and was in the end wiped out by the powerful states.

Three

Translation:

Song Keng was on his way to Chu. Mencius ran into him at Shi Qiu and asked him, "Where are you going, sir?" He replied, "I've heard that Qin and Chu are waging war against each other. I am going to see the king of Chu and persuade him to call it off. If he does not appreciate my arguments, I will go to the king of Qin and persuade him to call it off. I hope at least one of them will listen to me. Mencius said, "I do not wish to get into details, but what may I ask is the main focus of your argument? How would you try to persuade them?" "I would explain to them that waging a war is against their own interests," said Song Keng.

抱着利的觀念來彼此對待，這樣搞下去而國家不滅亡的，還沒有過。先生您如果以仁義來勸說秦楚二王，秦楚二王因喜歡仁義而撤回大軍，就會使大軍將士樂於罷兵，喜歡仁義。做臣子的，抱着仁義的觀念去侍奉君主，做兒子的，抱着仁義的觀念去侍奉父親，做弟弟的，抱着仁義的觀念去侍奉哥哥，就會使得君臣、父子、兄弟之間摒棄利的想法，抱着仁義的觀念彼此相待，如此這般還不能統一天下稱王的，還沒有過。您何必要說利呢？」

【時析】

孟子讚賞宋牼勸說秦楚止戰的志向，但是對他勸說的理由卻不同意。他認為，如果只是向秦楚二君指出打仗不利，從而罷兵，那以後秦楚覺得有利的時候，仍舊可能會打仗，因此，談利不能從根本上解決問題。只有向他們指出，仁義才能使他們國內有序，國際有治，天下太平。諸侯不是喜歡談利（實為兼併他國的私利、大欲）嗎？那就向他們指出根本「大利」，也即仁義，仁義才能王天下。一旦真正實行仁政，就不會以戰爭來兼併，而是憑道德感召力來令天下歸附，也就沒有必要發動戰爭了。這是孟子提出的一個通過軟實力實現「治平」的策略。

"Sir, I admire your lofty purposes, yet I doubt if your reasons are sound. If you succeed in persuading the kings of Qin and Chu to call off their armies for their own interests, then their armies would also be persuaded to retreat for their own interests. If an official served his ruler for the sake of his own interests, and likewise, a son served his father for the sake of his own interests, and a younger brother served his elder brother for the sake of his own interests, then the official and the ruler, the son and the father, as well as the younger and the elder brothers would treat each other for the sake of their own interests and forsake the virtues of benevolence and righteousness. The unavoidable consequence would be the downfall of the state.

If you persuade the kings of Qin and Chu to call off their armies on grounds of benevolence and righteousness, and they buy into it, then their armies would also buy into retreating on such grounds. If an official served his ruler on such grounds, and likewise, a son served his father on such grounds, and a younger brother served his elder brother on such grounds, then the official and the ruler, the son and the father, as well as the younger and the elder brother would treat each other out of concern for benevolence and righteousness rather than for their own interests. The ruler of such a state would for sure

　　孟子的論證方式，是說一個國家，如果人人都只講利（私利），則會帶來危害，如果講仁義，則會產生不同的效果。仁義將儒家的禮制秩序（孝悌、君臣）和國際政治（王天下）聯繫了起來。

　　其實，王天下是諸侯都嚮往的一種境界，孟子就是以「王天下」這個大利（孟子稱之為「仁義」，用詞不同而已），吸引諸侯實行仁政。這對於諸侯、百姓都有好處，當然，歸根結底是對百姓有最大好處。所以，孟子的談義不談利，並不像表面上那樣對立，反而是相通的。

四

　　齊宣王問曰：「齊桓、晉文之事可得聞乎？」

　　孟子對曰：「仲尼之徒，無道桓、文之事者，是以後世無傳焉；臣未之聞也。無以，則王乎？」

　　曰：「德何如則可以王矣？」

　　曰：「保民而王，莫之能禦也。」

become a king who unifies the world. Why must you speak of 'interests'?" (Chapter 12.4)

Contemporary interpretation:

Mencius praised Song Keng for his ambition to persuade the kings of Qin and Chu to end the war, yet he was opposed to the reasons Song Keng put forward. In his view, if the kings were persuaded to end the war out of their own interest, they might someday wage war again, when they came to think that waging war could be in their own interest. Such an argument, therefore, failed to solve the problem at its root. Instead, Mencius argued that it should be pointed out to them that only benevolence and righteousness could bring about domestic order, inter-state governance and peace throughout the world. Since the states all wanted to talk about interests (their own interests in annexing other states), Mencius advised them that "big interests" were in fact benevolence and righteousness that would make them the kings of the world. Once such benevolent governance was adopted, the kings would no longer need to annex other states by waging wars; instead, the other states would pay allegiance to them because of their moral appeal. Mencius defended a political scheme that used soft power to govern the state and manage the world.

曰：「若寡人者，可以保民乎哉？」

曰：「可。」

曰：「何由知吾可也？」

曰：「臣聞之胡齕曰，王坐於堂上，有牽牛而過堂下者，王見之，曰：『牛何之？』對曰：『將以釁鐘。』王曰：『舍之！吾不忍其觳觫，若無罪而就死地。』對曰：『然則廢釁鐘與？』曰：『何可廢也？以羊易之！』——不識有諸？」

曰：「有之。」

曰：「是心足以王矣。百姓皆以王為愛也。臣固知王之不忍也。」

王曰：「然；誠有百姓者。齊國雖褊小，吾何愛一牛？即不忍其觳觫，若無罪而就死地，故以羊易之也。」

曰：「王無異於百姓之以王為愛也。以小易大，彼惡知之？王若隱其

The reasoning behind Mencius's arguments is this: If everybody cares only about self-interest, damage will follow. If everybody cares about benevolence and righteousness, benefits will follow. The virtues of benevolence and righteousness offered the key for Mencius to link Confucian ritual and order (filial piety and fraternal respect) and inter-state politics (becoming the king of the world).

Indeed, all ruling powers of the vassal states aspired to become the king of the world. Mencius pointed out the "big interests" in becoming the king of the world (in other words "benevolent governance") and persuaded them to practice "benevolent governance" which would in fact serve the interests of the states and particularly the people.

Mencius talked about righteousness, not interests, but the two did not conflict with each other as it appeared on the surface. On the contrary, as we have seen, they were interconnected.

Four

Translation:

King Xuan of Qi asked, "Can you tell me about the stories of Duke Huan of Qi and Duke Wen of Jin?"

無罪而就死地，則牛羊何擇焉？」

王笑曰：「是誠何心哉？我非愛其財而易之以羊也。宜乎百姓之謂我愛也。」

曰：「無傷也，是乃仁術也，見牛未見羊也。君子之於禽獸也，見其生，不忍見其死；聞其聲，不忍食其肉。是以君子遠庖廚也。」

王說曰：「《詩》云：『他人有心，予忖度之。』夫子之謂也。夫我乃行之，反而求之，不得吾心。夫子言之，於我心有戚戚焉。此心之所以合於王者，何也？」

曰：「有復於王者曰：『吾力足以舉百鈞，而不足以舉一羽；明足以察秋毫之末，而不見輿薪。』則王許之乎？」

曰：「否。」

「今恩足以及禽獸，而功不至於百姓者，獨何與？然則一羽之不舉，

Mencius replied, "The disciples of Confucius did not speak of Duke Huan of Qi and Duke Wen of Jin, so the later generations had nothing to pass on. I therefore have no knowledge of them. May I talk to you of how to become a true king instead?"

"What sort of virtue must one have in order to rule as a true king?"

"If a man becomes a king by taking care of the people, no one can stop him."

"Could a man like me become a king by taking care of the people?"

"Yes, you could."

"How do you know I could?"

"I heard from Hu He that when Your Majesty was sitting in the hall, you saw someone bring an ox into the court below and asked, 'Where are you taking that ox to?' Your courtier said, 'Its blood is to be used to consecrate a newly cast bell.' And you said, 'Spare it. I can't bear to see it trembling like an innocent man being taken for execution.' Your courtier asked,

為不用力焉；輿薪之不見，為不用明焉；百姓之不見保，為不用恩焉。故王之不王，不為也，非不能也。」

　　曰：「不為者與不能者之形何以異？」

　　曰：「挾太山以超北海，語人曰，『我不能。』是誠不能也。為長者折枝，語人曰，『我不能。』是不為也，非不能也。故王之不王，非挾太山以超北海之類也；王之不王，是折枝之類也。

　　「老吾老，以及人之老；幼吾幼，以及人之幼，天下可運於掌。《詩》云：『刑於寡妻，至於兄弟，以禦於家邦。』言舉斯心加諸彼而已。故推恩足以保四海，不推恩無以保妻子。古之人所以大過人者，無他焉，善推其所為而已矣。今恩足以及禽獸，而功不至於百姓者，獨何與？」

　　「權，然後知輕重；度，然後知長短。物皆然，心為甚。王請度之！」

'Then should the consecration be called off?' You said, 'How can we do away with that? Use a lamb instead.' I wonder if this is a true story."

"Yes, it is."

"Your heart is sufficient for you to become a king. People all thought you had spared the ox because you were stingy, but I am certain that it was because you could not bear its distress." The King said, "You are right. That's just what they said. Qi may be a small state, but I am not quite so miserly about sacrificing an ox! It was because I couldn't bear its trembling like an innocent man being taken for execution, so I told them to use a lamb instead."

"Your Majesty should not be surprised that the people took you to be stingy, since you replaced a big animal with a small one. How could they know? But if you are distressed by the death of innocent animals, what difference would there be between an ox and a lamb?"

The King laughed. "Really, I wonder what was on my mind. I didn't replace the ox with a lamb because I was stingy. But I suppose it is natural for people to think that I am."

「抑王興甲兵，危士臣，構怨於
諸侯，然後快於心與？」

王曰：「否！吾何快於是？將以
求吾所大欲也。」

曰：「王之所大欲，可得聞與？」

王笑而不言。

曰：「為肥甘不足於口與？輕
暖不足於體與？抑為采色不足視於目
與？聲音不足聽於耳與？便嬖不足使
令於前與？王之諸臣，皆足以供之，
而王豈為是哉？」

曰：「否！吾不為是也。」

曰：「然則王之大欲可知已，
欲辟土地，朝秦楚，莅中國而撫四夷
也。以若所為，求若所欲，猶緣木而
求魚也。」

王曰：「若是其甚與？」

"There is no harm in what you did, it is how a benevolent man would respond. You had seen the ox, but you had not seen the lamb. For a gentleman, if he has seen an animal alive, he cannot bear to watch it die; if he has heard its cry, he cannot bear to eat its flesh. This is why gentlemen keep away from the kitchen!"

The King was pleased and said, "The *Book of Poetry* says: 'The heart belongs to others, I try to comprehend it.' This describes you perfectly well! For even though the action was mine, when I reflected on it, I failed to understand my own heart. Just now your words echoed perfectly with my feelings at the time. Can you tell me how such feelings enable one to become a king?"

Mencius said, "If someone said to Your Majesty, 'I am strong enough to lift half a ton, but not to lift a feather; I have eyesight good enough to see the tip of a hair, but not to see a load of firewood,' would you accept what he said?"

"No, I would not."

"Well then, how could one accept that Your Majesty's kindness can be extended to the animals but not to the people? A feather

曰：「殆有甚焉。緣木求魚，雖不得魚，無後災；以若所為，求若所欲，盡心力而為之，後必有災。」

曰：「可得聞與？」

曰：「鄒人與楚人戰，則王以為孰勝？」

曰：「楚人勝。」

曰：「然則小固不可以敵大，寡固不可以敵眾，弱固不可以敵強。海內之地方千里者九，齊集有其一。以一服八，何以異於鄒敵楚哉？蓋亦反其本矣。」

「今王發政施仁，使天下仕者皆欲立於王之朝，耕者皆欲耕於王之野，商賈皆欲藏於王之市，行旅皆欲出於王之途，天下之欲疾其君者皆欲赴愬於王。其若是，孰能禦之？」

王曰：「吾惛，不能進於是矣。願夫子輔吾志，明以教我。我雖不敏，請嘗試之。」

is not lifted because one doesn't use his strength; a load of firewood is not seen because one doesn't use his eyesight. Similarly, the people do not feel your care because you do not extend your kindness to them. Hence, whether or not you can become a king depends not on your ability but rather on your willingness."

"What is the difference in action between unwillingness and inability to perform an act?"

"In the case of taking Mount Tai across the Northern Sea, if you tell someone, 'I can't do it,' you genuinely mean you are unable to do so. However, in the case of bowing before an elder, if you tell someone, 'I can't do it,' it means you're unwilling to do it, not that you are unable to do so. That Your Majesty does not rule as a king is not a matter of taking Mount Tai across the Northern Sea, it is like being unwilling to bow before an elder.

"Treat one's aged kin with care and respect and do the same to the aged kinsmen of others; treat one's young kin with care and love and do the same to the young children of others. If one does this, one will be able to rule the world as though one rolls it in one's palm. The *Book of Poetry* says:

　　曰：「無恆產而有恆心者，惟士為能。若民，則無恆產，因無恆心。苟無恆心，放辟邪侈無不為已。及陷於罪，然後從而刑之，是罔民也。焉有仁人在位罔民而可為也？是故明君制民之產，必使仰足以事父母，俯足以畜妻子，樂歲終身飽，凶年免於死亡；然後驅而之善，故民之從之也輕。」

　　「今之制民之產，仰不足以事父母，俯不足以畜妻子；樂歲終身苦，凶年不免於死亡。此惟救死而恐不贍，奚暇治禮義哉？　」

　　「王欲行之，則盍反其本矣：五畝之宅，樹之以桑，五十者可以衣帛矣。雞豚狗彘之畜，無失其時，七十者可以食肉矣。百畝之田，勿奪其時，八口之家可以無饑矣。謹庠序之教，申之以孝悌之義，頒白者不負戴於道路矣。老者衣帛食肉，黎民不饑不寒，然而不王者，未之有也。」（卷一　梁惠王章句上・七）

'He set an example in his treatment of his wife and brothers. He ruled the state in the same way as he ruled his family.'

"In other words, nurture your own heart and devote it to them. Hence the one who extends his kindness can protect all within the Four Seas; the one who doesn't cannot even protect his family. The ancients surpassed the others just in one thing: their excellence in extending what they did. Now, how can it be possible that you extend your kindness to animals, but fail to benefit your people?

"It is by weighing a thing that its weight can be ascertained and by measuring it that its length be assured. It is so with all things, and particularly so with the heart. Your Majesty, please appraise your own heart!

"Or perhaps you find satisfaction only when you have waged a war, jeopardized your officials and incited the resentment of other rulers?"

"No, why should I find satisfaction in such acts? I only wish to pursue my great ambitions."

"May I be told what these are?"

【今譯】

齊宣王問：「齊桓公、晉文公的事情，可以給我講講嗎？」

孟子回答說：「孔子的學生輩，沒人談論齊桓公、晉文公稱霸的事，所以後來也沒有傳下來，我也沒有聽說過這些事情。我講不了，不如給您講講如何統一天下稱王的事吧！」

齊宣王說：「要達到怎樣的德行才可以稱王呢？」

孟子說：「保護好百姓，用仁政稱王天下，這樣就沒有人能阻擋得住您。」

齊宣王問：「像我這樣的，可以保護好百姓嗎？」

孟子說：「可以。」

齊宣王說：「您怎麼知道我可以呢？」

孟子說：「我聽胡齕說，您坐在堂上，有人牽着牛從堂下經過，您看到了，就問：『把牛牽到哪裏去？』那人回答說：『要用牠的血來塗鐘。』您說：『放了牠吧！我不忍看牠發抖哆嗦的樣子，好像沒有犯罪卻被送到了刑場。』那人

The King smiled but did not speak.

"Is it that the food is not tasty enough for your palate? Or that the clothes are not good enough for your body? Or perhaps the sights not beautiful enough for your eyes? The music not good enough for your ears? Your servants not good enough to serve you? Surely your officials know how to offer enough to meet your needs. These should not be what concern you."

"No," said the King. "These are not what concern me."

"In that case, may I know what Your Majesty's great ambitions are? Are they to expand your territories, to enjoy the homage of Qin and Chu, to rule over the Central Plain region and to bring peace to the four barbarian tribes? Yet to pursue these ambitions by the means you now employ is like trying to catch fish by climbing a tree."

The King said, "Is it as bad as that?"

"It might be worse. If you climb a tree in search of fish, though you will find no fish, no disaster will follow. But if you pursue your ambitions by those means that you employ, disaster will surely follow."

回答說：『那麼，要廢除用牛血塗鐘的儀式嗎？』您說：『怎麼可以廢呢？以羊來代替吧！』不知道有沒有這樣的事？」

齊宣王說：「有的。」

孟子說：「有這樣的心腸，就可以統一天下稱王了。百姓都以為您是吝嗇，我卻知道您是出於不忍之心。」

齊宣王說：「是的，確實有這樣的百姓。齊國雖然狹小，我也不至於吝惜一頭牛吧！我只不過不忍看牠那哆嗦可憐的樣子，就像一個人沒有犯罪卻要上刑場一樣，所以就用羊來代替牠。」

孟子說：「您不要怪百姓說您吝嗇。您用小羊換下了大牛，他們怎麼會知道您真實的想法呢？您如果心疼牛像無罪的人走上刑場，那怎麼就不心疼羊呢？牛和羊還有甚麼區別嗎？」

齊宣王笑着說：「是啊，我這到底是甚麼心理啊？我並非是因為愛財才用羊來代替牛的，也活該百姓說我吝嗇了。」

孟子說：「不要緊。您這種不忍之心正是仁

"May I be told more?"

"If the men of Zou and the men of Chu went to war, whom do you think would win?"

"The men of Chu would win."

"We can infer from this that the small one is no match for the big one, the side with few people is no match for the side with many, and the weak is no match for the strong.

"Among the states, there are only nine regions that cover up to a thousand square miles, and the territory of Qi makes up only one of these. To try to defeat eight with the strength of one, isn't that the same as Zou trying to beat Chu? This would not work, so we'd better go back to the fundamentals.

"Now if you were to rule the state with benevolence, then all the officials from other states would want to serve you, all the farmers would want to plough the fields in your state, all the merchants would want to do business at your marketplaces, all the travelers would want to journey on your roads, all those who had grudges about their rulers would want to lodge complaints before you. If such were the case, who could stop you?"

術，因為您當時只看見了牛而沒有看見羊。君子對於禽獸，看見牠們活着，便不忍心看見牠們死去；聽見牠們發出叫聲，便不忍心吃牠們的肉。所以君子總是離廚房遠遠的。」

齊宣王說：「《詩經》說：『別人有想法，我能揣測出。』說的就是先生您這樣的人啊！我只是這樣做了，反過來問自己為甚麼這樣做，卻想不出個所以然來。先生您這麼一說，我的心便有所啟發了。但您說我這種心理跟統一天下的王道相合，又是怎麼回事呢？」

孟子說：「如果有一個人對您說：『我的力氣舉得起三千斤的重物，卻舉不起一根羽毛。我的視力足以看清秋天鳥羽上的毫毛，卻看不見一車柴草。』這樣的話您信嗎？」

齊宣王說：「不信。」

孟子說：「現在，您的恩惠可以施及禽獸，百姓卻得不到您的恩惠，卻是為甚麼呢？這樣看來，一根羽毛都舉不起來，是因為不肯用力；一車柴草都看不見，是因為不肯用眼睛看；百姓得不到保護，是因為不肯施恩。所以您不行仁政統一天下，是因為您不肯，而不是您不能。」

The King said, "I am slow-witted; I can't follow your thought. May I ask you to assist me in my goals and instruct me in plain terms? I am not smart but would like to try out what you say."

"Only an educated man can have his heart rest assured without a stable means of livelihood. For the common people, if they cannot secure a stable means of livelihood, their hearts will not feel secure. If the people don't feel secure, they will go astray and turn evil, recklessly doing anything. In such cases, if the state does nothing other than to punish them when they have committed a crime, it is entrapping its people. How can this be deemed desirable if a benevolent man is in power? Hence, when a sensible ruler deliberates on the livelihood of his people, he would certainly ensure that they produce enough to serve their parents and nurture their wives and children, so that they will always have enough food in good years, and will not die of starvation in bad ones. Only then should he drive them towards goodness, and the people can easily follow.

"Yet the current livelihood policies don't provide them with enough to serve their parents or nurture their wives and children. They endure good years in bitterness and die from starvation in bad ones. When people have not enough energy

齊宣王說：「不肯和不能，兩者的表現有甚麼區別呢？」

孟子說：「把泰山挾在胳膊裏跳過渤海，跟人說『我不能』，這個是真的不能。對長者彎腰行禮，跟人說『我不能』，這是不肯，不是不能。所以您不行王道，並不是胳膊裏挾着泰山跳過渤海一類，而是對長者彎腰行禮一類。

「孝敬我家裏的老人，並推及別人家裏的老人，愛護我家裏的孩子，並推及別人家裏的孩子，如果能做到這一點，統一天下就會像拿個東西在手心裏轉動一樣容易了。《詩經》說：『先給妻子做出表率，再擴及兄弟，再擴及封邑和國家。』說的就是培育這仁義之心並施加到他們身上去。所以，推廣恩惠可以保四海，不推廣恩惠則連妻子兒女都保不了。古代聖賢之所以超過別人，沒有別的，只是善於推廣其善行罷了。如今您的恩惠可以推及禽獸，百姓卻得不到您的好處，這是為甚麼呢？

「稱一稱，就可以知道輕重；量一量，就可以知道長短。事物都是這樣，心腸更是如此。請您度量一下自己的心腸吧！

「難道說，您只有出動大軍，讓將士冒着危

even to survive, how can they spare time to learn rituals and duties?

"If Your Majesty wants to put it into practice, let's go back to the fundamentals. If mulberry trees are planted in every homestead with five *mus* of land, those aged fifty and over are able to wear silk clothes. When chicken, pigs and dogs are bred in a timely way, all who are seventy and older have meat to eat. If farmers in fields of a hundred mus are not taken from their work during the busy season, then even families with eight mouths to feed will never go hungry. Attention should be paid to teachings given by village schools: Expound the meanings of filial piety and fraternal respect so that no elderly person will ever have to carry heavy stuff along the roads. There has never been a king who failed to unify the world when he was able to let the elderly wear silk and eat meat, and save people from hunger or chill." (Chapter 1.7)

Contemporary interpretation:

Mencius stayed in Qi for six years and had quite a few conversations with King Xuan of Qi. This famous passage in *Mencius* offers a detailed account of the philosopher's thoughts on benevolent governance. Benevolent governance, as the kingly way to rule, seeks to win over the people by

險，跟諸侯結仇構怨，心裏才痛快嗎？」

齊宣王說：「不！我怎麼會以此為快呢？我這麼做，是為了滿足我大的欲望。」

孟子問：「您的最大欲望是甚麼，可以講給我聽嗎？」

宣王笑了笑，不說話。

孟子說：「是為了肥美的食物不夠吃，輕暖的衣服不夠穿？抑或是為了美色不夠眼睛看，樂音不夠耳朵聽，跟前的僕人不夠使喚？這些東西，您的大臣都能夠充分提供，您豈是為了這些東西？」

宣王說：「不。我不是為了這些東西。」

孟子說：「那您的最大欲望我可以知道了。您是想開疆闢土，使秦國和楚國來朝貢，統治中原地區，安撫蠻夷。不過，以您現在所做的，來求您所願的，卻好像爬到樹上去抓魚一樣。」

宣王說：「有這麼嚴重嗎？」

孟子說：「恐怕比這還嚴重呢！爬到樹上去

compassion. Mencius chose not to talk with King Xuan about how to realize his hegemonic ambitions because Mencius was against hegemonic rule that used force and people's fear to gain power. So how did Mencius persuade King Xuan to aspire to become a king instead of a hegemon? Mencius started the discussion by complimenting the king's compassion for the soon-to-be-sacrificed ox and made him aware of his own sensitivity over suffering and for caring about others. He further explained that if the king could extend his compassion to his people, he would be able to take good care of them. Mencius rejected King Xuan's ambition to unify the states by force and warned that it might in the end take his own state down a path to destruction. Instead, Mencius put forward the rule of benevolence under which people from other states would willingly pay allegiance, proposing that the commom people should be provided with a stable means of living so they felt secure; and public facilities should also be built so people could lead a contented life. Once people lived well, the government should educate them to become good people, thus engendering a positive ethos for all. Mencius even devised a detailed plan about how the land should be distributed for households and farming so that all the people could be well fed and become well behaved. For Mencius, this was the best way for a king to rule and manage the whole world.

抓魚，雖然抓不到魚，卻沒有災禍。以您的行為，來求您的所願，如果盡心盡力去幹，反而一定會有災禍。」

宣王問：「可以聽您說說嗎？」

孟子問：「鄒國人和楚國人打仗，您認為哪個會贏？」

宣王說：「楚人會贏。」

孟子說：「由此可知，小的確實敵不過大的，少的確實敵不過多的，弱的確實敵不過強的。海內的地方，方圓千里的共有九塊，齊國只是擁有其中之一。以一來征服八，這跟鄒國與楚國為敵有甚麼區別呢？這是行不通的，還不如回到根本上來。

「現在，您如果施行仁政，使天下搞行政的都想站在您的朝廷裏當官，耕田的都想在您的田野裏耕田，經商的都想在您的市場裏做買賣，旅行的都想在您的馬路上經過，各國痛恨本國君主的人都來您這裏訴苦，如果出現了這種局面，誰還能阻擋您呢？」

宣王說：「我腦子不夠用，到不了這麼高的

We can see from the above discussion that Mencius's views on humanity and politics are closely intertwined. Mencius, who upheld the intrinsic goodness of human nature, is generally criticized for overlooking the dark side of human nature and being too optimistic about humanity. In fact, in view of the extremely difficult livelihood people had at the time, caused by year after year of warfare, the best way to save people from the predicament may well have been to cease fighting, to focus on production and secure people's livelihoods. In order to convince the rulers of the states to accept his governance measures, Mencius had to come up with basic ideas acceptable to rulers of the vassal states. According to Mencius, human beings are all born with a sense of compassion — which is true of our own experience. He took such sense of compassion as the basis of his political thought as well as his doctrine of human nature. (Nowadays, neurologists claim that the human brain has evolved into three levels of functioning. The first and the most ancient one is about survival and reproduction. The second level, which evolved 120 million years, ago is the sub-cortical system that helps us protect and nurture our offspring, as well as to cooperate with others so as to foster survival. The third level, which has evolved since the Stone Age 25,000 years ago, is the neocortex that deals with our intellectual ability and self-awareness. Based on this demarcation, we can say the

層次。希望老先生您輔導我實現理想，明明白白地教導我。我雖然笨得很，也願意試一試。」

孟子說：「沒有穩定的財產卻有穩定的思想的，只有士能做到。至於百姓，就只能說若無穩定的財產，便無穩定的思想了。如果沒有穩定的思想，那麼胡作非為的事，沒有一件是做不出來的。等到他們犯了罪，再加以刑罰，這就等於是把他們趕到羅網裏去。哪有仁人當權，卻把百姓趕到羅網裏的呢？所以明智的君主規定人們的產業，一定要使他們上足以贍養父母，下足以撫育妻兒，豐收之年總能吃飽，荒欠之年不會餓死。有了這個基礎，再督促他們學好，他們遵從起來就比較容易了。

「現在呢，您規定的人們的產業，上不足以贍養父母，下不足以撫育妻兒，豐收之年都苦兮兮的，災荒之年更難免死亡。這種情況下，救自己的命都來不及，哪有閒工夫去學習禮義呢？

「您如果想施行仁政，何不從根本上着手呢？家家戶戶都分五畝地用作宅基地，周圍種上桑樹，那麼五十歲以上的人就可以穿上絲帛了。雞鴨豬狗這類家畜，都能按時得到餵養和繁殖，那麼七十歲以上的老者也可以吃上肉了。家家戶

moral sense that Mencius emphasized can be ascribed to the second level of functioning, that is, the unreflective and non-rational compassionate instincts or altruistic dispositions.)

King Xuan feeling pity for the ox showed that he was capable of compassion. No matter how rudimentary such a moral sense might seem, it was one that had been genuinely felt by the king. This offered a very good starting point for Mencius's arguments — one that may be backed up by our knowledge of human psychology. Why are human beings capable of compassion? Studies in neurology have revealed that there are biological and physiological factors that have given rise to human compassion — a naturally evolved feeling that has been formed during the long history of human evolution in support of the sustenance of the species. In fact, compassion is commonly seen in many social animals, such as ants and bees: in order to serve the group's common interest, some members of the group are willing to collaborate or to even sacrifice themselves. These animals seem to possess some form of altruistic gene. Would human compassion be yet another example of such genes? If humans are by nature self-interested, how can they enjoy long-term partnerships with others? Suppose King Xuan did possess an inborn sense of compassion, instead of restraining it he should let it develop

戶都分一百畝耕地，不佔用農忙時節，八口之家
也就可以不挨餓了。辦好學校教育，不厭其煩地
把孝悌的道理教給百姓，這樣鬚髮斑白的老人也
不至於馱着重物在道路上踽踽前行了。老人們能
穿上帛，吃上肉，百姓不挨餓，不受凍，實現了
這一步，還不能一統天下的，還沒有過。」

【時析】

　　孟子在齊國待了六年，與齊宣王有過多次對
話。這一節是《孟子》中的名篇，比較詳細地闡
述了孟子的仁政主張。仁政是王道，以仁愛吸引
天下歸心。反過來，霸主用的是武力殺人，令人
畏服，所以孟子不跟齊宣王談霸業。那麼，孟子
如何誘導齊宣王嚮往王道呢？孟子用齊宣王對將
要做犧牲的牛的同情心，來讓齊宣王切身地認識
到，他是有不忍人之心或惻隱之心（仁）的，只
要把這個仁心推廣開去，就能恩施百姓，這就是
「推恩保民」。齊宣王靠武力統一中國是不可行
的，反可能招來滅頂之災，如果他實行仁政，那
就會仁者無敵，天下歸心，王天下。作為仁政的
具體措施，孟子提出，應該對普通百姓予以恆產，
使他們有恆心 —— 搞好國內物質建設，使人民安
定，富而後教，使百姓有道德，民風良好。他甚
至制定一個儒家仁政的藍圖，宅基地、耕地多少

fully, simply by repeatedly reinforcing compassionate acts (such as stopping killing) that provoke positive reactions until compassion becomes his habitual response. Grounded in psychological principles and treating others as you would yourself, such a way may offer a more viable route towards the realization of benevolent governance.

We can see from other cultures how the sense of compassion has helped shape social norms as well as political measures. For example, the Old Testament commanded that when harvesting their crops farmers should leave a few bunches behind so that they can be picked by orphans and widows in need. The underlying humanitarianism is based upon a sense of compassion that connects us with those who suffer from poverty or mishap.

Five

Translation:

Mencius said, "No human being can bear the suffering of others. The ancient kings could not bear the suffering of others, and thus they practiced governance that bore no suffering of others. With a heart that cannot bear the suffering of others so as to practice governance that bears no suffering of others,

都規定了，總之讓人民能夠衣食無憂，彬彬有禮，做到這些後，就不難平天下了。

從這裏我們可以清楚地看出，孟子的人性論，跟他的政治學說是緊密相關的。一般說孟子持性善論，以為他沒有注意到人性中的陰暗面，對人性過於樂觀。其實，放在孟子的戰國時代，諸侯連年戰爭，生靈塗炭，最能從根本上救民於水深火熱之中的辦法，還是說服諸侯止戰，專心於生產，保障人民的生活。而這就需要找到諸侯能夠接受的基本信念，從那裏逐步推出整套邏輯。孟子認為，人的惻隱之心是先天就有的，可以從生活經驗中得到驗證。他把這惻隱之心作為他政治學說的基礎，也作為他人性論的基礎。（當代有的神經學專家認為，人類在進化過程中，腦進化出了三個層次。最古老的是只管生存和繁殖的層次；第二層次是一億二千萬年前的「邊緣系統」，主管保護和養育後代，及與其他個體合作團結，有助於生存；第三層次才是二萬五千年前舊石器時代演化出的「新腦」、〔新皮質〕，即理智能力和自我認知。如果根據這種神經學理論，孟子所說的良知大致可歸到第二層次，即無需理性反思的本能式的同情共感或利他反應。）

齊宣王可憐那頭牛，清楚地表明他有一種同

one can rule the world as easily as turning it in the palm of the hand. Why do I say no human being can bear the suffering of others? Suppose a man, all of a sudden, saw that a little child was about to fall into a well; he would certainly be startled and feel compassion, not because he wanted to befriend the child's parents, not because he wished to get compliments from neighbors and friends, nor because he was annoyed by the crying of the child. From this it can be seen that whoever has no compassion is not human, whoever feels no shame is not human, whoever displays no humility is not human, and whoever lacks a sense of right and wrong is not human. Compassion buds benevolence, shame buds righteousness, humility buds propriety, a sense of right and wrong buds wisdom. Man has four such budding senses just as he has four limbs. For a man who has these budding senses but still denies having such capabilities, he is blamable for crippling himself. For a man to deny that his ruler possesses such capabilities, he is blamable for crippling his ruler. For all who realize that these four budding senses are inherent in themselves, they will seek to develop them fully, just like tongues of flames starting to lick or a spring starting to flow. If a man develops these senses to the full, he can take care of the whole world; but if he fails, he will not even be able to take care of his parents." (Chapter 3.6)

情心，儘管這只是一個「端」，一個萌芽，但齊宣王確實真切地感受到了，因此孟子一系列的推論就有了一個很好的起點。從常識層面來說，孟子的人性論有心理事實作為依據。人的同情心來自於何處？今天腦神經科學揭示人類同情心是有其生物和生理基礎的。它也許是人類在長期的進化過程中演化出來的一種天然的情感，有益於群體的進化，可以合作共生。有一些社會生物，如螞蟻、蜜蜂等等，其中一些成員會有自我犧牲、自我奉獻的分工，牠們的行為是利他的。人的同情心，也許是利他基因在心理上的一個反映。如果基因或者人性都是自私的，那麼他們怎麼能夠長期合作呢？如果齊宣王有天生的同情心，並且不在後天被扼殺，而是反復地、多次地做有同情心的事（比如不殺生），就會形成一個正面的激勵機制，每做一次都帶來一種滿足感，從而使得同情心發揚光大，形成習慣行為。在這樣的心理基礎上推己及人，實行仁政措施，就比較容易了。

仁義之心帶來的禮制、政治措施，在別的文化中也有。比如，猶太教《舊約》就規定，收割麥子時，一定要留下一些麥穗不割，讓孤兒寡母可以藉此維持生計，其背後體現的是人道主義精神。對他人不幸命運、貧困生活的同情心理，是人道主義精神的重要的基礎。

Contemporary interpretation:

In this passage Mencius sought to link his doctrine of human nature with that of benevolent governance. In order to persuade the states to implement benevolent policies, Mencius drew on the inborn human conscience as the main premise in his argument. He pointed out that the compassion of not bearing the suffering of others is shared by every human being. If rulers can amplify their own compassion of not being able to bear the suffering of others, such compassion will lead to policies that would not allow the suffering of others (benevolent governance). In a similar way, an English monk named Pelagius in the late Roman period went to Rome and tried to convince those in power of the existence of free will. He argued that since man is endowed with the ability to choose between good and evil, he will be condemned or rewarded by God according to his choice. He therefore advised those in Rome to exercise their human freedom and choose to do good.

It should be noted that the case of the child about to fall into the well was meant to be an example instead of a proof. It did not seek to offer evidence to prove the intrinsic goodness of human nature; rather, it offered an example to show how we as human beings share the same response to such circumstances.

五

孟子曰：「人皆有不忍人之心。先王有不忍人之心，斯有不忍人之政矣。以不忍人之心，行不忍人之政，治天下可運之掌上。所以謂人皆有不忍人之心者，今人乍見孺子將入於井，皆有怵惕惻隱之心；非所以內交於孺子之父母也，非所以要譽於鄉黨朋友也，非惡其聲而然也。由是觀之，無惻隱之心，非人也。無羞惡之心，非人也。無辭讓之心，非人也。無是非之心，非人也。惻隱之心，仁之端也；羞惡之心，義之端也；辭讓之心，禮之端也；是非之心，智之端也。人之有是四端也，猶其有四體也。有是四端而自謂不能者，自賊者也；謂其君不能者，賊其君者也。凡有四端於我者，知皆擴而充之矣，若火之始然、泉之始達。苟能充之，足以保四海；苟不充之，不足以事父母。」（卷三 公孫丑章句上・六）

【今譯】

孟子說：「人都有不忍讓人遭難的心理。古代的聖王有不忍讓人遭難的心理，所以才實行不

As Mou Zong-san pointed out, "conscience manifests itself in experience."

Influenced by Mencius's thoughts, Chinese philosophers tend to regard "reason" and "feeling" as complementary elements in an argument, while in the Western tradition focus is placed on the use of "reason" and only a handful of philosophers discuss "sympathy."

According to Mencius, the sense of compassion can be developed into a full-fledged benevolent heart, and from there the governance of benevolence is made possible. In the same manner, the ideal in the Confucian tradition shared by Chinese intellectuals advocates firstly cultivating oneself, then putting one's family in order, then governing one's state, and finally managing the world. It can be reasonably doubted, however, whether he who cultivates himself can necessarily put his family in order. Whether he who can put his family in order is thus able to govern his state. And whether he who can govern his state can go on to manage the world.

In view of the vastly different roles these describe, not to mention the different professional skills required, a statement as sweeping as this may be rather oversimplifying the problem.

忍讓人遭難的政治。懷着不忍讓人遭難的心理，去實行不忍讓人遭難的政治，治理天下就會像手掌上轉動小球一樣容易。我之所以說人都有不忍讓別人遭難的心理，是因為有這種情況：比如當人們突然看到一個小孩子就要掉到井裏去時，都會產生驚懼和同情的心理。這種心理的產生，不是因為要和那個小孩的父母拉交情，不是因為想要在鄉鄰朋友中獲得讚譽，不是因為討厭那個小孩的哭聲。由此來看，沒有同情心的，不是人；沒有羞恥之心的，不是人；沒有推讓之心的，不是人；沒有是非之心的，不是人。同情之心，是仁的萌芽；羞恥之心，是義的萌芽；推讓之心，是禮的萌芽；是非之心，是智的萌芽。人有這四種萌芽，就跟他有四肢一樣。有這四種萌芽卻說自己沒有這方面能力的人，是自暴自棄者；說自己的君主沒有能力的人，是暴棄其君主者。凡是具有這四種萌芽的人，如果懂得把它們擴充起來，它們就會像剛燒起來的火，剛流起來的泉水。這四種萌芽，如果能擴充，就可以保有天下，如果不能擴充，則連父母也贍養不了。」

【時析】

　　這一節將人性論與仁政說結合起來，從中亦可看出孟子是為了在政治治理上鼓勵諸侯實行仁政，從他們天然良心上去找仁政的理論基礎的。

Six

Translation:

Mencius said, "When the Way prevails in the world, men of small virtue serve men of great virtue, men of little worth serve men of great worth. But when the Way is abandoned, the powerless men serve the powerful men, the weak men serve the strong men. Both are submitted to the will of heaven. Those who conform with destiny survive; those who go against destiny perish. Duke Jing of Qi said, 'Since on the one hand, we are unable to command, and on the other, we refuse to accept the command, we are destined to be exterminated.' In tears he gave his daughter to Wu as a bride. Now the small states emulate the big states, yet they feel ashamed of being commanded by the big states. This is like disciples feeling ashamed of learning from their masters. If one is ashamed, he'd better learn from the example of King Wen. He who has learned from him will be able to rule the whole world — in five years if he starts with a big state, and in seven years if he starts with a small state. The *Book of Poetry* says:

'The descendants of Shang,

Were so many, beyond tens of thousands,

But because the Lord above decreed,

They all submit to Zhou.

They all submit to Zhou,

他向他們顯示，人人都有不忍之心，如果他們身為諸侯或國王，能將不忍人之心放大，就可以變成不忍人之政（仁政）。這類似於當年羅馬帝國晚期時，英國修士佩拉糾跑到羅馬對那裏的達官貴人說，你們都有自由意志，有行善作惡的能力，也因此會受到上帝的賞罰，因此，發揮你們的能力從善吧。佩拉糾是在鼓勵他們行善。

孟子所舉孺子入井的例子，是一個示例，而不是例證。示例是向讀者顯示，如果你當時處於同樣情境下，也一定會有相似的心理。這也就是牟宗三所說的「良知是呈現」，而不是西方意義上的事實證據。

由於孟子的影響，中國哲學在重視「合理」之外，尚重「合情」。（在西方哲學中，重心放在「理性」上面，但亦有少部份人會談及「同情」。）

孟子認為，從惻隱之心可以向外擴充仁心，直到實行仁政。傳統儒家也一貫講修齊治平，成為中國知識份子的人生理想。但若從另一個側面分析，是否能修身，就能齊家？能齊家，就能治國？能治國，就能平天下？這裏涉及不同範疇的內容跳躍，亦涉及不同領域的「專業」技能，修齊治平這種簡單的一條鞭推論，可能將問題過於簡化了。

Because the Mandate of Heaven is not immutable,

The officials of Yin are fair and smart,

They assist at the libations in the Zhou capital.'

Confucius said, 'Benevolence has nothing to do with the number of people. If the ruler of a state values benevolence, he will be matchless in the whole world.' However, now you wish to be matchless in the whole world by any means but benevolence, it is like holding something hot while refusing to cool it with water. The *Book of Poetry* says:

'Who can hold something hot,

And not cool it with water?'" (Chapter 7.7)

Contemporary interpretation:

When morality prevails, people convince each other by moral reasoning, hence people of lesser virtue listen to those of greater virtue. When there is no moral order, people seek power by force, hence the less mighty obey those who are mighty. In troubled times, the ruler of a small state should seek to strengthen the state by emulating King Wen in imposing benevolent governance so that after a few years he can unify the world.

Mencius offered the governance of benevolence as the governance measure for small states under threat as well as big

六

孟子曰：「天下有道，小德役大德，小賢役大賢。天下無道，小役大，弱役強，斯二者，天也。順天者存，逆天者亡。齊景公曰：『既不能令，又不受命，是絕物也。』涕出而女於吳。今也小國師大國，而恥受命焉，是猶弟子而恥受命於先師也。如恥之，莫若師文王，師文王，大國五年，小國七年，必為政於天下矣。《詩》云：『商之孫子，其麗不億。上帝既命，侯於周服。侯服於周，天命靡常。殷士膚敏，祼將於京。』孔子曰：『仁不可為眾也夫！夫國君好仁，天下無敵。』今也欲無敵於天下，而不以仁，是猶執熱而不以濯也。《詩》云：『誰能執熱，逝不以濯？』」（卷七 離婁章句上・七）

【今譯】

孟子說：「若天下政治清明，道德低的人服從道德高的人，不太賢能的人服從非常賢能的人。若天下政治黑暗，力量小的就服從大的，弱的服從強的。這兩種情況，都是天意。順從天意

states which felt insecure. Mencius, as well as scholars from other schools of thought, sought solutions to the political chaos around them. In order to convince the rulers of the vassal states to accept their governance measures, they claimed the solutions were swift and thorough.

One may wonder how speedy his measures were. Mencius took King Wen as the model and believed that it took seven years for a small state and five years for a big state to unify the world with benevolent governance. Mencius's view may have had an influence on intellectuals of later generations.

For example, when Kang You-wei put forward his reform scheme to Emperor Guan Xu, he claimed that once the reform was implemented, a small change could be seen in three years, a big change could be seen in five years, and the whole country would be thoroughly reformed in ten years. Another example can be taken from Mao Zedong. Following his visit to Moscow to watch the Soviet Union's military parade for the first time, he devised the Great Leap Forward movement and other schemes which were intended to surpass Britain's status and catch up with America. Instead, the movement ended up starving to death over 10 million people. These examples reveal the common oversight shared by many passionate

者生存，逆反天意者滅亡。齊景公曾經說過：『既不能命令別國，又不能接受別國的命令，這是一條絕路啊！』因此流着眼淚把女兒嫁到了吳國。現在小國學習大國的樣子，卻以接受大國的命令為恥，這就跟當學生的以聽先生的話為恥一樣。如果真的以聽話為恥，那就不如向文王學習。向文王學習，大國只需要五年，小國只需要七年，就一定可以執掌天下了。《詩經》說：『商朝的子孫，數量何止十萬。上帝已經命令，都向周室臣服。都向周室臣服，可見天命無常。商朝士人漂亮聰明，都去周京助祭。』孔子說：『仁跟人多人少沒有關係。國君如果喜歡仁，就可以天下無敵。』現在您如果想天下無敵，卻又不願意施行仁政，這就好比熱得不行了卻不用水涼一下一樣。《詩經》說：『誰會在拿燙手的東西時，不先用水涼一涼呢？』」

【時析】

天下有道，以德服人，所以是用道德說話，道德差一點的服從好一點的，不賢的服從賢的；天下無道，以力服人，所以小的服從大的，弱的服從強的。當天下大亂，弱國小國的處世之道，在於奮發圖強，向文王學習，實行仁政，數年之間就可以一統天下。

and idealistic reformers who lack patience and a proper understanding of the real circumstances. Mencius had this problem. Confucius seems to have avoided such shortcomings. He said, "It takes time for satisfactory results." Likewise Deng Xiaoping showed patience in China's reform and opening-up and under his rule the country was able to boost economic development. In thirty years, he helped place China's GDP second in the world. This would not have been achievable by Mao Zedong who was impatient to get things done.

Seven

Translation:

Mencius said, "One who uses force in the name of benevolence will become a hegemon, but to do so he must first be the ruler of a big state. One who practices benevolence through virtue will become a king, and his success will not depend on the size of his state. Tang of Shang started with only seventy miles, and King Wen of Zhou with a hundred. When one rules by force, people are not convinced in their hearts but only succumb to might. When one rules on moral grounds, people are convinced with their hearts full of admiration. An example of this is the deference the seventy disciples have shown to Confucius. The *Book of Poetry* says:

　　孟子這是在為當時受欺負的小國和自感不安全的大國出謀獻策，勸他們接受儒家的仁政綱領，落實施政。實際上，孟子跟當時別的學派一樣，也是在為亂世求治開藥方，為了諸侯能夠接受，就把這藥說成速效且治病根的藥。

　　這個速效快到甚麼程度？孟子舉文王為榜樣，認為如果實行王政，小國七年、大國五年，就可以一統天下。這可能影響到了後來的一些知識份子。比如康有為在變法時，就對光緒皇帝誇下海口，只要實行變法，就能三年一小變，五年一大變，十年全變。毛澤東訪問莫斯科回國後便發起大躍進運動，要超英趕美，結果經濟民生遭受重創。這都是對實際情況估計不足，徒有熱情和理想，急於求成的毛病。這毛病在孟子時就有表現了。孔子似乎就沒有這個毛病。孔子說：事緩則圓。鄧小平搞改革開放，沒有着急的樣子，可是國家的經濟發展得很好，三十多年下來，GDP 就成了世界第二。這是當年毛澤東急也急不來的。

七

　　孟子曰：「以力假仁者霸，霸必有大國；以德行仁者王，王不待大，

'From West, from East,

From South, from North,

There was none who refused to submit.'

This describes well what I have said." (Chapter 3.3)

Contemporary interpretation:

During the Warring States period, only the ruler of Zhou was addressed as the king, rulers of the vassal states had titles such as "Gong" (prince), "Hou" (duke) and "Bo" (count). In 334 BC, Hui, the ruler of Liang went to Xuzhou to meet with Wei, the ruler of Qi, and addressed him as king. Not daring to be the only one addressed as king, Wei also addressed Hui as king.

This pair started the trend for the vassal rulers to address themselves as kings. Mencius did not oppose the title, rather he made good use of it in persuading King Hui to learn to become a benevolent king following the example of King Wen of Zhou.

In this passage we can be clear that all the vassal rulers aimed to make their states wealthy and powerful in order to rule over the whole world. In response to the situation, different schools of thought sought to convince the rulers to adopt their governance measures.

湯以七十里，文王以百里。以力服人
者，非心服也，力不贍也；以德服人
者，中心悅而誠服也，如七十子之服
孔子也。《詩》云：『自西自東，自
南自北，無思不服。』此之謂也。」

（卷三　公孫丑章句上・三）

【今譯】

孟子說：「憑着武力而打着仁義旗號的可以
成為霸主，稱霸一定要有國力的強大作為憑據；
而憑着美德推行仁義的卻可以成為聖王，成為聖
王並不以國家的強大為後盾。商湯憑着方圓七十
里，周文王憑着方圓一百里就成了聖王。憑着武
力使人服從的，人家並非心服，只是因為力量不
夠才不得不服從。因為美德而使人服從的，人家
是從心裏真的服從，就像孔子的七十個學生服從
孔子一樣。《詩經》說過：『從西從東，從南從北，
沒有不服的。』說的就是這種情況。

【時析】

戰國時，華夏地區只有周天子稱王，諸侯一
般只稱公、侯、伯。公元前334年，梁惠王到徐
州朝見齊威王，稱齊威王為王，齊威王不敢獨自稱
王，也承認梁惠王為王。他們兩人開了一個頭，以

In the same way, Mencius had no choice but to describe benevolent governance as a means: if you practice benevolent governance you'll acquire soft power (to convince people with virtues) and can then call on people throughout the world to follow you and to unify the world. Practicing benevolence will achieve genuine "big interests," through which the state will become powerful, orderly, more effective in governance, and thus gain the deference of the whole world. As a means, the rule of virtue is more effective than the rule of force. In fact, both share the same goal: to unify the world. The difference between them lies in the use of hard power (force) by the hegemon and the use of soft power (benevolence) by the king. As seen from the people's perspective, the rule of benevolence is definitely preferable and benefits them most. This is why Mencius adopted a people-oriented approach as the way out of conflict.

The struggle today between kingship and hegemony confronts international politics in the same way it did in the past. Concepts of hard power, soft power as well as sharp power have emerged in the political discourse. The powerful countries compete not only with their hard power, but also seek to beat others by soft power. This trend has prompted the hegemonic powers to increase their soft power by improving

後諸侯紛紛稱王。孟子對這個梁惠王稱王並沒有反對，而是因勢利導，勸其學周文王實行仁政稱王。

從這段話可以清楚地看出，當時，讓國家富強、一統天下，是所有諸侯的心願。各個學派為了說服諸侯，紛紛拿出自己的主張，吸引、說服這些諸侯採取自己的措施達到富強，一統天下。

孟子也不得不把仁政說得跟手段一樣，跟諸侯說你如果實行仁義，就能獲得軟實力（以德服人），就能召來天下人跟從，從而一統天下。做到仁義才是真正的「大利」，才會令國家強大，秩序井然，管治有效，天下歸心。從手段來說，以德服人比以力服人更有效。王與霸的目標是一致的，都是一統天下，只不過手段不同，霸是用硬實力（武），王是用軟實力（仁）。從百姓的角度說，王當然是更好的，百姓能獲得最大的好處。孟子是從民本主義立場上解決當時的王、霸問題。

今天，國際政治仿佛也面臨着當年王霸之爭。硬實力、軟實力、銳實力，不同的概念紛紛出籠。大國除了時不時秀秀硬實力的肌肉外，還要在軟實力上競爭，互相打擊對方的軟實力。這在無形中也促使各大霸主要搞好軟實力，塑造好

their global image and moral claim so that their leadership has more appeal to other countries. In the past, the United States and the Soviet Union competed against each other using their soft power. The Soviet Union failed in its domestic affairs and the people revolted; in the end it also lost in the international competition. It can clearly be seen from this case that the key to gaining recognition does not rest on propaganda and image building, instead it depends on whether people in your country and the world consider life there to be good, and where people enjoy freedom and justice.

It seems that Mencius did not refute hegemonic rule; he just pointed out that hegemony required hard power and the cost of such was high, while the rule of benevolence was cost-effective. This can be seen from the advice he gave to Duke Wen of Teng, a small state at the time — to practice benevolent governance.

In the past, the US projected an image of a superpower with its soft power of "democracy" and "freedom" in addition to dominating the world with its strong military hard power. Following his succession as US president, Donald Trump has favored the use of hard power and talked of an "America First" policy in a United Nations General Assembly session.

自己的形象，讓自己顯得講道義，讓別的國家口服心服。當年，美國和蘇聯爭軟實力，蘇聯內政沒有搞好，自己的人民先反了，國際競爭也落了敗。如果要當王者，在爭奪民心上，不單單要在宣傳和塑造形象方面，更要讓自己的百姓和世界上的人民都在你這裏覺得舒服，覺得自由公平。

孟子似乎並未否定霸，他只是指出，霸需要硬實力，成本高，王則可以本小利大。他建議小國的君主滕文公行仁政就是一例。

以前，美國除了以其稱霸全球的軍事硬實力君臨天下外，亦以民主自由為軟實力建立超級大國形象，但特朗普當上美國總統後，卻拋棄了這一套，到處只秀硬勢力，在聯合國大會上的發言宣講「美國優先」，令美國的軟實力大傷元氣，引來世界諸多國家媒體的奚落，可見只靠硬實力，是難以讓人心服口服的。

八

孟子曰：「不仁者，可與言哉？安其危而利其菑，樂其所以亡者。不

Such moves have damaged the reputation of the US and provoked criticism from media around the world. This shows that people are unwilling to accept hegemonic hard power.

Eight

Translation:

Mencius said, "How can one reason with a malevolent man? He treats danger as being safe and considers disaster as being advantageous; he delights in what will lead to his own destruction. If the malevolent man could be reasoned with, there would be no ruined states or broken families. There was a boy singing:

'If the blue water is clear

It is fit to wash my chinstrap.

If the blue water is muddy

It is fit to wash my feet.'

Confucius said, 'Listen to this, my young man. When clear, the water washes the chinstrap, when muddy it washes the feet; it is the water that brings this upon itself.' A man must have disgraced himself before others disgrace him. A family must have ruined itself before others ruin it. A state must have ravaged itself before others ravage it. Tai Jia said,

'When Heaven brings disasters,

仁而可與言，則何亡國敗家之有？有孺子歌曰：『滄浪之水清兮，可以濯我纓；滄浪之水濁兮，可以濯我足。』孔子曰：『小子聽之！清斯濯纓，濁斯濯足矣，自取之也。』夫人必自侮，然後人侮之；家必自毀，而後人毀之；國必自伐，而後人伐之。《太甲》曰：『天作孽，猶可違；自作孽，不可活』，此之謂也。」（卷七 離婁章句上・八）

【今譯】

孟子說：「不仁的人，聽得進別人的勸導嗎？他把危險當作安全，把災難當作有利，喜歡做讓自己滅亡的事。不仁的人，如果還能聽得進別人的勸導，他怎麼會有亡國敗家的事呢？有小孩唱道：『滄浪的水清啊，可用來洗我的帽纓；滄浪的水濁啊，可用來洗我的兩腳。』孔子說：『弟子們聽着！水清就洗帽纓，水濁就洗腳，這都是水質自己招來的。』所以人必是不自重，然後別人才輕慢他；家必是自己破壞，然後別人才摧毀它；國必是自相攻伐，然後別人才來攻伐它。《太甲》說『天降的災禍，還可以逃開。自己造成的災禍，逃無可逃，死路一條』就是這個道理。」

One can still hope to escape;

When man brings disasters upon himself,

He will inevitably perish.'

This describes well what I have said." (Chapter 7.8)

Contemporary interpretation:

Mencius observed that whenever benevolence is practiced, peaceful order exists whether it is in the individual, the family or the country. This results in improved relationships. If the individual, the family and also the country show no benevolence, it is hard to avoid chaos and internal conflicts. A country in such a predicament will be vulnerable to foreign aggression and invasion.

If a man looks down upon himself, others will look down on him also. In order not to be offended, we must learn to value and cherish ourselves. If a family lives in unity, others cannot easily harm it, but if it is divided and the married couple argues, betrayal often follows. The same applies to a country: if it is riven in antagonistic party politics, it may easily fall victim to foreign occupation. This happened in China in the Republic of China era. The country was torn apart by warlords and civil war broke out between the communists and the Nationalists, enabling Japan to take advantage of the chaos and invade.

【時析】

孟子看到，仁義的個人、家族和國家，都是內部較有秩序，對外關係也因此較好應對；不仁的個人、家族和國家，則會內部混亂，起內訌，擺不平，危機四伏，這種狀態，如果有外敵入侵就麻煩了。

對自輕自賤者，別人也賤視之。故人要自珍自愛自重，別人才不會冒犯。家裏團結，外人不能把你怎麼樣，如果家裏分裂，夫妻不和，第三者之類的事情就容易發生。國家內部分黨分派，外敵很容易拉一派打一派，然後併吞全國。比如民國時期的中國，軍閥混戰，南北對立，國共相殘，日本就可以順利入侵。

九

孟子曰：「求也，為季氏宰，無能改於其德，而賦粟倍他日。孔子曰：『求非我徒也，小子鳴鼓而攻之，可也。』由此觀之，君不行仁政而富之，皆棄於孔子者也，況於為之強戰？爭地以戰，殺人盈野；爭城以戰，殺人盈城，此所謂率土地而食人

Nine

Translation:

Mencius said, "When Ran Qiu served as the chief minister of the Ji family, he failed to improve the virtue of their governance and the grain-tax levy doubled. Confucius said, 'Qiu is no disciple of mine! Young men, you may beat the drums and attack him.' From this we can see that Confucius rejected those who helped a ruler to reap profits without putting benevolent governance into practice. How much more would he reject those who wage wars on the ruler's behalf? In wars over territory, men are slaughtered until corpses fill the fields; in sieges on a city, men are killed until corpses fill the city. This is what people say: 'They claim the land and devour the flesh of the people.' Death is too light a penalty for such crimes. Therefore, those who are keen on war must suffer the gravest punishment; next are those who forge war alliances among rulers; and finally come those who exploit unused land and levy taxes." (Chapter 7.14)

Contemporary interpretation:

Confucius condemned Ran Qiu for helping Count Kan of Ji to impose high taxes, thus harming the livelihoods of the common people. At that time, rulers of states often fought against each other in an attempt to annex more territory

肉，罪不容於死。故善戰者服上刑，連諸侯者次之，辟草萊、任土地者次之。」（卷七 離婁章句上·十四）

【今譯】

孟子說：「冉求做季康子的主管，沒有能使季康子變好，反而把稅收增加了一倍。孔子說：『冉求不是我的學生，你們可以大張旗鼓地討伐他。』由此看來，君主不實行仁政，下屬卻幫他斂財，這樣的下屬是孔子所唾棄的。何況那些為君主奮力打仗的人呢？以戰爭來搶奪地盤，殺死的人填滿了田野；以戰爭來搶奪城池，殺死的人填滿了城池，這就是人們所說的率領着土地來吃人肉，死刑都不足以懲罰他們的罪惡。所以善於打仗的人應該受最重的刑罰，搞合縱連橫的人應該受次一等的刑罰，主張開墾荒地依地收稅的人應該受再低一等的刑罰。」

【時析】

冉求幫季康子斂稅，侵害了百姓的利益，為孔子所批判。當時各諸侯為佔有更多的土地和人民，互相殺伐，死人如麻，大多是不正義的戰爭。孟子學說之提出，一個主要目的就是為了用仁政統一天下，實現和平，讓人民過上安寧的生活。

and swell their population. These incursions of war killed many people and were morally unjustifiable. In the hope of regaining peace and order, Mencius put forward his doctrine of benevolent governance. Mencius condemned as killers those rulers who waged wars, those strategists who forged alliances, as well as those Legalists who advocated exploitation of unused lands, and he called for their severe punishment. One may ask why those who advocated annexation of unused lands should face such retribution. The reason was that evil intentions lay behind the exploitation: land acquisition was not to better people's livelihoods but to maintain a long-term food supply for armies and to perpetuate a brutal war.

The politics of the Warring States period rendered that time in history far more destructive than the Spring and Autumn period through which Confucius had lived. Wars were more cruel, they expanded in scale and the death tolls were greater. How to end the wars and regain peace in the world became the most difficult question for thinkers of the time. Mencius sought to persuade rulers to employ the soft power of benevolence in their governance and advocate for just war. Would his doctrine be distorted, taken advantage of and used as a means or an excuse for war by the hegemons? In particular, in his "just war" theory, Mencius seemed to put "human rights" above

孟子認為發動戰爭的諸侯，搞合縱連橫的策士，和提倡開闢土地以盡地利的法家都是殺人者，應受嚴懲。為甚麼要懲罰提倡開闢土地以盡地利者呢？這是因為，這些人提倡這個並不是為了民生，而是為了戰爭作更好更長期的準備，使得戰爭更為持久而殘酷。

戰國時的國際形勢，要比孔子的春秋時代更為嚴峻，戰爭更加不擇手段，戰爭規模更大，死人更多；如何止戰，如何為天下謀和平，成了擺在所有思想家面前的一道難題。孟子以仁政的軟實力來吸引統治者，以正義戰爭解民於倒懸的主張，會不會被曲解利用，變成一種戰爭手段或藉口呢？尤其孟子那有點像「人權高於主權」的正義戰爭論，會不會被諸侯利用，打着拯救人民的旗號，行着霸佔天下之實呢？類似的主權與人權問題，在二十世紀末廿一世紀初，亦成為熱門議題，究竟是人權高於主權，還是主權高於人權？各有支持者。因此，更需要我們對二者的核心概念作深入分析，不是嚷嚷口號就能解決問題的。

十

齊宣王問曰：「交鄰國有道乎？」

"sovereignty." Would this stance be exploited by the vassal rulers using slogans about "saving neighboring peoples" in support of their aggressive wars? Similar heated debates on sovereignty and human rights have resurfaced in our time. Should one override the other? There are supporters on both sides of the debate. Perhaps we should probe deeper into the key concepts of the argument and not retort to empty words before coming up with solutions.

Ten

Translation:

King Xuan of Qi asked, "Is there a way for keeping up good relationships with neighboring states?"

Mencius replied, "Yes. Only a benevolent man can serve a state smaller than his own. In this way Tang was able to serve the Ge people and King Wen was able to serve the Kun Yi people. Only the wise man can serve a larger state than his own. In this way King Tai was able to serve the Xun Yu people and Gou Jian was able to serve Wu. A man who can serve a state smaller than his own is pleased with heaven's way; a man who can serve a state larger than his own is in awe of heaven's way. He who is pleased with heaven's way can keep the world; he

　　孟子對曰：「有。惟仁者為能以大事小，是故湯事葛，文王事昆夷。惟智者為能以小事大，故太王事獯鬻，勾踐事吳。以大事小者，樂天者也；以小事大者，畏天者也。樂天者保天下，畏天者保其國。《詩》云：『畏天之威，於時保之。』」

　　王曰：「大哉言矣！寡人有疾，寡人好勇。」

　　對曰：「王請無好小勇。夫撫劍疾視曰，『彼惡敢當我哉！』此匹夫之勇，敵一人者也。王請大之！

　　「詩云：『王赫斯怒，爰整其旅，以遏徂莒，以篤周祜，以對於天下。』此文王之勇也。文王一怒而安天下之民。

　　「書曰：『天降下民，作之君，作之師，惟曰其助上帝寵之。四方有罪無罪惟我在，天下曷敢有越厥志？』一人衡行於天下，武王恥之。

who is in awe of heaven's way can keep his state. The *Book of Poetry* says:
'Hold the majesty of heaven in awe
And thus be blessed.'"

The King said, "Your words are great! Yet I have a weakness. I am rather bold in character."

Mencius replied, "Then I beg Your Majesty not to be fond of petty boldness. To get offended and threaten with a sword, yelling, 'How dare that fellow oppose me!' is to show the boldness of the common man, enough only to match a single enemy. Your Majesty, you should make it something greater!
The *Book of Poetry* says:
'The King blazed in rage
And consolidated his troops
To stop the enemy from advancing on Ju
To expand the blessings of Zhou
In response to the wishes of the world.'
This was the courage of King Wen. In one outburst of rage, he brought peace to the people of the world.
And the *Book of Documents* says:
'Heaven sent the people down on earth
Give them a ruler

此武王之勇也。而武王亦一怒而安天下之民。今王亦一怒而安天下之民，民惟恐王之不好勇也。」（卷二 梁惠王章句下‧三）

【今譯】

齊宣王問孟子：「跟鄰國交往有原則嗎？」孟子回答說：「有的。只有仁愛的人才能以大國的身份服侍小國，所以商湯善待葛國，周文王善待昆夷。只有智慧的人才能以小國的身份侍奉大國，所以周太王（古公亶父）服從獫鬻，勾踐服從吳國。以大國的身份服侍小國的人，是以遵守天道為樂的人；以小國的身份服從大國的人，是敬畏天威的人。以遵守天道為樂的人能夠保護好天下，敬畏天威的人能夠保護好自己的國家。《詩經》上說：『敬畏天的威嚴，因此便得到保全。』」

宣王說：「說得真高明呀！可是我有個毛病，我喜歡鬥勇，恐怕不能服侍別國。」

孟子回答說：「那就請大王您不要鬥小勇。有人撫着把劍，瞪着眼睛說：『他哪敢抵擋我！』這只是匹夫之勇，只能對付一個人。請大王您鬥大勇！

And thereby a teacher

That he might assist God in loving them

In all the four quarters of the world, for the guilty and the innocent, the burden falls on me alone

Who in the whole world would dare to transgress?'

"Once there was a villain who bullied people around; King Wu of Zhou found it disgraceful. This was the valor of King Wu. In one outburst of rage, he too brought peace to the people of the world. Now if you too will bring peace to the people of the world in a single outburst of rage, then the people will fear only that you are not courageous enough." (Chapter 2.3)

Contemporary interpretation:

In this passage Mencius explains the diplomatic measures to be adopted based upon the principle of benevolent governance. The ruler of a big state should take pleasure in helping others in the same way heaven cherishes living things and treats the smaller states with benevolence. The ruler of a small state, instead of trying to challenge the order the big state brings, should revere the big state in the same way he reveres heaven and submit sensibly to the order set up by the big state. In this way, the big state, assisted by small states, can become the guardian of the world, while the small states that enjoy the

「《詩經》上說：『文王赫然發怒，於是整頓軍隊，阻擋徂國的兵馬，以增添周國的福祐，報答各國對周國的嚮往。』

「《尚書》說：『天降生了百姓，為他們設置了君主，也設置了教師，只是為了讓他們來幫助上帝寵佑百姓的。四方的百姓有罪還是無罪，都由我來負責，天下哪個敢越職胡作妄為呢？』當時有一人在天下橫行霸道，周武王以此為恥。這就是武王的大勇。武王也一怒而令天下百姓得到安寧。現在大王您如果也一怒而令天下百姓得到安寧，那天下百姓還惟恐大王您不好鬥勇呢！」

【時析】

在這一節，孟子根據王道或仁政原則來處理國際關係。對於大國來說，應該以天的好生之德為樂，以仁愛來善待小國；小國應該敬畏天的威嚴，理智地服從大國帶來的秩序，而不是挑戰這種秩序。這樣做，大國就可以得到小國的支援，保護天下；小國就可以得到大國支持，獲得安全。這樣，天下就能夠享有和平。否則，小國不服大國，大國不能保護天下；小國得罪大國，引來滅國之禍。

support of the big state can obtain security. Then the world can live in peace and mutual friendship. If, however, the small state refuses to obey the big state, the big state won't be able to protect the world; so, if the small state offends the big state, they both will face annihilation.

King Xuan thought that the governance measures suggested by Mencius were in principle good yet sounded impractical; he suggested using force to overpower other states. Mencius, once again, took a rhetoric detour with him to get back to the discussion of benevolent diplomatic principles. Mencius picked up his idea of "boldness" and revamped it into a noble moral emotion of "indignation." He then used King Wu's military intervention resulting from indignation as an example to illustrate the difference between the truly courageous action by force to save people from hardship and the reckless aggression fueled by antagonism. Mencius was not against wars in general, but his emphasis was always on people's livelihoods and he upheld the principle of humanistic intervention, which places human rights above sovereignty in any deliberation on military action.

Mencius's view on how big and small countries should treat each other still speaks to our times. It would have been self-

　　齊宣王提出勇，是認為孟子講的雖好，但不切實際，他齊宣王要用拳頭來作為外交的原則，威服他國。孟子的回應，是繞着圈子又把他引到仁政的外交原則裏，對「勇」這個詞作了一番改造，指出真正的「大勇」，是像周武王那樣的仁者之勇，使用武力只是為了討伐無道，救民於水火之中，而不是濫攻濫伐。孟子並不是一概反對戰爭的，他以民生為重，有「人權高於主權」的人道主義干預原則。孟子的大國小國相處之道，對今天仍然有啟發作用。像伊拉克、朝鮮這樣的小國，如果挑戰二戰後美國形成的秩序，便會受到懲罰，國破家亡為期不遠。即使像俄羅斯這樣的大國，如果挑戰或破壞既有秩序，也會遭來各國的封鎖。至於大國，像美國這樣，政策經常隨着總統換屆而變化無常，對一些小國不能做到有始有終，總會有小國不服它，因此它現在「保護」天下就越來越難了。至於孟子所說的以有道伐無道的「大勇」，「人權高於主權」式的正義戰爭論，在當代也有鮮活的例子。只不過在當今複雜的國際權力格局下，常常是越干預越亂而已。

十一

　　孟子曰：「桀紂之失天下也，

destructive for small countries like Iraq and North Korea to seek to challenge the order set up by the US after the Second World War. Even if a major political power like Russia sought to damage the existing order, other countries would join hands to boycott it. Even a powerful country like the US, whose policies always change on the change of presidents, now has many small countries doubt its integrity and goodwill. If these countries were gradually to lose their trust in the US, it would be very hard for the country to maintain its world order.

As for the just war theory put forward by Mencius advocating "great boldness" of just states fighting unjust states and placing "human rights above sovereignty," there are many vivid contemporary examples. However, the complicated nature of the struggles between countries these days seems to mean that the greater the intervention the greater the resulting chaos.

Eleven

Translation:

Mencius said, "Jie and Zhou lost the world because they lost the people, and the reason they lost the people was because they lost their hearts. The proper way to win the world is to

失其民也。失其民者，失其心也。得
天下有道：得其民斯得天下矣。得其
民有道，得其心斯得民矣。得其心有
道：所欲，與之聚之；所惡，勿施爾
也。民之歸仁也，猶水之就下，獸之
走壙也。故為淵驅魚者，獺也；為叢
驅爵者，鸇也；為湯、武驅民者，桀
與紂也。今天下之君有好仁者，則諸
侯皆為之驅矣；雖欲無王，不可得
已。今之欲王者，猶七年之病求三年
之艾也。苟為不畜，終身不得。苟不
志於仁，終身憂辱，以陷於死亡。
《詩》云：『其何能淑？載胥及溺。』
此之謂也。」（卷七 離婁章句上·九）

【今譯】

　　孟子說：「桀紂失去天下，是因為失去了百
姓的支持。失去百姓的支持，是因為失去了民心。
取得天下是有方法的：得到百姓的支持才能得到
天下。得到百姓的支持是有方法的，得民心才能
得百姓。得民心是有方法的：他們想得到的東西，
就為他們聚集，他們所反對的東西，就別施行。
百姓歸向仁政，就像水流到低處，獸走到曠野一
樣。所以為深淵把魚趕來的是水獺；為叢林把鳥

win the people. The proper way to win the people is to win their hearts. The proper way to win the hearts of the people is to give them what they want and not to impose on them what they don't. People are attracted to benevolent governance as water flows downward and as beasts head for the wilds. It is the otter that drives fish to the deep water, and the hawk that drives birds to the bushes: it was Jie and Zhou who drove the people to [King] Tang and [King] Wu. Now if there is one among the rulers of the states who values benevolence, the other rulers will drive the people to him. Even if he does not want to be the king of the world, he has no choice; whereas nowadays those who crave kingship of the world are in fact as inadequate as using artemisia dried only for three years to try and cure an illness suffered for seven years. If one does not store it early, one can never make good use of it. If a man has not set his heart on benevolence, he will suffer anxiety and shame all his life until he succumbs to death. The *Book of Poetry* says:

'How can they be doing any good?

They are drowning together.'

This describes well what I have said." (Chapter 7.9)

Contemporary interpretation:

In Mencius's view, the legitimacy of any regime rests on it

雀趕來的是鷹鸇；為商湯、周武王把百姓趕來的，是桀和紂。現在天下的君主中，如果有喜歡仁義的，那麼其他諸侯就會為他把百姓趕來，即使他不想一統天下也不行。不過現在想要一統天下的人，都好像患了七年的病，要用三年的陳艾來醫治。倘若平時不積蓄，那一輩子休想得到醫治。倘若無意行仁政，那就會一輩子都擔憂受辱，以至於完蛋。《詩經》說：『還能好到哪兒去？不過是大家一塊兒落水淹死罷了。』說的就是這種情況。」

【時析】

　　孟子認為，政權的合法性歸根結底在得民心與否，百姓所喜的事就做，百姓所惡的事就不做，百姓的需要要滿足，百姓的喜怒要考慮。孟子說「得其心斯得民矣」，講的是，要掌握民情、民意，以及獲得民心，才能做好管治。從孟子的所論可自然地得出，如果百姓「所欲」不僅包括民生內容，還包括其他方面，如言論自由、思想自由，那麼統治者也得滿足這些「欲望」。

十二

　　齊人伐燕，勝之。宣王問曰：「或

being recognized by the people. The ruler should do whatever pleases the people and refrain from doing whatever annoys them. The ruler should also seek to satisfy the people's needs and care about their likes and dislikes. Mencius said in the above passage, "The proper way to win the people is to win their hearts." The key to good governance is to have a good understanding of public feeling and public opinion, and to win the hearts of the people.

We can reasonably infer from Mencius's arguments that when people's desires go beyond livelihood issues and encompass other aspects such as freedom of speech and freedom of thought, rulers have an obligation to satisfy their demands.

Twelve

Translation:

The armies of Qi attacked and defeated Yan. King Xuan said, "Some advised me against annexing Yan, others asked me to do so. For a state of 10 thousand chariots to win a war against another 10 thousand chariots in just fifty days is something beyond the reach of human power. Yet if I do not annex Yan, heaven will send disaster for sure. What would you think if I decided to annex it?"

謂寡人勿取，或謂寡人取之。以萬乘之國伐萬乘之國，五旬而舉之，人力不至於此。不取，必有天殃。取之，何如？」

孟子對曰：「取之而燕民悅，則取之。古之人有行之者，武王是也。取之而燕民不悅，則勿取，古之人有行之者，文王是也。以萬乘之國伐萬乘之國，簞食壺漿以迎王師，豈有它哉？避水火也。如水益深，如火益熱，亦運而已矣。」（卷二 梁惠王章句下·十）

【今譯】

齊國人攻打燕國，打贏了。宣王問孟子：「有人勸我不要吞併燕國，有人勸我吞併燕國。以一個擁有萬輛兵車的大國去攻打一個同樣擁有萬輛兵車的大國，只用五十天就打了下來，光憑人力是做不到這個地步的。如果不吞併燕國，老天一定會降下災禍，不如把它吞併了，如何？」

孟子回答說：「如果吞併了燕國而它的百姓很高興，那麼就吞併它吧。古代的人有這樣做的，

Mencius answered, "If the people of Yan will be pleased by your annexation, then do it. There were ancient rulers who followed this course of action; King Wu was one example. If the people of Yan will not be pleased by your annexation, then don't do it. There were ancient rulers who followed this course of action; King Wen was one example. When a state of 10 thousand chariots attacks another of 10 thousand and its armies are met by people welcoming them with food and drink, what other reasons can there be? They are turning towards that state hoping to flee from flood or fire. But if the flood turns out to be deeper and the fire hotter in that state, they will surely turn back." (Chapter 2.10)

Contemporary interpretation:

In the fifth year of King Xuan of Qi (315 BC), King Kuai of Yan was influenced by others to abdicate and gave his throne to his minister Xian Zi Zhi. The incident caused civil unrest and the state of Qi took this chance to wage a war against Yan. King Xuan claimed victory and asked Mencius whether he should annex Yan. Mencius advised him to follow the principle of benevolent governance and put the desires and wishes of the people of Yan as his highest concern in his deliberation over annexation. Mencius said if the people of Yan wished to be annexed, then it would be good to do so; on the other hand, if

周武王就是這樣。如果吞併了燕國但它的百姓不高興，那就別吞併。古代的人有這樣做的，周文王就是這樣。擁有萬輛兵車的齊國去攻打擁有萬輛兵車的燕國，燕國的百姓卻用竹筐裝着飯、用壺盛着酒漿來歡迎您的軍隊，這難道還有別的原因嗎？百姓這麼做只是為躲避水深火熱的處境罷了。如果水更深，火更熱，那他們也就只好再跑掉了。」

【時析】

　　齊宣王五年（前 315 年），燕王噲受禪讓思想影響，將權力讓給臣相子之，結果引發內亂。齊國趁機出兵，大獲全勝。齊宣王諮詢孟子，是否可以兼併燕國。孟子說了兼併的幾個條件，是從仁政出發，將燕國的民心民意作為兼併與否的前提。如果燕國百姓樂意被兼併，那就兼併；如果他們認為齊國比以前更糟，那就不要兼併。

　　孟子以民意為準則，當然有其崇高的理想。但是，民意如何體現？如何量化？如何能夠比較客觀地證明民心向背？孟子卻沒有提出解答。如果民意只是一個抽象概念，又焉知齊國不能操縱燕國民意，或者分化燕國民意，使之為我所用，

the people of Yan thought that annexation would make things worse for them, then annexation was not desirable.

For Mencius, to take the people's desires as the criterion for annexation is undeniably a righteous thought. However, how do the people's desires express themselves? Are there quantifiable or objective measures to verify the people's desires? For these questions, Mencius didn't offer an answer. If "the people's desires" remained an obscure concept, the state of Qi might have used it to justify its annexation ambition — by manipulating or splitting the opinions of the Yan people.

The modern international political system has its origins in the Thirty Years' War which took place from 1618-1648. The treatises signed in Westphalia as a result of the war established the inviolable sovereignty of the state. In our times, the Kosovo War marked the Western powers' change of position on the principle of sovereignty and advocacy of "human rights above sovereignty." This could end up opening a back door for superpowers to forcefully intervene in other countries.

In chapter 2.11 of *Mencius*, it is told that after King Xuan of Qi annexed Yan, other states joined hands in preparing to fight against the annexation. King Xuan thus sought advice from

從而使佔領合法化？

現代國際體系，源於歐洲新舊教各國在 1618-1648 三十年戰爭，於德國威斯特伐利亞所簽訂的條約，承認主權第一，不得侵犯。當代科索沃戰爭，西方轉倡「人權高於主權」，對主權原則作了調整，但也可能為後來強國武力干涉他國留下後門。

在《孟子》梁惠王 2.11，齊宣王佔領燕國後，諸侯團結起來準備武裝干涉，對齊不利。宣王召見孟子問對策，孟子建議他在燕國實行仁政，想燕國百姓之所想，而不是燒殺搶掠，毀人宗廟。孟子建議，與燕國人一起選立一位君主然後撤兵，這樣各國也就沒有了干涉的藉口。

但孟子的仁政主張齊宣王沒有聽從，結果「燕人畔」（反叛），後來燕人在樂毅的帶領下攻入齊國，齊國幾乎亡國，元氣大傷，從此走上下坡路，不復往日的強盛。從孟子的建議可以看到，在仁政理念的主導下，他的正義戰爭論的一個主要元素，就是要看民意，以人民是否安定幸福為宗旨，這和掠奪、殖民戰爭是不同的。

Mencius. Mencius advised him to adopt benevolent governance and rule in accordance with the wishes of the people, and not to kill and plunder or ruin Yan's ancestral temple. Mencius proposed that he should elect a new ruler together with the Yan people and then withdraw his troops, so that other countries had no excuse for intervention. However, King Xuan did not follow Mencius's advice. In the end, Le Yi led the army of Yan to invade Qi. Qi was nearly annihilated and from then on, the state's power declined and never recovered. Mencius's advice to be guided by benevolent governance shows that whether a war is just or not depends on the will of the people and whether it is likely to lead to long-term stability and happiness for the people. We should be careful not to confuse the idea of a just war with those who regard wars merely as the means to plunder or colonize other countries.

In our times, even for a country as powerful and as experienced at battles as the US when facing small nations like Afghanistan and Iraq, without a Mencius-style just war theory — lacking support by the people and being unable to withdraw troops in a timely manner after the election of new leaders in the occupied country — it will find it costly to sustain the war and difficult to achieve its initial aims. As a result, the country's own national strength will be undermined

當代，即使是美國這樣經常打仗的大國，面對阿富汗、伊拉克這樣的小國，沒有孟子式的正義戰爭理論，不遵從民意，不在被佔國選出新領導人後及時撤走，維持的成本也會非常高昂，而且很難達到原有的目的，反而耗掉了自身的國力，犧牲了本國人民的福祉。小布希時期美國花了五六萬億美元打阿富汗戰爭、伊拉克戰爭，卻所獲不多，反而成為美國實力由巔峰下落的轉捩點。

十三

孟子曰：「天時不如地利，地利不如人和。三里之城，七里之郭，環而攻之而不勝；夫環而攻之，必有得天時者矣，然而不勝者，是天時不如地利也。城非不高也，池非不深也，兵革非不堅利也，米粟非不多也，委而去之，是地利不如人和也。故曰：域民不以封疆之界，固國不以山溪之險，威天下不以兵革之利。得道者多助，失道者寡助。寡助之至，親戚畔之；多助之至，天下順之。以天下之所順，攻親戚之所畔，故君子有不

and the welfare of its own people hurt. That was the case with President G.W. Bush who spent almost 6,000 billion US dollars on the war in Afghanistan and Iraq but did not gain much from it. In fact, it marked a watershed in the downturn of US power from its peak.

Thirteen

Translation:

Mencius said, "Heaven's timely weather is not as critical as the environmental advantages benefited from the earth, and the environmental advantages benefited from the earth are not as critical as the harmony among people. Suppose an army encircled a city with a three-mile inner wall and a seven-mile outer wall, and still failed to capture it. During such a siege there should be time of fair weather, yet it still failed. This shows that the weather is not as critical as environmental advantages benefited from the earth.

At other times, even though the walls of the city are high and the moats are deep, the weapons are sharp and armor is strong, and the supply of food is plentiful, the defenders, nevertheless, abandon the city. This is because the environmental advantages are not as critical as the harmony among people.

戰，戰必勝矣。」（卷四 公孫丑章句下‧
一）

【今譯】

　　孟子說：「天時比不上地利，地利比不上人
和。譬如一座小城，內城邊長只有三里，外城
邊長只有七里，敵人圍攻它卻攻不下。他們圍攻
它，一定能得到有利的天時，但卻勝不了，這表
明天時比不上地利。又譬如另一城，城牆不是不
高，壕溝不是不深，兵器不是不鋒利，糧食不是
不多，城裏的人卻棄城而逃，這說明地利比不上
人和。所以說：圈住人民不靠邊疆的界限，保護
國家不靠山河的險峻，威服天下不靠兵器的鋒
利。得到道義的，支持的人就多；失去道義的，
支持的人就少。少到極致，連內親外戚都會背叛
他；多到極致，全天下的人都會歸順他。用天下
所歸順的優勢，來攻打連親戚都背叛的劣勢，哪
還有不勝的？所以君子要麼不打，一打就必定勝
利。」

【時析】

　　這一段話是孟子的名篇。說明決定戰爭勝負
的關鍵是民心向背，得民心者得天下，仁者無
敵。諸侯讀了這段話，估計都會想一想要不要實

"Therefore, it is said: it is not boundary markers that retain one's people; it is not mountains and ravines that secure one's state; it is not fine weapons and armor that inspire awe around the world. Those who have mastered the Way will have many supporters, while those who have lost it will have just a few. In extreme cases, those who have few supporters might be abandoned even by their own families, while those with many supporters will be submitted to by the whole world. Hence, a gentleman does not go to war unless it is certain for him to win; for the whole world is willing to submit to him while his opponent is being abandoned even by his own family." (Chapter 4.1)

Contemporary interpretation:

This passage is one of Mencius's most famous texts. It serves to illustrate how the support of the people is the key to winning wars. If a ruler wins the hearts of the people by benevolence, he will become the king who unifies the whole world and in doing so become matchless. Having read this passage, rulers of the vassal states would give great thought to the practice of benevolent governance.

A ruler can win the hearts of his own people, or he can win

行仁政了。

得民心有在國內的，有在國外的。統治者在國內得民心，人民和他一條心，支持他，上下團結一心，就擁有強大的力量。

國外得民心，就能獲得一些國家的同情，甚至獲得外援。比如在二戰期間，蘇聯政府改變了對僑民的政策、對宗教的政策，緩和了內部矛盾，使國內團結，同時對英、美示好，與之結盟，爭取援助，最終與盟國一起打敗了德國納粹。

薩達姆，對內鎮壓民眾，大搞裙帶關係，將一個兩伊戰爭前繁榮的伊拉克變成了一個凋敝的國度，對外侵佔科威特，終於招來美國的攻打。大敵當前，薩達姆的發言人還狂吹反美，說伊拉克軍隊牢不可克，結果剛一開打，高級將領就紛紛投降，薩達姆的親信全都背叛了他。原來他們早就被美國出錢買通，早已作好稻粱謀了。這就是一個活生生的「親戚之所畔」的例子。

如果不仁，在內將人民分成敵我，讓他們互相殘殺，在外干涉，到處搞顛覆，就會招來敵人，內不悅，外不來。

the hearts of people of other countries. Winning the hearts of his fellow countrymen may help to unify his people and strengthen his power, while winning the hearts of foreigners may gain sympathy or even assistance from other countries. For instance, during the Second World War, the government of the Soviet Union revised its policies on overseas citizens and religion and succeeded in alleviating tensions among people. At the same time, it showed goodwill to Britain and America, allied with and got assistance from them, leading to the defeat of Nazi Germany. In notable contrast, Saddam Hussein of Iraq repressed his people and engaged in nepotism, pushing the once prosperous Iraq into withering decline. Ignoring the turmoil in the country, he invaded Kuwait and thus provoked the attack by the US. Worse still, facing such a powerful enemy, his spokesman expressed strong anti-American views and boasted about the strength of the Iraqi Army. Soon after the war broke out, many of his top officials surrendered and Saddam Hussein was betrayed by his own confidants who had long been bribed by America. What a case of abandonment by family!

We can now see how a tyrant might split the people internally and have them kill one another, while externally he might intervene and subvert other countries, thus making enemies

十四

萬章曰：「堯以天下與舜，有諸？」孟子曰：「否，天子不能以天下與人。」「然則舜有天下也，孰與之？」曰：「天與之。」「天與之者，諄諄然命之乎？」曰：「否，天不言，以行與事示之而已矣。」曰：「以行與事示之者，如之何？」曰：「天子能薦人於天，不能使天與之天下；諸侯能薦人於天子，不能使天子與之諸侯；大夫能薦人於諸侯，不能使諸侯與之大夫。昔者堯薦舜於天而天受之，暴之於民而民受之。故曰，天不言，以行與事示之而已矣。」曰：「敢問薦之於天而天受之，暴之於民而民受之，如何？」曰：「使之主祭而百神享之，是天受之。使之主事而事治，百姓安之，是民受之也。天與之，人與之，故曰：天子不能以天下與人。舜相堯，二十有八載，非人之所能為也，天也。堯崩，三年之喪畢，舜避堯之子於南河之南。天下諸侯朝覲者，不之堯之子而之舜；訟獄者，不之堯之子而之舜；謳歌者，

everywhere and creating hostility within and beyond his borders.

Fourteen

Translation:

Wan Zhang said, "Is it true that Yao gave the world to Shun?"

Mencius said, "No. The Son of Heaven cannot bestow the world upon anyone."

"In that case, who gave the world to him?"

"Heaven bestowed it upon him."

"You say heaven bestowed it upon him, but did heaven give him repeated instructions?"

"No," said Mencius. "Heaven does not speak. It simply reveals itself through acts and deeds."

"How does heaven reveal itself through acts and deeds?"

Mencius said, "The Son of Heaven may recommend a

不謳歌堯之子而謳歌舜；故曰『天』也。夫然後之中國，踐天子位焉。而居堯之宮，逼堯之子，是『篡』也，非『天與』也。《泰誓》曰：『天視自我民視，天聽自我民聽。』此之謂也。」（卷九 萬章章句上・五）

【今譯】

萬章問：「堯把天下給了舜，有這回事嗎？」孟子說：「沒有的事，天子是不能把天下給人的。」萬章問：「那麼舜得有天下，是誰給他的呢？」孟子說：「是天給他的。」萬章問：「天給他，是說天親口叮囑告訴他的嗎？」孟子說：「不是，天不說話，天只是以行動和事蹟顯示而已。」

萬章問：「以行動和事蹟顯示，是怎麼回事？」孟子說：「天子可以向天推薦人選，但不能強使天把天下交給這個人選；諸侯能向天子推薦人選，但不能強使天子賜予這人諸侯的爵位；大夫能向諸侯推薦人選，但不能強使諸侯賜予這人大夫的職位。從前堯向天推薦舜，天接受了舜，堯把舜公示給了百姓，百姓接受了舜。所以說：天不說話，只是以行動和事蹟顯示其意志罷了。」

successor to heaven but cannot make heaven bestow the world upon him. The rulers of the states may recommend their successors to the Son of Heaven, but they cannot make him bestow their states upon them.

Ministers may recommend successors to the rulers of the states, but they cannot make their rulers bestow their ranks upon them. In the past, Yao recommended Shun to heaven and heaven accepted him; he presented him to the people and the people accepted him. That is why we say heaven does not speak, and it simply reveals itself through acts and deeds."

"May I ask how Shun was recommended to heaven and how do we know heaven accepted him? And how was Shun presented to the people and how do we know the people accepted him?"

Mencius said, "He was asked to conduct the sacrifices and all the gods accepted them gladly; this shows heaven accepted him. He was asked to manage public affairs, and public affairs were kept in order and the people were satisfied; this shows the people accepted him. Heaven gave the world to Shun and the people gave the world to Shun. This is why I say that the Son of Heaven cannot bestow the world upon anyone."

　　萬章問：「請問向天推薦而天接受，向百姓公示而百姓接受，是怎麼回事？」孟子說：「堯讓舜主持祭祀而百神享受了，這表明天接受了舜。堯讓舜主持事務而事務辦好了，讓百姓安寧，這表明百姓接受了舜。這是天給了他，百姓給了他，所以說：天子不能私相授受，把天下給人。舜給堯當臣子，有二十八年之久，這不是一般人能夠做到的，一定是出自於天意。堯逝世了，舜守了三年的喪，之後為避開堯的兒子而到了南河以南。天下朝覲天子的諸侯，不去找堯的兒子而來找舜；要訴訟的人，不去找堯的兒子而來找舜；歌頌的人，不歌頌堯的兒子而歌頌舜。所以說這是『天意』。這之後舜才回到京城，登上天子的寶座。如果他當初就搬進堯的宮殿，趕跑堯的兒子，那就是『篡奪』，而不是『天賜』了。《泰誓》說：『老天所見來自我百姓所見，老天所聞來自我百姓所聞。』就是這個意思。」

【時析】

　　孟子和萬章關於政權禪讓的討論，很可能跟當時燕王噲讓國於相子之引起的悲劇有關。噲受當時禪讓思潮的影響，把權力讓給臣相子之，結果引起內亂，召來齊國干涉，最終搞得家破國亡。這對禪讓思潮是一大打擊。孟子圈子裏也就此展

"Shun assisted Yao for twenty-eight years, man alone cannot achieve such a thing — it was heaven's deed. Yao died, and after observing the three-year period of mourning Shun withdrew to the south of Nan He in order to leave the way open to Yao's son. But the rulers of the states did not attend the court of Yao's son, and went instead to Shun; people who had disputes did not seek advice from Yao's son, but went instead to Shun; ballad singers did not sing praises to Yao's son, but sang instead of Shun. This is why I say it was the deed of heaven. Only afterwards did Shun return to the central states and mount the throne. Had he simply moved to Yao's palace at the beginning and ousted his son, it would have been usurpation, not the gift of heaven. Tai Shi says:

'Heaven sees through my people's sight,

Heaven hears through my people's ears.'

This describes well what I said." (Chapter 9.5)

Contemporary interpretation:

The discussion between Mencius and Wan Zhang on the abdication of political power might have been provoked by the tragic story of King Kuai of Yan, who was persuaded to offer his throne to his chief minister, Zi Zhi. His abdication, however, resulted in civil war and invasion by the state of Qi, and eventually Yan's annihilation. The case of King Kuai was a

開了討論，關鍵是權力合法性的來源問題。

孟子認為，天子只是代替天管理、經營天下（相當於管家的職務），因此不能私相授受，把天下轉讓給別人，一定要經過天的同意。但是天無言，怎麼知道天是不是同意呢？那就得從天（所選者）的行為和事件（事蹟）去領會天的意思了。如果人民都接受，那就證明這是天所選的天子。

這裏，民意是最重要的、決定性的因素。也就是說，「天視自我民視，天聽自我民聽」，天是根據民心民意選擇天子的，不管這個天子是不是前任天子的兒子（這只是一個形式）。

問題在這個民心「民意」（可換算成「天意」）如何體現，在小社會裏比較容易瞭解大多數的意見，在資訊未能流通的大國家裏，人數眾多，就較難掌握民意，更有甚者是操縱或偽造民意。

民國初年，袁世凱不就是根據偽造的「民意」當皇帝的嗎？德國希特勒不就是通過操縱方法激發出來的民意發動戰爭的嗎？當代試圖通過所謂

big blow to the support of the idea of abdication and prompted Mencius's associates to discuss the topic of legitimacy of political power.

According to Mencius, the Son of Heaven only manages the world on behalf of heaven (equivalent to the work of a butler) and does not have the power to offer the state to others. To do so, he must seek consent from heaven. Yet heaven never speaks, so how can we know if heaven gives consent or not? Mencius claims that heaven's consent can be grasped via the deeds of the chosen one: if the people accept the governance of the ruler, then this proves that he is the chosen one. For Mencius, the preference of the people serves as the factor of utmost importance for the selection of the ruler. "Heaven sees through my people's sight, heaven hears through my people's ears," the one who can win the people's heart and is thus preferred by the people is the one to be chosen by heaven as the Son of Heaven. Whether or not the successor of the throne is the son of the previous ruler is irrelevant to his legitimacy of power.

Doubt, however, might arise about how the opinions of the people can be represented. In a small community, decisions can be made according to the opinion of the majority. In

「科學的」方法搞「民意調查」，到底有多少準確性呢？相對來說，現代的發明——選票——可能是一個較好的辦法，它以和平的方式替換領導人，終結了以往的暴力循環史。

在孟子的時代，天以「行和事」來確立天子，也就是以政績和名望來選領導人，含有今天所謂「政績合法性」或「政績認受性」的意思。舜就是一個典型例子。在當代中國也仍是如此，這是跟西方選票制不同的選舉法，前幾年一些中國學者將這稱為「禪讓制」，還是有一些道理的。

十五

齊宣王問曰：「湯放桀，武王伐紂，有諸？」

孟子對曰：「於傳有之。」

曰：「臣弒其君，可乎？」

曰：「賊仁者謂之『賊』，賊義者謂之『殘』。殘賊之人謂之『一

a large country with poor communications and a huge population, it is difficult to gauge the opinion of the people. In such situations, public opinion may even be manipulated or forged. Wasn't it true that in the early years of the Republic of China, Yuan Shi-kai proclaimed himself as emperor based on falsified public opinion? Wasn't it true that Germany's Hitler manipulated public opinion to launch war? We may even question the accuracy of the so-called "scientific" opinion polls. Perhaps, the modern invention of "voting" offers us a better method of enabling the peaceful change of political leadership, and in this way ending the violent cycles of history that traditionally accompanied the change of reigns.

In Mencius's era, the ruler established his heaven-bestowed authority through his actions and conduct. In other words, political achievement and the reputation of the candidate were seen as important criteria for choosing the ruler, and the enthronement of Shun offers a classic example. The method may be rephrased in modern terms as "political legitimacy by political achievement," which is still applicable to the modern Chinese selection of political leadership — an alternative to the Western vote-based election system. This is why some Chinese scholars named the modern change of political power in China as "the abdication system."

夫 』。聞誅一夫紂矣，未聞弒君也。」

（卷二 梁惠王章句下・八）

【今譯】

齊宣王問：「商湯趕跑了夏桀，周武王討伐了商紂王，有這樣的事嗎？」

孟子回答說：「史書上有這樣的記載。」

宣王問：「臣子殺害自己的君主，可以嗎？」

孟子說：「危害仁的人叫做『賊』，危害義的人叫做『殘』。既『殘』又『賊』的人叫做『獨夫』。我只聽說過周武王誅殺了獨夫紂，沒有聽說過他殺害了他的君主。」

【時析】

孟子被一些知識份子稱為「儒家左派」，革命性很強。這段話據說也曾被明朝皇帝朱元璋刪除過。由於孟子將仁政強調到極致，因此為了百姓得到仁政，不惜支持用暴力手段處理政權轉移問題。以仁政之暴易虐政之暴，以王道之暴易霸道之暴，但由於一些觀念缺乏嚴格的定義，或者

Fifteen

Translation:

King Xuan of Qi asked, "Is it true that Tang banished Jie and that King Wu attacked Zhou?" Mencius replied, "It is so recorded in history books." "Is it permissible for an official to murder his ruler?" Mencius said, "A man who ruins benevolence is called a culprit; a man who ruins righteousness is called a brute. A man who is both a culprit and a brute is called a villain. I have heard of the execution of a villain named Zhou, and yet I have not heard of any murder of a ruler." (Chapter 2.8)

Contemporary interpretation:

Some scholars call Mencius the "Confucian leftist," implying that he is remarkably revolutionary in spirit. Some say that this passage was once removed by the Ming emperor Zhu Yuan-zhang. Although Mencius placed utmost emphasis on the governance of benevolence, he was still in support of using necessary forceful means to overthrow tyrant regimes in order for benevolent governance to be carried out. Nevertheless, as his idea for just wars was not well delineated, it could hardly be put into practice without the risk of being misused. As we see from history, his idea was used by hypocrites or tyrants as a pretext for overthrowing and killing monarchs.

說，只能定性，難以操作，所以在後世反而給一些偽善者或暴君提供了造反左弒君的藉口。

　　推翻前朝統治的革命，在中國每隔兩三百年就要來一次，被人們稱作「王朝循環」，實際上是由家族專權造成的。從商湯革命開始，到周武伐紂，孟子已領會革命的原因和革命成功的條件，就是民心問題，但他不可能分析到民心背後的政治、經濟、社會結構的總體問題。民心只是一時的心理或情緒反應，而王朝興衰、革命發生是有長時段的歷史規則的。每一朝代都由革命而來，針對前朝弊端進行改革，前幾代君主大都能奮發有為，官吏較為清廉，中間幾代就開始歌舞昇平，吏治腐敗，矛盾越積越多越深，最後幾代就事故頻生，社會全面潰爛，一旦內部或外部哪個環節出了問題，來不及修補應對，革命又起，舊朝亡，新朝立，又開始新一輪循環。

　　孟子強調以革命手段換掉暴君，但是，誰來作這個判斷？誰有權來決定這個君是「一夫」並得以「誅」之？這往往就成了一個道德藉口，缺乏嚴格的準則。後世軍閥發動戰爭時（如三國，如隋唐之際），往往都要把自己標榜為「仁義之師」，將討戰檄文寫得特別道德化，說自己是王

In ancient China, revolutions broke out against hegemonic rulers every two to three hundred years. People refer to this phenomenon of clan-based hegemony as "Cycles of Dynasties. Mencius learned from past revolutions, such as the Shang Tang Revolution and King Wu's defeat of Zhou, and he concluded that popular sentiment was a major factor in any successful revolutionary attempt. However, it was not possible for him to see the problems of the social, political and economic infrastructure involved. Public sentiment just reflects emotional reactions at a particular time, while dynastic destiny and revolution follow long-term historical patterns. While every dynasty was born of an uprising and aimed to cure the ills of the previous dynasty, its early emperors were mostly enterprising and the government was comparatively uncorrupted. After a few generations of peace and affluence, however, government officials succumbed to corruption, conflicts of interest accumulated and grievances were heard everywhere. During the last years of a dynasty, society was in turmoil and the slightest problems on domestic or external fronts — if not dealt with at once — would trigger a revolt leading to the collapse of the old order and the establishment of a new one. And in such a way, the cycle continues.

While Mencius endorsed the use of force against tyrants, the

者之師，來討伐「無道」的昏君。史書寫改朝換代，對其原因也常常沒有清晰的、深入的、客觀的探討，往往是以道德語言來代替分析，譴責無道、歌頌有道了事。

西方以前也有朝代更替，改朝換代也常常以武力進行，但隨着進入現代化，改用政黨輪流坐莊制或投票制這類較文明的民主方法，就基本告別了以暴易暴的政權更替方式，免除了流血衝突和大規模的生產力破壞。如果孟子能看到投票制，他會感到很欣慰的。

從民主的現實成效看，得到票數多的黨派並不意味着會有更理想的執政效果，這還要視乎很多外緣條件，選民質素是重要的因素。在有的文化裏，沒有規則和遵守契約的意識，比如在拉美，投票後失敗的少數派往往不服，要搞抵抗，造成社會長期動亂。在由傳統向現代過渡的社會裏，投票選舉便常常造成不穩定的狀態，有時還會引致倒退。這也從側面解釋了為甚麼當代新儒家希望能將孟子的民本思想轉化為民主思想，以避免上述由傳統向現代過渡可能出現的亂局。但很可惜，到現時為止，新儒家似乎還未找到能讓人信服的方法。

questions remained: Who was to judge? Who had the power to decide who the tyrant was and why he deserved to be killed? Since there were no clear standards for making such a decision, it easily became a moral pretext for evil actions. History shows us that all feudal lords (such as those in the Three Kingdoms period, and the period between the Sui and Tang dynasties) when waging war against the existing power claimed that they were fighting a just war against a corrupt tyrant. Even when we look into historical records, we can only find moralistic narratives instead of clear, critical and objective analyses of the real causes of the change of dynasties.

In the West, dynastic changes were also once carried out in a violent manner. However, since the modern era, most Western countries have adopted more civilized and democratic means to achieve regime change. Use of the electoral system and the rotation of different political parties in government has generally meant that changes in power do not result in violence, bloodshed and large-scale destruction. If Mencius were here, he would surely be gladdened to see the electoral system at work.

If we look at the actual outcomes of the democratic electoral system, we discover that the party which gets the most votes might not be the one to bring about the most desirable

　　當然，民主體制本身亦非完美無瑕，即使老牌的民主社會亦無法避免各類體制上的問題，比如：政黨輪換頻繁，未能有長久的國策規劃；口水戰政治秀華而不實，爭取選票時說得天下無敵，到執政時卻有心無力。無論如何，在民主制度的運作中，「民意可塑造、指導以及控制身為僕人而不是主人的部長」。這裏引述的英國首相丘吉爾的話與孟子的看法作比較，「英雄所見略同」。

governance. This situation results from many external factors. Among them, the civic quality of the voters is a significant one. In some cultures where there is a lack of sense of abiding by rules and contracts, such as happens in Latin America, the candidates who lose in the elections often boycott the results and bring about long-term social chaos. During the transition from a traditional to a modern political system, the electoral system often causes instability and sometimes regression. This explains why contemporary Neo-Confucians want to import Mencius's "people-centered" philosophy to modern democratic theories, in the hope that transitional chaos can be avoided. Unfortunately, they are yet to offer any convincing solutions to achieve this.

The democratic system is not perfect. Even long-established democratic societies are not without their own structural problems. Long-term national policy planning can be made difficult because of the frequent rotations of ruling parties; and while politicians may make great claims during electoral campaigns, their performance when in power often falls short of achieving them. However, it is a system whereby public opinion can "shape, guide, and control the actions of ministers who are their servants and not their masters." Winston Churchill's words here echo those of Mencius.

治國方略 *Governance Measures*

一

　　孟子曰：「民為貴，社稷次之，君為輕。是故得乎丘民而為天子；得乎天子為諸侯；得乎諸侯為大夫。諸侯危社稷，則變置；犧牲既成，粢盛既潔，祭祀以時，然而旱乾水溢，則變置社稷。」（卷十四　盡心章句下・十四）

【今譯】

　　孟子說：「百姓最寶貴，土地神和五穀神其次，君主排末尾。所以得到百姓擁護的可成為天子，得到天子支持的可成為諸侯，得到諸侯支持的可成為大夫。諸侯如果危害到土地神和五穀神，那就換掉諸侯。如果供品已經準備好了，祭品也很乾淨，祭祀的時間也很正確，但還是鬧旱災澇災，那就換掉土地神和五穀神。」

【時析】

　　孟子這一節非常著名，集中體現了他的民本思想。後來有些君主特別痛恨這一節，如朱元璋，就命令把這一節刪掉。雖然沒有設想人類出現君主的歷史過程（像霍布斯或盧梭那樣），但是，孟子卻說明了君主產生的理由，或君主存在的合

One

Translation:

Mencius said, "The people are the most important; the gods of the earth and grain come next; the ruler is the last of all. Therefore, the man who gains the support of the common people will become the Son of Heaven, the man who gains the support of the Son of Heaven will become a vassal state ruler, and the man who gains the support of the vassal state ruler will become a minister. When the vassal state ruler endangers the gods of the earth and grain, he should be replaced. When the animals being offered are well prepared, the grain being given is cleansed, and the ceremonies are performed when required, and yet droughts and floods still occur, then the gods should be replaced." (Chapter 14.14)

Contemporary interpretation:

This well-known passage in Mencius is an iconic text of his people-centered democratic thought. Some later rulers (such as Zhu Yuan-zhang) so vehemently disliked this passage that they ordered it to be deleted. Unlike Hobbes or Rousseau, who offered historical accounts for the rise of sovereigns, Mencius explained the cause for a sovereign's rise to power and his legitimacy of rule as being grounded in serving the people's interests. If a ruler fails to benefit the people, he should be

法性，在於為百姓服務，為百姓做事。如果君主做不到，不能為百姓帶來福祉，那麼，就可以把君主換掉，換一個能為百姓帶來好處的有能耐的君主。

古代帝王或諸侯建國時，都要立壇祭祀「社」、「稷」，所以，「社稷」又作為國家的代稱，如果換了君主也不能為百姓謀福利，那就連國家也可以換掉。有人把孟子叫做儒家左派，或儒家革命派，是有道理的。

孟子的說法，用在今天也不過時。現今民主講的就是重視民眾的意願，並用選舉的方法表達出來，從重視民眾的角度而言，是與民本思想一致的。就算以現代商業主要形式的企業來說，一般都重視其對社會的貢獻與價值。民本思想應用於企業經營，就是要求它們重視社會的利益。如果企業與其管理層沒有實現對社會的承擔，就會被社會揚棄。

二

　　滕文公問為國。孟子曰：「民

replaced by one who is capable of bringing happiness to his people. In ancient times, when a king or a ruler of a vassal state founded a nation or state, one of his very first duties was to build altars for the "gods of the earth" (_she_) and "gods of grain" (_ji_). Later, the term "_she ji_" was used to represent the state. If a ruler fails to serve the interests of the people, then his state should be overthrown. This explains why Mencius is considered a Confucian leftist or a Confucian revolutionist. Mencius's idea is still applicable to our society today. Contemporary democracy is about paying attention to the people's will, and to express it through elections. From the perspective that both ideas place emphasis on the people's will, democracy and people-oriented thought are comparable. Nowadays business enterprises generally consider that it is their responsibility to make a contribution and add value to society. Applying people-centered thought to the running of enterprises is to demand that they promote the interests of society. If enterprises and their management fail to do so, they will be rejected by society.

Two

Translation:

Duke Wen of Teng asked about governance.

事不可緩也。《詩》云：『晝爾於茅，宵爾索綯。亟其乘屋，其始播百穀。』民之為道也，有恆產者有恆心，無恆產者無恆心。苟無恆心，放辟邪侈，無不為已。及陷乎罪然後從而刑之，是罔民也。焉有仁人在位罔民而可為也？是故賢君必恭儉禮下，取於民有制。陽虎曰：『為富不仁矣，為仁不富矣。』

「夏后氏五十而貢，殷人七十而助，周人百畝而徹。其實皆什一也。徹者，徹也；助者，藉也。龍子曰：『治地莫善於助，莫不善於貢。』貢者，校數歲之中以為常。樂歲，粒米狼戾，多取之而不為虐，則寡取之；凶年，糞其田而不足，則必取盈焉。為民父母，使民盻盻然，將終歲勤動，不得以養其父母，又稱貸而益之，使老稚轉乎溝壑，惡在其為民父母也？夫世祿滕固行之矣。《詩》云：雨我公田，遂及我私。』惟助為有公田。由此觀之，雖周亦助也。

Mencius said, "The business of the people must be taken care of without delay. The _Book of Poetry_ says:
'By day they gather up the reeds,
By night they weave them into ropes,
They hasten to repair the roof,
Then off they go sowing the grains.'
This is the way of the common people: the hearts of those with a stable means of livelihood will feel secure, while the hearts of those who cannot secure a stable means of livelihood will not feel secure. If their hearts don't feel secure, they will go astray and turn to evil, recklessly doing anything. In such cases, if the state does nothing other than to punish them when they commit a crime, the state is entrapping its people. How can this be deemed desirable if a benevolent man is in power? Hence a good ruler should be respectful, thrifty, courteous and humble, and exercise lawful restraint whenever he has to take from his subjects. Yang Hu said, 'One who pursues wealth will not be benevolent; one who pursues benevolence will not be wealthy.'

"Under the Xia's rule, each family was allotted fifty _mus_ of land, and they paid tax according to the _gong_ system. Under the Yin's rule, each family had seventy mus of land, and they paid tax according to the _zhu_ system. Under the Zhou's rule,

「設為庠序學校以敎之。庠者養也，校者敎也，序者射也。夏曰校，殷曰序，周曰庠，學則三代共之，皆所以明人倫也。人倫明於上，小民親於下。有王者起，必來取法，是為王者師也。《詩》云：『周雖舊邦，其命維新。』文王之謂也。子力行之，亦以新子之國。」

使畢戰問井地。孟子曰：「子之君將行仁政，選擇而使子，子必勉之。夫仁政必自經界始。經界不正，井地不均，穀祿不平。是故暴君污吏必慢其經界。經界既正，分田制祿，可坐而定也。夫滕壤地褊小，將為君子焉，將為野人焉。無君子莫治野人，無野人莫養君子。請野九一而助，國中什一使自賦。卿以下必有圭田。圭田五十畝，餘夫二十五畝。死徙無出鄉，鄉田同井，出入相友，守望相助，疾病相扶持，則百姓親睦。方里而井；井九百畝，其中為公田。八家皆私百畝，同養公田。公事畢，然後敢治私事，所以別野人也。此其

each family had one hundred mus each, and they paid tax according to the _che_ system. Basically, all three systems were designed to tax at a rate of about one-tenth. The term 'che' means 'it is implemented throughout the country'; the term 'zhu' means 'to have the aid of.' Long Zi said, 'In managing the land, there is no better system than the zhu and no worse system than the gong.' In the gong system, the tax due was calculated on the average yield over several years. Thus, in good years, harvested rice was so plentiful that it went to waste, yet the government didn't take more as tax payment even though it caused no hardship for the people; while in bad years, when making effort to fertilize the fields there was still not enough yield, the government still insisted on collecting the average quota in full. If the ruler, who claimed to be the parent of the people, forced them to work non-stop, but they still could not feed their aged parents and their children; and if he forced them to take out loans to pay tax, and the elderly and young died in ditches, what was the use of having a ruler who claimed to be the parent of the people? In fact, the system of hereditary income has long been practiced in Teng. [Yet why cannot people get an income from the fields?] The _Book of Poetry_ says:

'May it rain on the common fields,

And also on our private fields.'

大略也。若夫潤澤之，則在君與子矣。」（卷五 滕文公章句上・三）

【今譯】

滕文公問怎麼治理國家。孟子說：「民生事務不能拖延。《詩經》說：『白天割茅草，晚上搓草繩。屋篷快搭好，就要播種了。』人民的基本情況，是有穩定產業才有穩定的思想，沒有穩定產業就沒有穩定的思想。倘若沒有穩定的思想，就會放縱胡來，甚麼事都幹得出。等他們犯了罪，再加以刑罰，這就等於把百姓往羅網裏趕。哪有仁愛的人做了國君，卻做這種讓百姓投入羅網的事呢？所以賢明的君主必定謙恭節儉，按禮義對待臣民，向百姓收取賦稅要有合理的制度。陽虎說過：『要想富，就不會仁，要想仁，就不會富。』

「夏朝每家五十畝地實行『貢』法，商朝每家七十畝地實行『助』法，周朝每家一百畝地實行『徹』法。名稱雖有不同，實質都是抽取十分之一。『徹』，是『通行』的意思；『助』，是『藉助』的意思。龍子說過：『治理土地，沒有比「助」更好的，沒有比「貢」更不好的。』貢，是比較若干年的收成求得一個平均數，將之作為

Only the zhu system designated common fields to families. This is why even the Zhou practiced the zhu system.

"Institutes such as _xiang, xu, xue_ or _xiao_ have been set up to educate the people. 'Xiang' means 'to nurture'; 'xiao' means 'to teach'; 'xu' means 'archery training.' During the Xia, schools were called xiao; during the Yin, they were called xu; and during the Zhou they were called xiang. The term xue ('to learn') was a common name used in these three dynasties, for their schools all served to enlighten the people about human relationships. When human relationships are properly understood by people in power, the common people will be kind to one another. Should a king arise, he will surely take this educational system as his model and you will become the teacher of a king. The _Book of Poetry_ says:
'Though Zhou was an old state
Its mandate is new.'
Here it refers to King Wen. If you wholeheartedly adopt this, you will surely renew your state."

The Duke sent his minister Bi Zhan to ask about the "well-field system." Mencius said, "Your ruler plans to implement benevolent governance and has selected you for this purpose. You must try your best. Benevolent governance always starts

不變的抽稅根據。豐收之年，糧食到處堆放，多徵收點也不算暴虐，卻並不多收；欠收之年，即使努力施肥，收成也不夠吃，卻一定要收滿那平均數。國君號稱百姓父母，使百姓整年不停地辛苦勞動，卻不能養活其父母，還得借貸來補齊賦稅，使老人小孩都餓死了拋屍露骨於山溝之中，那麼，號稱百姓父母的，其作用何在？貴族爵位俸祿的世襲，滕國早已實行，（可為甚麼百姓就不能有一定的田地收入呢？）《詩經》上說：『先給我們的公田下雨吧，再下到我們的私田裏！』只有『助』的稅制才有『公田』可言。由這點來看，就是周朝也是實行『助』的稅制的。

「（人民能吃飽飯後）國家要設立庠、序、學、校來教化人民。『庠』是『培養』的意思，『校』是『教導』的意思，『序』是『射箭』的意思。夏朝說『校』，商朝說『序』，周朝說『庠』，『學』則三個朝代都這麼說，都是用來讓人民懂得人間倫常的。上面的人把倫常搞明白了，下面的老百姓自然就會彼此親愛。如果有聖王興起，一定會來您的國家（滕國）效法取經，那（您）就可以成為聖王的國師了。《詩經》說：『周雖然是一個舊邦，其天命卻是新的。』這說的是周文王的情況。您如果力行這樣的制度，也

from the setting of land boundaries. If boundaries are not properly drawn, the division of land according to the well-field system will be not be even, and the salaries paid to officials will also be unequal. This is why a tyrant and corrupt officials always ignore the boundaries. Once the boundaries are properly set, the allocation of fields for the people and the salaries for officials can be easily settled.

"Now Teng is a very small state, but still there has to be a gentleman who rules it, and some common people who live off the fields. Without rulers there would be no way to bring order to the common people, and without the common people there would be no way to sustain the rulers. I recommend that those living in the countryside be taxed at a rate of one-ninth according to the zhu system, while those who live in the capital city be taxed at a rate of one-tenth out of what they produce. Ministers and lower officials should own fifty mus of land for sacrificial purposes. For ordinary households, each family can be given twenty-five mus more land for each extra person providing manpower. Whether for burial of those who have passed away or for resettlement, no one will go beyond his village boundary; all who live within the same well-field system will befriend each other, help each other to keep watch and take care of each other in illness. In such a way

可以使您的國家煥然一新。」

　　滕文公派畢戰來向孟子詢問井田制的問題。

　　孟子說：「您的國君想要實行仁政，選派了您來，您一定要好好幹。實行仁政，一定要從劃分田地的邊界開始。邊界劃分得不正確，井田的大小就會不均勻，官員的俸祿就會不公平，所以暴君和貪官就會放鬆對邊界的管理。邊界劃正確了，給人民分配田地，給官員制定俸祿，就容易作出決定了。滕國國土雖然狹小，卻也得有官員，有平民。沒有官員，就沒有人來管理平民。沒有平民，就沒有人來供養官員。我建議，郊野用九分抽一的『助』稅制，城市用十分之一的『貢』稅制。公卿以下的官員一定要有供祭祀的圭田，每家五十畝。如果他家還有剩餘的勞力，便每一勞力分二十五畝。無論是死了埋葬還是搬遷，都不離開本鄉。共一井田的各家，平時出入，相互友善，防禦盜賊，彼此幫助，有人生病，則加以扶持，這樣，百姓之間就親愛和睦了。方圓一里是一井，一井有九百畝田，中間的那一百畝是公田。八戶人家各有一百畝私田，他們一起耕種公田。公田裏的事情幹完後，才敢打理私田的事，這是用來區別平民的辦法。我只是說了一個大

the people will live together in peace and harmony. A unit of land according to the well-field system measures one square *li* or nine hundred mus. The central plot is owned by the state, while the eight outer plots, each of a hundred mus, are owned and farmed privately by eight households, who also join hands in farming the central state-owned plot for the state. Only when their work on the state-owned plot is done do they dare to turn to their private affairs. This is how the common people are treated.

"All of the above is just a brief outline. As for its refinement and details, I leave those to your ruler and you." (Chapter 5.3)

Contemporary interpretation:

In this passage, Mencius discusses government policies and the well-field system. Teng was a small state located to the south of Lu. When Duke Wen of Teng came to power, he wanted to strengthen the state and therefore consulted Mencius about governance. In Mencius's view, when the common people have a "stable means of livelihood their hearts will feel secure." It is therefore important to see that the people have such stable means. As far as a taxation policy was concerned, Mencius believed that the system of zhu should be adopted in the cities, where people pay one-tenth of their

略，至於怎麼調整改善，那就要靠國君和您的努力了。」

【時析】

內文這一節討論治國措施和井田制。滕國是魯國南面的一個小國，滕文公即位後，有意發展國家，就找孟子諮詢治國策略。孟子認為百姓的特點是「有恆產者有恆心」，讓百姓有產業很重要。在賦稅制度上，他認為在城裏助法（收什一稅）較好，在鄉下，實行井田制（九分之一抽稅）較好。他還提出設立學校，搞好教化。孟子把井田制理想化了，跟歷史上的井田制不完全相符。

孟子為甚麼推崇井田制？從經濟上說，光抽什一稅或九一稅亦未嘗不可。孟子可能是考慮到井田制的政治與社會功能。井田制中間的公田需要眾人一起耕種，它可以起到凝聚家族、族群、社區的作用，形成一個共同勞動的空間，有益於公共意識的建立。公田的背後可能還有人道主義的關懷，比如對孤兒寡母、弱勢群體的關心。從儒家傳統上推崇公田來說，儒家自身是含有一些社會主義成份的。當然，孟子並不是社會主義者，並不是主張公有制。他還是主張要讓百姓有穩固的私產，認為這樣才有「恆心」，才能保障社會

private produce as tax, while the well-field system should be adopted in rural areas, where villagers deliver one-ninth of their agricultural yield to the government as tax. Mencius also proposed the setting up of schools for education. But if we look into historical accounts of the well-field system, we will know that the system as depicted by Mencius was far more idealized than that which was actually implemented.

Why did Mencius think highly of the well-field system? Economically speaking, it was indeed plausible for the government to set the tax rate at one-tenth or one-ninth, but what Mencius had in mind may have been something else — the political and social functions that can be served by the system. The central plot in the well-field system was a state-owned public plot to be attended to by all members of the community. This may have been seen as helping to create a public domain of labor where social awareness could be nurtured through the collaboration within and beyond families. The system could even perhaps serve humanitarian purposes, such as offering communal assistance to those in need, including orphans, widows and other locally disadvantaged. Knowing that the well-field system had been so well-received by Confucians, we spot a socialist spirit in people's minds. Of course, in the case of Mencius, he was not

安定。井田制中的公田,為了防止各家各戶自私自利,忙完私田後才去耕公田,因此規定先一起把公田耕好。

雖然井田制後來沒有實行,但是在宗法制度下,宗族的公田制卻有遺留。宗族除了各個小家之外,還要維護整個宗族的團結和親情,比如為孤兒寡母、為考科舉的族人提供幫助,公田作為族產就起到了一定的作用。比如在徽州,族規裏就對公田的維持與管理作了規定。

但是作為族產的公田,會不會發生西方所謂「公地悲劇」呢?其實所謂公田跟公地還是有分別的。公田是由族長或長老管理的,跟沒有人專門管理的「公地」不一樣。另外,孟子特別強調要分清界限,防止慢其經界,發生侵吞、責權不明等現象,有權者不能用權侵犯別人田界,這有限制權力之意。清晰產權對大家都有好處,如果產權不清晰,就會公權私用,化公為私。

大陸改革開放近四十年,國力增長迅速,GDP 目前已居全球第二。改革開放伊始,即分開公有資產的所有權、經營權、使用權,責、權、利規定清楚,讓百姓有機會租借公有財產經營或

a socialist and he did not support public ownership. Instead, he claimed that only when the people have their own stable private property, so that their hearts will feel secure, can society as a whole remain stable. The obligation requiring everyone to work on the public plot first can be seen as a means of restraining human selfishness that might jeopardize the community as a whole.

Even though the well-field system was in the end not realized, the public field system remained as a part of the patriarchal clan system. Apart from attending to their own families, the clan members were obliged to promote unity and kinship of the bigger family, like taking care of orphans and widows as well as supporting those members who sat for the imperial examination. The public fields commonly owned by all clan members did offer an effective way to serve those purposes. For example, in Hui Zhou, the clan rules made stipulations on the management of public fields.

One may wonder whether the clan's shared ownership of the public fields might have given rise to the "tragedy of the commons," as happened in the history of the West. However, there are at least two differences that set them apart. First, the public fields were managed by the head or the senior members

使用獲利，發揮了百姓的創造性和主動性，創造
出中國經濟持續快速增長的奇跡。

　　隨着中產階級的逐漸出現，中國承認房屋等
屬於私有財產，相當於使人民有了「恆產」。人
民安居樂業，就有「恆心」，就不會天天發牢騷，
天天想着鬧革命了。在一些城市，近年來修建了
很多大型廣場，公眾可以在裏面跳舞娛樂，這也
可以說是建設社區文化和凝聚力的一種公共空間
吧。在胡溫執政期間，農民已無需交納公糧，農
村裏的老人還能每個月領到幾十元的養老金，農
村也逐漸實現了醫保，可以說，這是繼承了中國
古代「小康」的政治理念的。

三

　　子產聽鄭國之政，以其乘輿濟人
於溱、洧。孟子曰：「惠而不知為政，
歲十一月徒杠成，十二月輿梁成，民
未病涉也。君子平其政，行辟人可
也；焉得人人而濟之？故為政者，每
人而悅之，日亦不足矣。」（卷八・離
婁章句下・二）

of the clan, whereas the common land, in such as England, did not have any assigned management team. Second, Mencius stressed the importance of having clear boundaries to the land to prevent the abuse of power, so that with properly drawn boundaries problems such as infringement of property rights or unsettled ownership rights could be avoided. This is why having clearly drawn and stated property ownership rights is beneficial not only to individual property owners but to all members of a community because public properties will not then easily fall into unlawful hands.

Since China started her reform and opening-up efforts forty years ago, her economic strength has developed so rapidly that she has become the second largest economy in the world in terms of GDP. One of the reform measures introduced at the beginning of the opening-up program was to demarcate clearly the ownership, operating rights and usage rights of public assets so that the rights and responsibilities were properly clarified. This measure made people willing to exercise their operating and usage rights in order to create wealth, thus bringing about China's miraculous economic development and growth. With the rise of the middle class in China, more and more people now buy their own homes, and their ownership rights are acknowledged by the government. Once the people

【今譯】

　　子產主持鄭國的政務，用所乘的車輛幫助人們渡過溱水和洧水。孟子說：「這是小恩小惠，他也太不懂政治了。如果十一月修成過人的橋，十二月修成過車的橋，百姓就不會為過河發愁了。執政的君子只要把該管的政事管好了，出行時讓百姓避讓也可以；哪能幫人一個個地過河呢？如果執政的要一個一個地討好百姓，那他的時間就太不夠用了。」

【時析】

　　政治家做事，要從大處着眼，要有頂層設計，要有為人民謀福利的大規劃，而不要陷於具體事務，尤其不能為個人聲望討好人民而做政客，做鄉愿，用小恩小惠籠絡人心。仁政不是眉毛一把抓，而是要做好當務之急，弄清各個事項的輕重緩急，揀重大的做。如果一個領導人天天穿着一件穿了四十年的舊衣服，以顯示自己樸素，國家卻被他治理得一團糟，怨聲載道，他就是一個失職的領導人。如果一個領導人把國家治理得蒸蒸向上，欣欣向榮，只要他沒有貪贓枉法，他就是出入都坐豪華轎車，經常打高爾夫球，工資拿得高一點，生活奢侈一點，那又有甚麼關係呢？

have attained a "stable means of livelihood" and enjoy a contented life, their hearts will feel secure; and since no one will have grievances about the way they are governed, there will be little desire to overthrow the government. In recent years, mega malls have been built in more and more cities where people can entertain themselves in many ways. This seems to have become a new form of public space by means of which a local community culture and sense of belonging are gradually established among people. During the rule of (President) Hu Jintao and (Premier) Wen Jiabao, farmers no longer needed to pay tax with grain. What is more, the elderly in the villages got a small pension from the government each month and more villages were covered by medical insurance. These improvements show that the ancient political ideal of a *xiaokang* (moderately prosperous and peaceful) society is being realized in modern China.

Three

Translation:

When Zi Chan served as the chief minister of the state of Zheng, he used his carriage to take people across the Zhen and the Wei Rivers. Mencius said, "He gave people small favors, yet he did not know how to administer a government.

現在香港、澳門、新加坡這些地區和國家，有些年頭會退稅派錢，一人能發個數千元。有人說，這可以說是對人民的恩惠，政治清明，派下去的錢還是會被人們花掉，促進當地經濟；也有人說，這不過是小恩小惠，一個人幾千塊錢隨便也就花了，還不如集中起來，搞大工程，利於本地長遠發展。誰是誰非，就要看對治理哲學有怎樣的理解了。

四

孟子曰：「仁言，不如仁聲之入人深也。善政，不如善教之得民也。善政民畏之；善教民愛之。善政得民財；善教得民心。」（卷十三 盡心章句上·十四）

【今譯】

孟子說：「仁愛的言論不如仁愛的聲望更深入人心，良好的政治不如良好的教化更能獲得民心。良好的政治，百姓是出於畏懼才服從；良好的教化，百姓是出於愛好而跟從。良好的政治能贏得百姓的財富，良好的教化卻能贏得百姓的心。」

If footbridges are built by the eleventh month and carriage bridges are built by the twelfth month, no one will be distressed about how to get across rivers. If a gentleman in power runs the government properly, the people will not mind clearing the road for him to pass. Why should he have to ferry all the people across the rivers? When the one in power seeks to please everyone, he will not find enough time to perform his own proper duties." (Chapter 8.2)

Contemporary interpretation:

In order to be a good politician, a man should not preoccupy himself with trivial matters, in particular, by offering small favors to people in exchange for personal fame and support. A good politician should be able to think big and look far, so that he can make comprehensive plans in the interest of all people. Benevolent governance requires the political leader to be sensible and perceptive in judgments, knowing what is best to do in which particular situation.

If the leader wears the same old clothes for years just to show that he is a thrifty person, yet under his leadership the country runs into a mess, then we can be certain that he is inadequate as a leader. On the contrary, if a leader leads his country towards prosperity and happiness and does so with integrity,

【時析】

有些統治者在世時推出大量語錄、著作，但生前人們記不住，死後也就成了過眼雲煙。相反，仁愛的聲望往往是以身作則的結果，形象比言語更加深入人心。

一個是硬措施，一個是軟實力，後者以德感人，贏得民心。百姓活在現有政治體制中，不得不納稅支持國家，但大多是出於無奈，但如果領袖有威望，國家有魅力，國家利益與人民利益一致，教化起來也就容易讓人民信服，人民自願地支持國家，國家執行起政策來也就容易很多。

從歷史來看，政和教有時是不同步的。比如，印度在古代常常存在成百上千個小國家，但是印度教使這些國家人民的心理基礎相似，有着相近的價值觀，因此，現代印度統一起來也就比較容易。

這段引文中，有人把「仁聲」理解成「仁的音樂」，即雅樂，指一種「樂教」。言論進大腦，但音樂進心靈。比如當代西方教會中，靈恩派的音樂就很有感染力，對於薰陶人心是有一些作用

no one will bother whether he earns a substantial salary and enjoys a relatively lavish lifestyle.

Nowadays, in some Asian cities, such as Hong Kong, Macau and Singapore, people benefit from tax refunds or even cash handouts from the government every year. Some say that this is a beneficial policy backed up by an upright government, and the money will eventually be spent and will boost the local economy. At the same time, there are others who think that the social impact of such cash handouts is in no way comparable to the long-term impact of investing the whole fund into major infrastructure projects. As for the question of who is right and who is wrong, that may well depend on which philosophy of governance a person espouses.

Four

Translation:

Mencius said, "One's benevolent words do not touch people's hearts as deeply as one having a benevolent reputation. Good governance does not win over the people as thoroughly as good education. With good governance, the people submit to the ruler in awe; with good education [from him], they support the ruler out of admiration. Good governance wins over the

的。孔子也說過樂教的作用巨大。鄭衛靡靡之音大概也就是亡國之音了。

至於「善教」的內容，孟子在這裏沒有細談，結合他的主旨，應該是教給百姓儒家的道德規範。現在中國大陸所倡導的社會主義核心價值觀，共有24字如下：「富強、民主、文明、和諧，自由、平等、公正、法治，愛國、敬業、誠信、友善」。不知你能否記住？再如「八榮八恥」，也比較難記。

相比之下，新加坡的核心價值觀共有40個字，但非常有條理，簡明精要，主旨突出，記起來也容易：「國家至上、社會為先；家庭為根、社會為本；關懷扶持、尊重個人；協商共識、避免衝突；種族和諧、宗教寬容。」

五

莊暴見孟子，曰：「暴見於王，王語暴以好樂，暴未有以對也。」曰：「好樂何如？」

孟子曰：「王之好樂甚，則齊國

wealth of the people; good education wins over their hearts."
(Chapter 13.14)

Contemporary interpretation:

Some rulers like to have people read a lot of their quotations
and works during their lifetime, yet most often people do not
remember them and soon after they die their words die away,
too. On the contrary, those leaders who have a reputation of
benevolence lead by deeds, and they impress others with their
actions rather than their words. While one way is to impose
ideas through propaganda, the other is to win the people
by touching their hearts with virtuous achievements. Under
modern political systems, most people pay taxes to support
their government because it is mandatory. If, on the other hand,
the moral authority of leaders can be established, and their
government serve the interests of the public wholeheartedly,
then the people will be convinced of their ability and willingly
support their government in carrying out their policies.

Looking back at history, we may see that political and
educational development do not always go hand in hand. Let's
take the case of India as an example: in the past, hundreds
of small states co-existed in India, yet Hinduism meant the
people of these states shared a common mentality and values,

其庶幾乎？」

他日，見於王曰：「王嘗語莊子以好樂，有諸？」

王變乎色，曰：「寡人非能好先王之樂也，直好世俗之樂耳。」

曰：「王之好樂甚，則國其庶幾乎，今之樂猶古之樂也。」

曰：「可得聞與？」

曰：「獨樂樂，與人樂樂，孰樂？」

曰：「不若與人。」

曰：「與少樂樂，與眾樂樂，孰樂？」

曰：「不若與眾。」

「臣請為王言樂。今王鼓樂於

facilitating the establishment of a unified India in more modern times.

Some people take *ren sheng* (benevolent reputation) in this passage as meaning "benevolent music," since "sheng" in Chinese literally means "sound." If we adopt this interpretation, "benevolent music" would refer to an education in music, and the passage can be read in an alternative light: as words are for our brains to comprehend, music is for our hearts to be touched. An example can be drawn from the use of music in the modern Charismatic Christian tradition, which is infectious and is useful for nurturing the spiritual mind. Confucius also emphasized the importance of a musical education for the cultivation of character. That is why it was said, when decadent music was playing in the state of Zheng, it was a signal for its collapse.

Mencius did not explain in detail in this passage what makes a good education, which, in its context, should mean the education of moral virtues as espoused by Confucian tradition. Nowadays, China is promoting twenty-four socialist core values, which include prosperity, democracy, civilization, harmony, freedom, equality, justice, legality, patriotism, respect for one's profession, integrity and friendliness. Can you remember them all? There

此，百姓聞王鐘鼓之聲，管籥之音，舉疾首蹙頞而相告曰：『吾王之好鼓樂，夫何使我至於此極也？父子不相見，兄弟妻子離散。』今王田獵於此，百姓聞王車馬之音，見羽旄之美，舉疾首蹙頞而相告曰：『吾王之好田獵，夫何使我至於此極也？父子不相見，兄弟妻子離散。』此無他，不與民同樂也。

「今王鼓樂於此，百姓聞王鐘鼓之聲，管籥之音，舉欣欣然有喜色而相告曰：『吾王庶幾無疾病與，何以能鼓樂也？』今王田獵於此，百姓聞王車馬之音，見羽旄之美，舉欣欣然有喜色而相告曰：『吾王庶幾無疾病與，何以能田獵也？』此無他，與民同樂也。今王與百姓同樂，則王矣。」（卷二　梁惠王章句下・一）

【今譯】

　　齊國的大臣莊暴來見孟子，說：「我被國王召見，國王對我說他喜歡音樂，我不知道該怎麼

are also "eight honors and eight shames," which might be harder still to recall. In contrast, the core values of Singaporeans sound concise and precise: "Nation before community and society above self; family as the basic unit of society; community support and respect for the individual; consensus, not conflict; racial and religious harmony."

Five

Translation:

Zhuang Bao went to see Mencius and said, "I met with the king and he told me he loved music. I didn't know how to respond. Is it good to love music?" Mencius said, "If the king wholeheartedly loves music, then the governance of the state of Qi is not bad!"

On another day, when Mencius met with the king he said, "You told Zhuang Zi that you loved music. Is that true?" The king blushed and said, "I'm not capable of appreciating the music of the former kings. I just love popular music."

"If Your Majesty wholeheartedly loves music, then the governance of the state of Qi is not bad! The music of today is like the music of the past."

回答。」又說：「喜歡音樂好嗎？」

孟子說：「國王特別喜歡音樂，那齊國的治理就差不多了。」

後來有一天，孟子見到了齊王，孟子說：「您曾告訴莊先生說您喜歡音樂，有這回事嗎？」

國王的臉色都變了，說：「我喜歡不了古代君主的音樂，我只是喜歡世俗的音樂而已。」

孟子說：「只要您非常喜歡音樂，那國家的治理就差不多了。今天的音樂跟古時的音樂是一樣的。」

齊王問：「可以聽您說說嗎？」

孟子說：「一個人欣賞音樂，和跟別人一起欣賞音樂，哪個更快樂？」

齊王答：「跟別人一起。」

孟子問：「跟少數人一起欣賞音樂，和跟多數人一起欣賞音樂，哪個更快樂？」

"May I hear more about this?"

Mencius said, "Which gives you more joy: enjoying music alone or enjoying it in the company of others?" The king said, "In the company of others."

Mencius said, "Which gives you more joy: music in the company of a few or in the company of many?" The king said, "In the company of many."

Mencius said, "Let me tell you about enjoyment. Suppose you were having a musical performance here, and when the people heard the sound of the bells and drums, the notes of the pipes and flutes, they all frowned and said to each another, 'How come our king who loves music so much is putting us in such distress? Fathers and sons cannot see each other, and brothers and wives disperse.' Or suppose you were hunting here, and when the people heard the sound of your chariots and horses and saw your magnificent banners, they all frowned and said to each another, 'How come our king who loves hunting so much is putting us in such distress? Fathers and sons cannot see each other, and brothers and wife disperse.' The reason for their distress would simply be that you have failed to share your joy with the people.

齊王答：「跟多數人一起。」

孟子說：「請讓我跟您談談音樂（娛樂）的事情。假設國王您在這裏演奏音樂，百姓聽到了鳴鐘擊鼓，笙簫齊響，卻全都覺得頭痛，愁眉苦臉，彼此議論說：『我們國王這麼愛好音樂，卻為甚麼使我苦到這個地步呢？父子不能相見，兄弟妻子東逃西散！』假設國王您在這裏打獵，百姓聽到您車馬路過的聲音，看到了儀仗的華麗，卻都頭痛，愁眉苦臉，彼此議論說：『我們國王這麼愛好打獵，卻怎麼讓我苦到這個地步呢？父子不能相見，兄弟妻子東逃西散！』這沒有別的原因，是因為您沒有與民同樂。

「假使國王您在這裏鼓樂喧天，百姓聽到了您鳴鐘擊鼓，笙簫齊響的聲音，都興高采烈，眉開眼笑，彼此談論說：『我們的國王應該沒有生病吧，不然怎麼能鼓樂呢？』假使國王您在這裏打獵，百姓聽到您車馬經過的聲音，見到您儀仗的華麗，都眉開眼笑，興高采烈，彼此談論說：『我們的國王應該沒有生病吧，不然怎麼能打獵呢？』這沒有別的原因，只是因為您與民同樂啊！如果國王您與民同樂，就可以成為聖王征服天下了。」

"Now, suppose you were having a musical performance here, and when the people heard the sound of the bells and drums, the notes of the pipes and flutes, their faces all beamed with joy and they said, 'Our king must be in good health, otherwise how can the music be played?' Or suppose you were hunting here, and when the people heard the sound of your chariots and horses and saw your magnificent banners, their faces all beamed with joy and said, 'Our king must be in good health, otherwise how can he go hunting?' The reason would simply be that you have shared your joy with the people. "Now if Your Majesty shares your joy with the people, you become a king." (Chapter 2.1)

Contemporary interpretation:

This passage records the dialogue between Mencius and the king of Qi. The "king" referred to in the text was King Xuan of Qi.

Confucius admired the refined music of the past and condemned the popular music of Zheng as "decadent." That is why King Xuan felt uneasy when he told Mencius that he loved popular music. Mencius, nevertheless, replied, "The music of today is like the music of the past." Such a reassuring response made King Xuan willing to listen to his further

【時析】

這裏的「王」應該是指齊宣王，是孟子在齊國時與齊宣王的一番對話。

對於音樂，孔子推崇古代的雅樂，反對鄭國的流行音樂，認為「鄭聲淫」，所以齊宣王承認自己喜歡流行音樂時覺得不好意思。孟子為了推行自己的主張，說「今之樂猶古之樂也」，讓齊宣王寬心，流行音樂沒甚麼不好的，只要與民同樂就好。孟子急於匡救時弊，而不計較雅樂俗樂之別。孟子說，俗樂沒問題，沒甚麼好譴責的，同樣地，「人欲」也不要緊，人人都有欲望，關鍵是要與民同樂。只要你也想到百姓跟你欲望相同，能滿足百姓的欲望，你就有了群眾基礎，能得到人民擁護。

清朝時，皇家宮殿及別墅（如圓明園、避暑山莊）都是皇家禁苑，民眾不得入內。所以，圓明園被英法聯軍燒毀時，百姓並不覺得多麼痛惜，因為他們認為這是皇帝家的房子，與己無關——皇家從來沒有跟他們分享過。周圍的一些百姓反而進去偷走一些東西。相比之下，現今英國皇家做得好一些，其花園有時會對公眾開放。香港禮賓府（即以前的港督府）每年有一天是開

thoughts on the topic. In Mencius's view, so long as a ruler was willing to share the joy of music with the people, he (Mencius) didn't care about the difference between refined and popular music. In the same way, it is fine for a ruler to satisfy his personal desires, so long as he also shares the joy of satisfaction with the people, which means he is willing to satisfy the people's desires as if they are his own. In so doing, the ruler will be recognized and supported by the people.

In China's Qing dynasty, all the royal palaces and villas (such as Yuan Ming Garden and Chengde Mountain Resort) were highly restricted places and the people were prohibited from entering them. So when Yuan Ming Garden was burned down by the Anglo-French allied force, the people did not lament the loss — actually it was none of their business since the garden was owned by and exclusively enjoyed by the royal family. Some people even took the opportunity to break into it and take some items away. In comparison, the British Royal Family in contemporary times has managed to do better because many of its gardens are open to the public on quite a few occasions. Government House in Hong Kong (the Governor's House in the past) is open to the public on a certain day each year so that citizens have a chance to enjoy the beauty of its gardens and buildings. This is indeed a good way to

放日，市民能夠自由進入參觀，有分享和參與的機會，認識其美好後，比較容易有珍惜的感覺。

大陸這些年發展快，貧富差距拉大，一些富人蓋起豪華別墅，豪華高爾夫球場，在西湖等名勝區也搞起高級會所，只有富貴人才消費得起；公地私用，大眾享受不起，自然產生仇富心理。習近平上台後，主張走群眾路線，要跟群眾打成一片，西湖的會所也走向大眾化，首先是價格大眾化，讓普通遊客都能消費得起。這就叫與民同樂，平民不僅不會仇視，反而有可能會自覺維護那些設施。

六

孟子告齊宣王曰：「君之視臣如手足，則臣視君如腹心；君之視臣如犬馬，則臣視君如國人；君之視臣如土芥，則臣視君如寇讎。」王曰：「禮，為舊君有服。何如斯可為服矣？」曰：「諫行言聽，膏澤下於民；有故而去，則使人導之出疆，又先於其所往；去三年不反，然後收其田里。此之謂三有禮焉。如此則為之

strengthen the bond between the people and the government. In recent years, with the economic boom in China, luxurious villas and extravagant golf clubs have been built everywhere, even in renowned scenic areas like Hangzhou's West Lake. Many of these facilities, which are built on public land, are only enjoyed by the privileged few because most people simply cannot afford the outrageously expensive services offered. This has contributed to an animosity towards the rich in China. Since Xi Jinping came to power, he has advocated getting close to the masses. The recreational clubs in the West Lake area have been made accessible to ordinary people as the prices now charged are reasonable. This serves as an example of sharing the joy with people, which not only helps alleviate the problem of animosity towards the rich, but also enhances public awareness of the need to preserve public properties.

Six

Translation:

Mencius said to King Xuan of Qi, "When a ruler looks upon his officials as his hands and feet, the officials look upon the ruler as their belly and heart. When a ruler looks upon his officials as though they were his dogs and horses, the officials look upon the ruler as just another countryman. When a ruler

服矣。今也為臣，諫則不行，言則不聽，膏澤不下於民；有故而去，則君搏執之，又極之於其所往；去之日，遂收其田里。此之謂寇讎。寇讎何服之有？」（卷八 離婁章句下‧三）

【今譯】

孟子告訴齊宣王說：「如果君主把臣子視如手足，那臣子就會把君主視如腹心；如果君主把臣子看作狗馬，那臣子就會把君主看作路人。如果君主把臣子看成泥巴和雜草，臣子就會把君主看成仇敵。」宣王說：「按照禮制，臣子對老君主是要服喪的。怎麼樣才能做到服喪呢？」孟子說：「臣子所勸阻的，君主當實行，臣子的建議，君主當聽從，讓他們的恩惠施於百姓。臣子因某些原因辭職離去，君主要派人護送他平安走出邊疆，並且派人先到他要去的地方把一切安頓好。離開三年還不回來，才收回賜給他的田地房屋。這可以說是三大禮數。君主做到這幾點，臣子就應為他守喪。可是今天做臣子面對的是怎樣的呢？勸阻，不實行；建議，不聽從；恩惠，落不到百姓頭上。因某種原因要離開，君主就逮捕他，並先派人在他要去的地方斷他的後路。離開的當天，就沒收當初賜給他的田地房屋。這不是仇敵

looks upon his officials as mud and weeds, the officials look upon the ruler as an enemy."

The King said, "According to the rites, officials wear mourning for a late ruler. What should a ruler do to deserve this?"

Mencius said, "The ruler should accept criticism from his officials and take their advice so that the people can benefit from his governance. When an official has decided to resign and leave the state, the ruler should send guards to escort him to his destination and help him settle down. If after three years, he does not return, then his allotted properties can be taken back. This is called the three courtesies. If a ruler behaves like this, he deserves that his officials wear mourning for him. However, nowadays officials' criticisms are not accepted and their advice is not taken; as a result, the policies do not benefit the people. Instead, when an official wants to resign and leave the state, the ruler detains him by force and sends people to his destination to impede his move. Moreover, his properties are confiscated on the day of his departure. This is what is meant by 'enemy.' Who would mourn his enemy?" (Chapter 8.3)

Contemporary interpretation:

In comparison with the time of Confucius more than a

是甚麼？對仇敵，還服甚麼喪？」

【時析】

從孔子到孟子，過了一百多年，仕的地位已大不如昔。

諸侯對仕的態度，由尊重（對等）變成不平等。孟子這裏說的諸侯對辭職者的做法表明了這一變化。這可能是由於當時國家數目少了，仕（多是知識份子）可以出售主張的市場選擇沒有那麼多，買主減少了，君主也自信可以掌控知識份子。

在孔子那裏，君臣父子夫婦的關係常是對等的，到了大一統漢代的《白虎通義》，就弄出了三綱五常，將君、父、夫的地位固定為統治的、高高在上的一方，而將臣、子、婦的地位固定在服從的、在下的一方。孟子可能正處在向這個方向過渡的階段。

今天許多城市、公司展開了人才大戰。內地以前只有國家和集體兩個老闆，現在有無數多的老闆，對於勞動者來說，只要有聰明才智，做事勤快，就可以擁有選擇的自由，選擇的自由可以帶來經濟自由，雖然經濟自由不一定帶來其他自

hundred years earlier, the status of officials had significantly diminished by Mencius's time. The attitude of the vassal state rulers towards officials had changed from recognition to belittlement. The treatment of the resigning official quoted by Mencius here reveals such a change. The decrease in the number of states might have led the rulers to believe that they had more power over the officials (mostly intellectuals) since there were not as many states that needed their advice as before.

Back in Confucius's day, the relationship between ruler and official, between father and son, and between husband and wife were more egalitarian. However, since the grand unification achieved in the Han dynasty, as described in the book _Bai Hu Tong Yi_, the roles of the ruler, the father and the husband were given a higher, more authoritative status, whereas the roles of the official, the son and the wife were considered submissive ones and lower in status. We may say Mencius lived in a transitional phase during a major shift from an egalitarian morality to an authoritative one.

In today's world, there has been a craving demand for talent: companies and cities compete for talented people. In the past in mainland China, there were only two bosses — the

由，但是沒有經濟自由，就很難取得其他自由。

七

孟子曰：「離婁之明，公輸子之巧，不以規矩，不能成方圓。師曠之聰，不以六律，不能正五音。堯舜之道，不以仁政，不能平治天下。今有仁心仁聞而民不被其澤，不可法於後世者，不行先王之道也。故曰：徒善不足以為政，徒法不能以自行。《詩》云：『不愆不忘，率由舊章。』遵先王之法而過者，未之有也。聖人既竭目力焉，繼之以規矩準繩，以為方圓平直，不可勝用也。既竭耳力焉，繼之以六律正五音，不可勝用也。既竭心思焉，繼之以不忍人之政而仁覆天下矣。故曰：為高必因丘陵，為下必因川澤。為政不因先王之道，可謂智乎？是以惟仁者宜在高位。不仁而在高位，是播其惡於眾也。上無道揆也，下無法守也；朝不通道，工不信度；君子犯義，小人犯刑，國之所存者幸也。故曰：城郭

government and the collectives; but nowadays, there are numerous bosses to choose from. One just needs to be smart and diligent to get a good job. We can see that people now enjoy a greater freedom in their career choices and therefore can enjoy greater economic freedom. Even though economic freedom does not necessarily bring forth freedom in other aspects, the lack of economic freedom is definitely a hindrance to achieving other freedoms.

Seven

Translation:

Mencius said, "Even if one had the keen eyes of Li Lou and the skillfulness of Gong Shu Zi, without the compass and try [carpenter] square one could not make perfect squares and circles. Even if one had the sharp ears of Shi Kuang, one could not adjust the five notes of the scale without the six pitch pipes. Even if one knew the conduct of Yao and Shun, one could not manage well the world without implementing benevolent policies. There are rulers who have benevolent hearts and good reputations, yet their benevolence still cannot benefit the people nor set a good example for future generations. This is because they do not put into action the proper way of the former kings. Therefore, it is said, 'Good intentions alone are

不完，兵甲不多，非國之災也。田野不闢，貨財不聚，非國之害也。上無禮，下無學，賊民興，喪無日矣。《詩》曰：『天之方蹶，無然泄泄。』泄泄猶沓沓也。事君無義，進退無禮，言則非先王之道者，猶沓沓也。故曰：責難於君謂之恭，陳善閉邪謂之敬，吾君不能謂之賊。」（卷七　離婁章句上・一）

【今譯】

孟子說：「就是有離婁那麼好的視力，公輸班那麼好的技巧，如果沒有圓規和曲尺，也劃不出方形和圓形。就是有師曠那麼好的聽力，如果沒有定音的六律，也無法校正五音。就是有堯舜那麼好的道，如果不行仁政，也不能管理好天下。現在有些諸侯，雖有仁愛的心腸和仁愛的名聲，百姓卻得不到他的恩澤，也無法成為後世效法的楷模，之所以如此，就是因為不實行前代聖王的道。所以說，光有好心還不足以搞政治，光有好法也不行，好法不會自動運轉。《詩經》說：『不犯錯，不忘事，一切按舊規章辦。』遵守前代聖王的法度而犯錯，這樣的事還從來沒有過。聖人已經用盡他們的目力，又以圓規、曲尺、水平儀、

not sufficient for governance; laws alone are pointless because they can't operate themselves.'

The *Book of Poetry* says:

'Do not overstep and do not overlook;

follow the established rules.'

"One would never go wrong if he followed the examples set by the former kings. The sages have exerted the best of their eyesight to create the compass, the try square, the level and the plumb line, which can be used to make endless straight lines, squares and circles. They have exerted the best of their hearing to create the six pitch pipes, which can be used for endless tuning of the five notes. They have also exerted the best of their thinking to establish governance that will not support the suffering of others so that the whole world can be sheltered by the benevolent man's compassion. Hence it is said, 'To erect something high one should make use of the hilltops, to dig deep one should make use of the wetlands.' Can one be considered wise if one does not make use of the Way of the former kings? Therefore, only the benevolent man is suitable for holding high office. If a malevolent man were to hold high office, his wickedness would inevitably be spread among the people. When those above have no guiding principles, those below have no laws to follow: the courts do

墨繩，來製作方、圓、平、直的東西，使它們用
都用不完；聖人已經用盡他們的聽力，又用六律
來校正五音，使音調的變化無窮無盡；聖人已經
用盡他們的思想能力，又創造了不忍讓人遭難的
政治制度，使仁道無遠弗屆。所以說，築高台一
定要憑藉山陵，挖深池一定要憑藉沼澤；搞政治
卻不憑藉前代聖王之道，能說是聰明的嗎？因
此，只有仁人才應該坐在高位上，不仁的人在高
位上只會把他的惡傳播給眾人。上面的人沒有道
德規範，下面的人沒有法律操守，在朝廷的不相
信道義，做工匠的不相信尺度，有社會地位的君
子違犯道義，沒社會地位的老百姓違犯刑法，這
樣的國家還能生存下來的，只能說是僥倖。所以
說，城牆不牢固，軍備不充分，算不上國家的災
難；荒野沒有開墾，錢財沒有集中，也不是國家
的禍害。如果在上的不守禮儀，在下的沒有教養，
違法亂紀的人多起來，國家滅亡也就沒幾天了。
《詩經》說：『天正在運轉，沒有一絲懈怠。』
懈怠就是不負責任。事奉君主不講道義，進退
之間不講禮儀，說起話來就詆毀古代聖王之道的
人，就是不負責任的人。所以說，用難做的事情
（行仁政）來要求君主是『恭』，向君主陳說正
道堵塞邪路是『敬』，認為君主沒有行仁政的能
力，就是『賊』。」

not believe in justice and craftsmen do not trust the measures; the gentlemen violate righteousness and the folk violate laws. In such circumstances, it would be sheer luck if the country were still to survive. Thus it is said, 'It is not broken city walls and inadequate armor that bring disaster to a state, nor is it unreclaimed wastelands and unaccumulated wealth that cripple a state. When those above scorn the rites, those below refuse to learn, villains arise and the state will be on the point of collapse. The _Book of Poetry_ says:

'Heaven is revolving,

Do not be so sluggish!'

Sluggishness implies negligence. When a man shows no uprightness in his service to the ruler and shows no respect for the rites in his deeds, he is indeed defying the Way of the former kings, and thus we call him negligent. Hence it is said: 'One who condemns his ruler for his wrongdoing is being reverent; one who advises his ruler to do good and avoid evil is respectful; one who says his ruler is not capable of benevolent rule is a betrayer.'" (Chapter 7.1)

Contemporary interpretation:

In this passage, Mencius elaborated on benevolent governance. He took the Way of the former kings as the exemplary governing practice and emphasized the equal importance of

【時析】

這一節論述治國時應該「善」「法」並重，要遵守已經十分完善的「先王之道」，也即仁政。孟子認為，「徒善不足以為政，徒法不能以自行」，光是有好心還不足以成就好政治，光是制定規矩還是不行的，因為規矩是死的，需要人主動地去遵守實行。

孟子還提出「仁者宜在高位」，好人治國，好人要有官位，德位相配。這是由仁政的本質決定的。如果高位者都不仁，難以想象他們制定的政策會好到哪裏去，任用的幹部會好到哪裏去。

八

淳于髡曰：「男女授受不親，禮與？」孟子曰：「禮也。」曰：「嫂溺，則援之以手乎？」曰：「嫂溺不援，是豺狼也。男女授受不親，禮也；嫂溺，援之以手者，權也。」曰：「今天下溺矣，夫子之不援，何也？」曰：「天下溺，援之以道；嫂溺，援之以手——子欲手援天下乎？」（卷七 離婁章句上·十七）

"goodness" and "lawfulness." According to Mencius, "Good intentions alone are not sufficient for governance; laws alone are pointless because they can't operate themselves." Good governance cannot be achieved just with good intentions, neither is it possible to achieve with the formulation of laws alone because laws need to be observed and executed by people in order to take effect. Mencius also pointed out that only the benevolent man is suitable for holding high office. This means that a man's political power should match his virtue so that the governance of the state is put into the hands of the virtuous man. This is essential for carrying out benevolent governance. If those in power are malevolent, it is impossible to imagine that they can enact good policies and attract good people to assist them.

Eight

Translation:

Chun Yu Kun said, "Is it prescribed by the rites that men and women should not touch each other in giving and receiving?"

"It is," said Mencius.

"If one's sister-in-law is drowning, should one reach out his hand to help?"

【今譯】

淳于髡說:「男女之間,不親手交接東西,這是禮制嗎?」孟子說:「是禮制。」淳于髡說:「如果嫂子掉進水裏,那應該用手去拉她嗎?」孟子說:「嫂子掉進水裏還不去拉她,這簡直是豺狼。男女不應該親手交接東西,這是禮制;嫂子掉進水裏應該用手去拉她,這是權變。」淳于髡說:「現在天下人都掉進水裏,先生還不去拉一把,是為甚麼呢?」孟子說:「天下人掉水裏,就應該用仁義之道去拉他們;嫂子掉水裏,就應該用手去拉她——你是希望我用手去一個一個地拉天下人嗎?」

【時析】

這段話涉及經與權的關係。做人以至治國一方面要堅持原則,另一方面要根據情況加以適度的變通,不至拘泥死守原則,食古不化,貽誤時機。孟子也重視用對的方法做事,如用道去拉天下。不過,「權變」到底能達到哪個程度?是否有一定的限度?還有,誰來設定這個限度?這似乎是高度依賴情境的,有時就難免陷入靈活無度的陷阱。故此,開「權變」的後門要謹慎,若人人都可以說根據權變不講規則,實際上就等於沒有規則,社會的法制就會被破壞。

Mencius said, "A man who does not give a drowning sister-in-law his hand is but a beast. It is prescribed by the rites that men and women should not touch each other, yet when one's sister-in-law is drowning, he must use his discretion in deciding to reach out his hand to help."

"Now the world is drowning. Sir, why don't you reach out your hand to help?"

"When the world is drowning, one saves it with the Way; when a man's sister-in-law is drowning, he saves her with his hand — do you wish me to save the world (one by one) with my hand?" (Chapter 7.17)

Contemporary interpretation:

This passage is a deliberation on the use of "principle" and "discretion." On the one hand, one should hold on to one's principles for conducting oneself as well as providing good governance. On the other hand, one needs to display flexibility according to circumstance in order to reach timely decisions and not be rigidly bound by principles. It must be noted, however, that Mencius always stressed using the right way in doing things, and that was why he insisted on the (benevolent) Way as the guiding principle to save the world.

九

孟子曰：「楊子取『為我』，拔一毛而利天下，不為也。墨子『兼愛』，摩頂放踵利天下，為之。子莫『執中』，執中為近之。執中無權，猶執一也。所惡執一者，為其賊道也，舉一而廢百也。」（卷十三 盡心章句上・二十六）

【今譯】

孟子說：「楊子主張『為我』，你讓他拔下一根毫毛來有利於天下，他也不幹。墨子主張『兼愛』，即使幹活搞得從頭頂到腳跟都受傷了，只要有利於天下，他也會幹。子莫主張『執中』就是中道。主張中道就差不多了，但光講中道而不講權變，那就跟執着於一點一樣了。人們反對執着於一點，這是因為它有損正道，它只抓住一點而不計其餘。」

【時析】

孟子認為，楊朱利己和墨子利他都走向了極端，只有執中才比較合理。但是執中也不能死守，而要根據情境有所權變。問題是這個「權變」高度依賴情境，有時會走向主觀，過於靈活就難以

Nonetheless, one may still wonder to what extent one should exercise discretion. Is there any limit? If so, who is there to set the limit? It may be true that our deliberations must allow a certain extent of flexibility in the face of circumstantial variations. It is, however, also true that the use of discretion might turn into an arbitrary violation of principles. Therefore, we must be cautious in "opening the backdoor of discretion" since if people defy rules and regulations because of discretion there will be no rules and regulations. The result of such action would jeopardize the legal system.

Nine

Translation:

Mencius said, "Yangzi supports egoism; even if he could benefit the world by plucking out a single hair, he would not do it. Mozi defends egalitarian altruism; he would dedicate himself from head to toe solely for the sake of benefiting the world. Zi Mo advocates a midway stance; he thinks halfway between the two extremes is the best way out. Yet going after the middle ground without discretion is not different from upholding one of the extremes. These extremist views are annoying because they cripple the Way through holding on to one view at the expense of all others." (Chapter 13.26)

說明到底如何才是合理的。

　　說到執中，常常就變成了取中間數。比如很多貨物和服務的定價，現在都有指導價，給出一個區間，比如在 1 至 100 元之間，以禁止惡意傾銷和壟斷暴利。那麼，價格就常常定在 50 元。權變可能就是指，根據當地消費水準和供銷情況再適當調高調低一點。

　　我們知道，西方的法律規定嚴格，而中國的法律彈性較大，「權變」的機會較多。比如，近年來打擊的蒼蠅、老虎不少，但我們看到判刑的輕重相差懸殊。同樣貪一千萬，有的判七年，有的判死刑，這就太「權變」了吧！

十

　　有為神農之言者許行，自楚之滕，踵門而告文公，曰：「遠方之人，聞君行仁政，願受一廛而為氓。」文公與之處。其徒數十人，皆衣褐，捆屨、織席以為食。陳良之徒陳相與其弟辛，負耒耜而自宋之滕。曰：「聞君行聖人之政，是亦聖人也，願為聖

Contemporary interpretation:

According to Mencius, Yang Zhu's egoism and Mozi's altruism both go too far, and it is more reasonable to hold the middle ground. Still, one should always leave room for the use of discretion in response to circumstantial needs. The problem with such a view, however, is that there seems to be no criterion other than the immediate circumstance for the exercise of discretion. As a result, decisions taken might be quite arbitrary and choices made may be hard to justify.

The middle ground is often taken as the median between two points. For example, nowadays a prescribed price (such as 50 yuan is the prescribed price for marketable prices between 1 to 100 yuan) is often set for goods and services in order to prohibit malicious dumping or monopolization. In these cases, the use of discretion may mean fine-tuning adjustments of the prescribed price according to local levels of consumption and sales figures.

We all know that the rules and regulations of Western countries are far stricter than those of China where discretion is exercised more often. For example, in recent years both big and small corruption cases have been targeted, but the disparity in sentences is huge. When two people are prosecuted for

人氓。」陳相見許行而大悅，盡棄其學而學焉。

陳相見孟子，道許行之言曰：「滕君則誠賢君也；雖然，未聞道也。賢者與民並耕而食，饔飧而治。今也滕有倉廩府庫，則是厲民而以自養也，惡得賢？」孟子曰：「許子必種粟而後食乎？」曰：「然。」「許子必織布而後衣乎？」曰：「否，許子衣褐。」「許子冠乎？」曰：「冠。」曰：「奚冠？」曰：「冠素。」曰：「自織之與？」曰：「否，以粟易之。」曰：「許子奚為不自織？」曰：「害於耕。」曰：「許子以釜甑爨、以鐵耕乎？」曰：「然。」「自為之與？」曰：「否，以粟易之。」「以粟易械器者，不為厲陶冶；陶冶亦以械器易粟者，豈為厲農夫哉？且許子何不為陶冶，舍皆取諸其宮中而用之？何為紛紛然與百工交易？何許子之不憚煩？」曰：「百工之事，固不可耕且為也。」「然則治天下獨可耕且為與？有大人之事，有小人之事。

bribery over the same amount of bribe, say 10 million yuan, one is sentenced to seven years in prison while the other gets the death penalty. Don't such cases demonstrate the use of too much discretion?

Ten

Translation:

A man called Xu Xing, who was an advocate of the doctrines of Shen Nong (Divine Farmer), came to Teng from Chu. He went to the court gate and spoke to Duke Wen saying, "I, a man from a distant land, have heard that you, my lord, govern with benevolent policies. I wish to be offered a place to reside here so that I may become one of your subjects."

Duke Wen provided him a place. Xu had a few dozen followers and they all wore clothes made of coarse hemp and earned a living by making sandals and mats.

Chen Xiang, a follower of Chen Liang, went to Teng from Song with his brother Xin, both carrying ploughs upon their backs. He said, "I have heard that you, my lord, follow the sages' footsteps in your governance. This makes you a sage as well, and it is my wish to become a subject of the sage."

　且一人之身，而百工之所為備。如必自為而後用之，是率天下而路也。故曰：或勞心，或勞力。勞心者治人，勞力者治於人。治於人者食人，治人者食於人——天下之通義也。」

　　「當堯之時，天下猶未平，洪水橫流，氾濫於天下；草木暢茂，禽獸繁殖；五穀不登，禽獸逼人；獸蹄鳥跡之道，交於中國。堯獨憂之，舉舜而敷治焉。舜使益掌火；益烈山澤而焚之，禽獸逃匿。禹疏九河，瀹濟、漯而注諸海；決汝、漢，排淮、泗，而注之江，然後中國可得而食也。當是時也，禹八年於外，三過其門而不入，雖欲耕，得乎？后稷教民稼穡，樹藝五穀，五穀熟而民人育。人之有道也，飽食暖衣，逸居而無教，則近於禽獸。聖人有憂之，使契為司徒，教以人倫：父子有親，君臣有義，夫婦有別，長幼有序，朋友有信。放勳曰：『勞之來之、匡之直之、輔之翼之，使自得之；又從而振德之。』聖人之憂民如此，而暇耕乎？堯以不得

Later, Chen Xiang met Xu Xing and was so delighted with his teachings that he discarded all he had learned before and became Xu Xing's student.

When Chen Xiang met Mencius, he spoke to him of Xu Xing's teachings. "The lord of Teng is certainly a good ruler. Yet he still has not grasped the Way. A truly good ruler farms and eats together with his people; he rules while he cooks his own meals. Now as we can see, there are granaries and treasuries in Teng. This shows that the Duke exploits his people in order to let himself be fed. How can this be good?"

Mencius said, "Does Master Xu eat only what he himself has planted?" "Yes." "Does he wear only clothes that he himself has sewn?" "No," said Chen Xiang. "He wears hemp."

"Does he wear a cap?" "Yes." "What kind of cap?" "It is of plain silk." "Did he weave it by himself?" "No, he traded grain for it."

"Why didn't Master Xu weave it himself?" "Because it would have interfered with his farm work."

"Does he cook with pots and steamers and work his land with

舜為己憂；舜以不得禹、皋陶為己憂。夫以百畝之不易為己憂者，農夫也。分人以財謂之惠，教人以善謂之忠，為天下得人者謂之仁。是故以天下與人易，為天下得人難。孔子曰：『大哉，堯之為君！惟天為大，惟堯則之。蕩蕩乎民無能名焉！君哉舜也！巍巍乎有天下而不與焉！』堯舜之治天下，豈無所用其心哉？亦不用於耕耳。」

……（陳相說）「從許子之道，則市賈不貳，國中無偽；雖使五尺之童適市，莫之或欺。布帛長短同，則賈相若；麻縷絲絮輕重同，則賈相若；五穀多寡同，則賈相若；屨大小同，則賈相若。」

曰：「夫物之不齊，物之情也；或相倍蓰，或相什百，或相千萬。子比而同之，是亂天下也。巨屨小屨同賈，人豈為之哉？從許子之道，相率而為偽者也，惡能治國家？」（卷五滕文公章句上·四）

an iron plowshare?" "Yes." "Does he make these things by himself?" "No, he trades grain to get these things."

"Then to trade grain for tools cannot be exploiting the potter and the blacksmith, and when the potter and the blacksmith exchange their wares for grain, neither do they exploit the farmer. Actually, why doesn't Master Xu work as a potter and a blacksmith so that he will be able to get from within his own home everything that he needs? Why does he bother himself with such a variety of exchanges with various craftsmen? Isn't he annoyed?"

"It is impossible to craft so many kinds of things and at the same time plough the fields."

"Well, then, isn't ruling the world an exception that one can take while ploughing the fields? There are affairs of great men and affairs of ordinary men. Besides, it is necessary for every one of us to rely on crafts and tools made by others in order to lead an ordinary life. If a man had to make all the tools for himself, the whole world would be marching down the road to exhaustion. Hence it is said, 'Some work with their minds, some work with their strength.' Those who work with their minds govern those who work with their strength, and those

【今譯】

有個研究神農學說的人，叫做許行，他從楚國來到滕國，上門跟滕文公說：「我是遠方來的人，聽說您施行仁政，希望您賜給我一個居處，做您的僑民。」文公給了他居所。他有幾十個徒弟，都穿着粗麻衣服，以編鞋織席為生。陳良的徒弟陳相和他弟弟陳辛，都扛着農具，從宋國來到滕國，對滕文公說：「聽說您施行聖人的仁政，那您也是聖人，我們願意成為聖人的僑民。」陳相見到了許行，大喜，就拋棄他以前學到的東西，跟從許行學習了。

陳相見到孟子，轉告許行的話說：「滕文公確實是賢明的君主；雖然如此，卻還未懂得真理。賢人要跟百姓一起自耕自養，親自做飯，同時搞好管理工作。現在滕國還有穀倉財庫，可見還在剝削百姓來養活自己，怎麼能說賢明呢？」孟子說：「許先生一定是吃自己種的糧食嗎？」陳相說：「是的。」孟子問：「許先生一定是穿自己織的布嗎？」陳相說：「不是的，許先生穿粗麻布衣。」孟子問：「許先生戴帽子嗎？」陳相說：「戴的。」孟子問：「哪種帽子呢？」陳相說：「白綢帽。」孟子問：「是他自己織的嗎？」陳相說：「不是的，是以糧食換來的。」孟子問：

who work with their strength are governed by those who work with their minds. Those who are governed provide for those who govern, those who govern are provided for by those who are governed. This is a principle universally recognized by the world.

"In the time of Yao, the world was not yet settled. The great flood raged across the lands, inundating vast areas of the world. Plants grew thick, and birds and beasts multiplied; the grains did not ripen, and the birds and beasts attacked people, leaving traces of their destruction all around the Central Plains. Yao was particularly worried, so he appointed Shun to tackle the problems. Shun told Yi to be in charge of fire, and Yi lit fires in the mountains and valleys and the birds and beasts fled into hiding. Yu dredged the nine rivers and channeled the Ji and Ta Rivers into the sea; he unblocked the Ru and Han Rivers and diverted the Huai and Si Rivers to the Yangzi River. Only then the people of the Central Plains could [cultivate the fields and] have enough food to eat. During those times, Yu spent eight years away from home, and passed the door of his home three times without entering. Even if he wished to work in his fields, could he have done so?

"It was Hou Ji who taught the people how to farm and plant

「許先生怎麼不自己織呢？」陳相說：「耽誤他耕地。」孟子問：「許先生是用鍋和甑做飯、以鐵器耕地嗎？」陳相說：「是的。」孟子問：「這些東西他是自己造出來的嗎？」陳相說：「不是，是用糧食換來的。」孟子說：「用糧食來換炊具和農具的人，不能說是剝削了陶匠和鐵匠；陶匠和鐵匠也用炊具和農具來換糧食，怎麼能說是剝削農夫呢？還有，許先生何不自己製陶打鐵，讓家裏甚麼都有，隨時備用，他怎麼不這麼做？怎麼反而忙前忙後地跟各類工匠交換產品？他不嫌麻煩嗎？」陳相說：「各種工匠的事，本來不是可以一邊耕地一邊兼顧的。」孟子說：「這麼說，獨獨就可以一邊治理天下一邊耕地嗎？事情分官吏做的事和平民做的事。

光是一個人，他的生活就需要各個工種的產品，如果所有東西都要親自製造才能用得上，那會把所有人都累死。所以說：有的出智，有的出力。出智的管理人，出力的被管理。被管理的供養管理者，管理者被人供養，這是天下的普遍原則。

孟子說：「在堯的時代，天下還沒有平定，洪水亂竄，到處氾濫；草木茂盛，五穀不豐，禽

the five types of grain. As the grains ripened, people could feed themselves. There is a way that the common people follow: when they are well fed, warmly clothed and comfortably lodged, yet do not receive any education, they soon become almost like the beasts. The sage was worried about this, so he appointed Xie to be the Minister of Education to teach people about proper human relationships: love between father and son, righteousness between ruler and official, the different roles of husband and wife, precedence of elders over the young, and trustworthiness to friends. Yao said, 'Motivate them, correct them and support them, let them thrive; then inspire them to attain a fruitful life.' When a sage is so deeply worried about his people, how can he have time to work in his fields? Yao's worry was not being able to find someone like Shun; Shun's worry was not being able to find someone like Yu and Gao Tao. A man who only worries about the hard work of ploughing a hundred acres of land explains why he is a mere farmer.

"To share one's wealth with others is generous; to teach others to be good is devoted; to find the right leader for the world is benevolent. It is easy to hand the world over to someone else; however, it is hard to pick the right man for it. Confucius said, 'Yao was indeed a great ruler! Heaven's greatness is

獸眾多，把人嚇跑，中原一帶路上印滿鳥獸的腳印。對此唯有堯憂心忡忡，他提拔了舜來管理。舜讓伯益來主管火政。

伯益把山野沼澤圍起來，用火焚燒，禽獸被趕跑，到處躲藏。禹疏通九條河，治好了濟水和漯水，把它們引到海裏；挖開汝水和漢水，攔截淮河和泗水，把它們注到長江，然後中原一帶才可能耕上地，吃上飯。在那個時候，禹八年在外工作，三次經過自家門前而不進，他雖然想耕地，可是行嗎？后稷教人民種莊稼，栽種五穀，五穀成熟，養育百姓。人性也是有規律的，吃飽了，穿暖了，住好了，如果缺乏教化，那就跟禽獸差不多。

聖人又憂心忡忡了，就讓契掌管教育，把人倫的道理教給人民：父子之間要有親愛，君臣之間要有道義，夫婦之間要有分工，長幼之間要有秩序，朋友之間要有誠信。堯說：『督促他們，糾正他們，幫助他們，使他們各自學有所得，然後加以提攜和教誨。』聖人為百姓操心到這等地步，哪還有時間去耕地啊！堯擔心的是得不到舜這個人才，舜擔心的是得不到禹、皋陶這樣的人才。擔心耕不好一百畝地，這是農夫。把財產分

unsurpassable, and only Yao can emulate it. His greatness, like a river, was so boundless that the people could find no name for him! What a ruler Shun was! He was so lofty like a mountain that he had the whole world under his command, yet he had absolutely no craving for it!' How would it have been possible for Yao and Shun to have governed the world without using their minds? It is only that they did not use their minds on ploughing fields."

"If we adopt Master Xu's approach," Chen Xiang said, "market prices will be fixed and there will be no fraud in the state. Even if you sent a mere boy to the market, no one would cheat him. For equal lengths of cloth or silk, the price will be the same; for equal weights of raw hemp, flax or silk, the price will be the same; for equal quantities of the five grains, the price will be the same; for sandals of the same size, the price will be the same."

Mencius replied, "It is a fact that all things are not identical. Some are worth twice or five times as much as others, some ten or a hundred times, or even a thousand and ten thousand times. If you insist that they be treated as equal, you are causing confusion in the world. If a pair of roughly woven sandals are sold at the same price as those that are finely

給別人叫作惠，把好思想教給別人叫作忠，為天下物色人才叫作仁。因此，把天下送給人容易，為天下物色到人才困難。孔子說：『堯作君主，真是偉大啊！最大的莫過於天，只有堯能效法天。他如江河之水無窮無盡，百姓找不到詞來形容他。舜也是位偉大的君主啊！他如高山巍峨，雖擁有天下，卻不佔有它。』堯舜治理天下，難道沒有用心思嗎？他們只是不用去耕地而已……」

陳相說：「如果聽從許先生的主張，市場上的價格就不會有兩樣，國中沒有欺詐現象。即使是打發才五尺高的小孩去市場，也沒有人會欺騙他。麻布和絲綢的長短一樣，價錢便一樣；麻線和絲線的重量一樣，價錢便一樣；糧食的多少一樣，價錢便一樣；鞋子的大小一樣，價錢便一樣。」

孟子說：「事物的品質各不相同，這是事物的實情。有的相差一倍五倍，有的相差十倍百倍，有的相差千倍萬倍。你要將它們並列在一起，等而同之，是要搞亂天下的。如果好鞋和壞鞋賣一樣的價錢，人們還會去做鞋嗎？如果聽從許先生的主張，那就會讓人們彼此造假，怎麼能治理好

woven, who would make fine sandals anymore? To adopt Master Xu's approach is to lure each other into deceitful acts. How can one govern a state in this way?" (Chapter 5.4)

Contemporary interpretation:

If Xu Xing were to become a ruler, then the state under his rule would for certain regress into a primitive society. There everyone would be counted equal, and yet no one would have enough to eat or to wear because cultivating the fields alone would be such a consuming task that people would have no time for any other activities.

Division of labor is essential for human society to develop into an organic whole. Different individuals, communities and regions have their distinctive strengths in different industries and therefore they can contribute as well as benefit from the mutual exchange of products fulfilling the needs of all.

Xu Xin and Chen Xiang might have set out to fight the alienation of the ruling power from the people; however, it was their insistence that the ruler also engaged in manual labor, thus rejecting the division between work of strength and work of mind, that made them vulnerable to Mencius's severe attack on their thinking.

國家呢？」

【時析】

　　如果讓這個許行來當國君，那國家肯定要退到原始社會，雖然人人平等，但人人都會吃不飽，穿不暖，因為光是每個人耕地打糧食就很難，哪還有時間去幹別的事呢？

　　人類社會能發展，靠的是分工，分工使整個社會成為一個有機體。每個人、每個群體、每個地區都有其優勢，從事的工種效率高，出的產品比別人的好，這樣通過互相交換，大家就都能獲得自己需要的產品，滿足生活各方面的需要。

　　許行、陳相的本意，可能是針對統治者權力異化，脫離群眾，但他們要求統治者也從事體力勞動，就否定了勞心勞力的分工，被孟子抓住辮子，批得體無完膚。

　　現代民主國家領導人通過選舉上台，可上可下，一切言行置於公眾的監督之下，除了分工的不同外，私人並沒有甚麼特權。而普通公民也有參與社會治理的權利。當然，這些在孟子的時代是做不到的，他只能根據他那個時代的政治模式

Nowadays, the political leaders of democratic countries gain power through elections, and their words and deeds are under constant scrutiny by the people. Apart from their assigned political duties they do not have any privileges over other citizens. Besides, the citizens of democracies all hold a stake in public administration. Since this modern political system was not available at Mencius's time, the division of labor that he envisaged can only be understood within the political framework of his time.

In modern times, even for illiberal democratic governments such as in Singapore, its political leader does not enjoy any privileges other than those necessary for carrying out his duties. Singapore has regular elections, though its ruling party has been in power for a long time and there are relatively tight restrictions on the people's liberties, but the country is, nevertheless, governed under the rule of law. Its leader has to observe the law and government officials are under strict regulations; this results in a near absence of corruption. If we seek to develop Mencius's doctrines on people-centered governance and division of labor to the extreme, adding in the modern elements of public monitoring and the rule of law, we may in the end attain a system similar to the Singaporean model: while the political leader is responsible for running

去解釋社會分工。

在當代，不自由的民主國家如新加坡，雖然領導人分工與大眾不同，但享受不了甚麼特權。新加坡有正常選舉，但一黨長期執政，人民的自由受較大限制，但它是個法治國家，領導人也要遵守法律，官員的管理非常嚴格，幾乎沒有貪污腐敗現象。如果我們把孟子的民本主義和分工論發展到極端，再加上對領導層的嚴格監督或法治化，也許就會得到一個新加坡這樣模式的國家。領導人的分工是管理（勞心者，治人者），百姓是勞力者和治於人者，這只是分工的不同而已。這樣一個分工明確，各就各位的「有機」國家，大概是孟子夢想的國家吧。

在內地現行的制度設計中，人民代表大會是立法機構，政治協商會議是最高諮詢機構，人大代表和政協委員都不是專職的，都是業餘的，是本職工作以外的。這還沒有實現專業化，跟西方立法機構裏的專職議員是兩碼事。按照傳統的解釋，人大代表和政協委員不專職，不脫離生產，表示未脫離群眾。但這種未專業化，使得很多事情不能深入討論。比如一個叫申紀蘭的九十歲的老代表，幾十年基本上就做了一件事，投贊成票。

the entire society, the common people are responsible for contributing their strengths and efforts in their different social roles. This is an "organic" state in which all have a role in the clear division of labor and a prescribed duty. This may well be the ideal state envisaged by Mencius.

In the current political system of China, the National People's Congress is the legislature and the Chinese People's Political Consultative Conference is the top advisory body. Since all of their members are part-time, their participation and professionalism cannot be compared with Western professional politicians. The apparent rationale for the Chinese arrangement is that such composition can ensure that the members of the advisory body are not detached from their work and the common people. Nonetheless, this composition is unprofessional and has prevented members from discussing many issues at stake in any depth. For instance, there is an elderly delegate named Shen Jilan whose main service over the past several decades has been to cast affirmative votes in meetings. His membership has become a mere honor, instead of an opportunity to have genuine participation in governance and consultation, and in the improvement of livelihood and democracy. This is one shortcoming of the current political system in China.

把開會當成一種榮譽，而不是真正參政議政、改善民生民主的機會，是這個體制的一個弊端。

十一

公孫丑曰：「《詩》曰：『不素餐兮。』君子之不耕而食，何也？」孟子曰：「君子居是國也，其君用之，則安富尊榮；其子弟從之，則孝悌忠信。『不素餐兮』，孰大於是？」（卷十三　盡心章句上‧三十二）

【今譯】

公孫丑問：「《詩經》上說：『不白吃飯。』君子不耕地卻吃飯，為甚麼呀？」孟子說：「君子住在一個國家，如果君主任用他，就會平安、富足、尊貴、光榮；如果少年子弟跟從他，就會孝順父母、敬重兄長、忠誠信實。說到『不白吃飯』，還有能比他做得更好的嗎？」

【時析】

一個社會的運行，需要各方面的人才，其中管理人才、知識份子是很重要的。管理得法，小至公司，大至國家，都能運行得井井有條；知識

Eleven

Translation:

Gong Sun Chou said, "The *Book of Poetry* says:

'He eats no food unearned.'

Then why does the gentleman accept food when he does not farm?"

Mencius said, "When a gentleman lives in a state, the ruler uses his service and the state becomes peaceful and prosperous; the young men come to learn from him, and they become filial, brotherly, faithful and trustworthy. Could 'he eats no food unearned' be better exemplified?" (Chapter 13.32)

Contemporary interpretation:

The smooth functioning of a society relies on capable people from a wide variety of professions, among which management experts and intellectuals are two of those who make important contributions. Good management keeps an organization in good order, be it small like a company or big like a country. Intellectuals are signposts for the high level of culture and intellectual activism of a country. An active intellectual community fosters advancement in science and technology and serves as the nurturing ground for a productive and prosperous society. However, despite their contribution to

份子多代表國家文明程度高，思想活躍，科技發達，生產力水準高，經濟繁榮昌盛。但是，由於管理人才和知識份子屬於勞心者，一般不從事體力勞動，因此，如果把勞動這個概念狹窄化，只認體力勞動為勞動，那就會認為腦力者不勞而獲，對他們拿着高薪忿忿不平。等而下之者甚至把腦力勞動者，尤其管理者當作剝削者和寄生蟲，予以懲罰和驅逐，造成社會治理水準大倒退。

在中國內地文革期間，當權者把知識份子和管理人員視作寄生蟲，或不是真正的勞動者，要把他們改造成跟農民、工人一樣的體力勞動者，把他們下放到農村、工廠去勞動，並且改造他們的思想，使他們成為服服帖帖的寫字工具。無論是下放勞改，還是知識青年上山下鄉，都耽誤了整整一代人正常的學習，使他們的人生荒廢了。

在當代，「勞心者」可以說是經濟發展的火車頭。一個科技發明、一家科技企業就可以創造數億、數十億、數百千億的價值，因此許多國家、城市都掀起了對「勞心者」的人才爭奪戰。當北京、上海限制人口流入的時候，杭州、廣州、武漢、西安紛紛到各大高校搶人，送戶口。當年馬雲沒有去深圳，而選擇了杭州，現在馬雲每年給

society, managers and intellectuals are often stigmatized as "people who reap without sowing" just because their mental efforts are not as visible as the physical efforts made by those who labor in the fields, for example. Such narrow understanding of "labor" has led many to hold grudges against those who earn a better living by mental effort; some of the aggrieved may even accuse white-collar workers of economically exploiting the laborers and thus seek to penalize or expel them. Such incidences, unfortunately, have caused serious regression in social development.

During the time of the Cultural Revolution in China, intellectuals and management officials were labeled as social parasites or pseudo-laborers. They were sent to remote villages or factories to be "reformed" through intense physical labor and also to have their thoughts "re-molded," with the aim of turning them into talking parrots of the propagated ideology. Both the "Reform through Labor" and the "Down to Countryside" movements ended up depriving a whole generation of their youth and their prime time for learning.

It can clearly be seen that those working with their minds have been the driving force for the economic development of recent years. With just one technological invention, a technological

杭州貢獻多少億的稅收？這就是「勞心者」作為企業家、發明家的價值，一個人可以雇傭數千數萬人。

所以到底「勞心者」和「勞力者」究竟是誰養活誰，還真不好說。

enterprise may create over millions' or even billions' worth of market value. Therefore, many cities and countries are competing for talented minds, while xenophobic countries still cling to their outdated restrictive immigration policies. If we look at Chinese cities, while Beijing and Shanghai restrict the inflow of population, other cities such as Hangzhou, Guangzhou, Wuhan and Xian have sent officials to tertiary institutes in other provinces to recruit young people to work and grant them residence in their cities. Years ago, when the entrepreneur Jack Ma was declined residency rights by Shenzhen, Hangzhou seized the opportunity to get him there and the city now receives billions in tax revenue from him every year. This serves as an example of how people working with their minds, including entrepreneurs and inventors, can contribute to the national economy — just one talented mind can support the livelihood of many thousands of people. Whether those "working with their strength" feed those "working with their mind" or vice versa is a chicken or egg question to which no one can give a satisfactory answer.

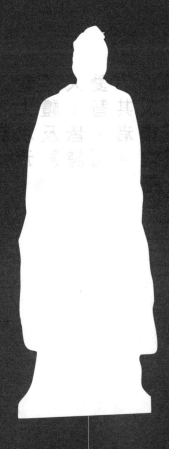

君子自處 *Refinement of the Gentleman*

一

孟子曰：「愛人不親，反其仁；治人不治，反其智；禮人不答，反其敬。行有不得者，皆反求諸己。其身正而天下歸之。《詩》云：『永言配命，自求多福。』」（卷七　離婁章句上·四）

【今譯】

孟子說：「你愛人，人卻不親你，那你得反問自己，我的仁有甚麼問題？你管別人，卻管不好，那你就得反問自己，我的智有甚麼缺欠？你禮待別人，卻得不到回應，那你就得反問自己，我的敬有沒有毛病？你做了事卻得不到效果，那就要反過來從自己身上找原因。你自己做端正了，天下的人就會歸附。《詩經》說：『做事總要符合天的旨意，幸福要靠自己的努力。』」

【時析】

孟子是個道德主義者，把周朝的「以德配天」之德強調到極點。在這裏，孟子強調君子要有自我反省的精神，時時檢討自己的言行，別人對我不好、事情辦得不好、事情沒有回報，一定是我

One

Translation:

Mencius said, "When those you love do not respond with affection, reflect on your own benevolence. When you fail to govern well, reflect on your own wisdom. When those you treat with courtesy do not return it, reflect on your own respectfulness. Whenever your actions do not yield good results, reflect upon yourself. The world will follow you when you are upright in character. The _Book of Poetry_ says:

'Always strive to follow Heaven's Mandate

Then you will be seeking your own happiness.'" (Chapter 7.4)

Contemporary interpretation:

Mencius is a moralist who placed utmost emphasis on the Zhou dynasty idea of the virtue of "following heaven's way through virtuous actions of one's own." In this passage, Mencius underscored the importance for the gentleman to be self-reflective. In circumstances where others are unkind to us, or things do not work out well, or we are not rewarded for what we have done, it is likely there are some issues concerning ourselves that need attention. Self-reflection, of course, is beneficial for our own moral practice. However, we must be careful not to push this to an extreme and become a pan-moralist and consider all failures as arising from our

自己有甚麼問題。這麼做當然是好的，有益於促進自己的德行。但是切忌將這種觀點推到極端，將一切失敗、責任都推到自己德行虧欠上，則犯了泛道德化的錯誤。因為很多事辦不成，很多人待你不好，並非一定是你的原因，可能是別人的原因、環境的原因、際遇的原因等等。

人生常常不如意，德福常常不一致，只要自己盡了力，對不同結果能坦然面對就好。

佛教看到今生難以德福一致，遂將之推往來世，因此總是給人下輩子以希望。基督教看到今生好人不一定有好報，壞人反而得好報（《約伯記》），因此把德福一致推到末日大審判，給人以永遠的希望。墨子理解很粗糙，講究現報，因此與經驗不符，學生中間就有人不信。儒家沒有來世永世的觀念，只有今生的觀念，因此，在不能保證有德必有福的實際情況下，有些人只好說德自身有福。

道家老子是哲學家，他說「天道無親，常與善人」，把德福一致說成一個大概率事件，這個解釋較為圓滿。至於後來的道教和民間宗教，則把現世延長到後代，認為「積善之家，必有餘慶。

own moral faults. We must be aware of the fact that some of the mishaps that happen to us may be caused by factors other than our own actions, whether actions by other people, the environment, or simply a sheer lack of luck. Life can be tough at times, and often despite our best efforts we cannot guarantee success. Yet, if we have already exerted that effort, it may be best for us to take whatever happens in our stride.

Observing the unlikelihood of life being filled with virtues and happiness, Buddhism has made it possible for us to hope to have the happiness we desire and think we deserve in our next life. Christianity, as the Book of Job has made it clear, teaches that in the present life, while it is not necessarily only the good guys who get rewarded but the bad guys also, the eternal hope of the righteous to live forever in happiness is granted by God on the Day of Judgment. Mozi, believed in instant retribution, which is rather contradictory to common experience and was held in doubt even by his own students. In Confucianism, there is no concept of reincarnation or eternal life because Confucian thinking is most concerned about how one can live to the fullest in the present life. Confucians observed from experience that being virtuous did not necessarily bring about happiness, some Confucians saying instead that it was virtuous actions that could bring forth happiness.

積惡之家，必有餘殃」。你行的德你收不到福報，但會報給你的後代；你作的惡你未受到懲罰，但會落到你後人頭上。可以說，在追求德福一致的動機背後，其實是人對於「正義」的嚮往，是一種「等價」回報的要求。

二

　　孟子曰：「自暴者，不可與有言也；自棄者，不可與有為也。言非禮義，謂之自暴也；吾身不能居仁由義，謂之自棄也。仁，人之安宅也；義，人之正路也。曠安宅而弗居，舍正路而不由，哀哉！」（卷七　離婁章句上・十）

【今譯】

　　孟子說：「自己害自己的人，跟他沒法交流；自己放棄自己的人，跟他沒法一起成事。說話不符禮義，這叫自己害自己；自身不能堅持仁義，這叫自己放棄自己。仁，可以說是人舒適的住宅；義，可以說是人正確的道路。把舒適的宅子空着而不去住，把正確的道路放棄而不去走，可悲呀！」

The Taoist philosopher Laozi may have offered the most satisfactory answer to the relationship between virtue and happiness. He said, "Heaven's way never favors anyone, it is always on the side of the good man." Hence, he preferred to see the concurrence of virtue and happiness as a matter of great probability. At a later time, Taoist and other folk religions developed this line of thinking into a kind of moral inheritance: "The charitable family will have joyful things follow. The malevolent family will have disastrous things follow." This means that even if the man who has led a good life doesn't receive blessings during his lifetime, they will be passed on to his descendants. In the same way, if a man has done evil, though he might not be punished for it in his life, his descendants will receive punishment in his place. Perhaps what underlies the desire to have a life filled with virtues and happiness is actually a pursuit of justice and a yearning in the retributive sense: good exchanged for good, and bad for bad.

Two

Translation:

Mencius said, "One cannot speak with those who harm themselves, and one cannot collaborate with those who forsake themselves. People speaking not in compliance

【時析】

如果承認孟子性善說這一前提，那麼上面的這些話就很容易理解。在西方的自然法傳統中，也有跟孟子性善說相類似的成份。比如中世紀的湯瑪斯・阿奎那，人的天性中有上帝印下的自然法則，包括人會行善避惡，保存自己的生命，與人為善，不會無緣無故得罪身邊的人，追求真知等等。

現代法國天主教哲學家馬利坦認為，上帝造出萬物，萬物都有其本來的一個「應當是」的樣子，這也就是它的自然法。比如，馬被造出來，有它的特有的功能（善跑），有它的正常的生長過程（由小馬長成大馬），母馬到了一定的年齡會交配生育，生出健康的小馬，等等。這都是「馬性」之「應當」，也即正常的馬的性理。

當然，有個別的馬會生病、發生畸形的情況，比如瘸腿，跑不了或跑不快，達不到一匹正常的馬應該達到的功能。還可用人造的鋼琴來類比。鋼琴被人造出來是為了彈出好聽的音樂，這是它受造的目的，它的「應該是」。如果鋼琴壞了，它就不成其為鋼琴，沒有達到它的正常的目的。

with rites and righteousness will harm themselves; people thinking themselves as incapable of becoming benevolent will forsake themselves. Benevolence is man's safe haven and righteousness his proper path. How sad it is to see people leaving their safe havens and wandering away from their proper paths!" (Chapter 7.10)

Contemporary interpretation:

If we accept Mencius's claim about intrinsic goodness, the outcome this passage describes is logical. Similar claims can be found in the traditional natural law theory from the West. For example, in the Middle Ages, Thomas Aquinas claimed that God's natural law was imprinted in human nature, and such as doing good and avoiding evil, self-preservation, compassion, not offending others without a reason and the desire for the truth was inborn. In modern times, French Catholic philosopher Jacques Maritain put forward a similar account of natural law. He claimed that since all beings on earth are the creation of God, each being is created with a purpose in God's mind that will become their nature. For example, the horse is created as an animal that will grow from a foal to a mature horse; it can run fast; and it can start to reproduce once it reaches maturity. These characteristics constitute the nature of the horse and serve as their purpose of being a

馬利坦認為人被上帝造出來，也有這樣一個目的，有正常的功能。在人的天性中，有行善避惡、自我保存、樂群、求真知等傾向，這是人「應該」的樣子。

人如果能把這種天性正常地發揮出來，那就可以形成較完美的社會。價值和事實應該是統一的，但是由於受到罪、壞習俗等等因素的影響，人實際上並沒有達到自然法要求他達到的事，沒有達到「應該是」的那個樣子。

在這個出錯誤的過程中，人的理性和自由意志也可能作出錯誤的判斷，選擇錯誤的方向，從而造成人偏離了本來的天性。就認為人天性中有好的東西、「應該是」的東西來說，天主教的自然法學說跟孟子的思想有相似之處。

三

孟子曰：「道在邇，而求諸遠；事在易，而求諸難。人人親其親、長其長，而天下平。」（卷七 離婁章句上‧十一）

horse. Nonetheless, there exist horses that fail to possess these attributes. There are those that are sick, deformed, or cannot run fast. These become dysfunctional horses that are unable to serve their purpose of existence.

Let us take as another example an object made by man. The piano is created for the purpose of producing good music, and a typical piano ought to serve this function. However, if the piano becomes damaged, it can no longer serve its function as a piano and thus is no longer a true piano. According to Maritain, man as a creation of God also serves his unique purposes as contemplated by God. In principle, man is by nature disposed to do good and avoid evil, he is also good at self-preservation, peacefully co-existing with others, as well as seeking truth. If man can realize his nature to the fullest extent, he can help make society perfect. Yet, in reality man often fails to serve his purposes and live up to his ideal self because he is corrupted by his sins as well as bad customs. Maritain believed that it may also be the misuse of man's reasoning and free will that has mistakenly led him away from realizing his human nature prescribed by natural law.

These Catholic doctrines on natural law bear a considerable resemblance to Mencius's doctrine on intrinsic goodness.

【今譯】

孟子說：「道路就在近處，人們卻到遠處尋找；事情本來很容易，人們卻從難處着手。其實只要人人都親愛自己的父母，尊敬自己的長輩，就天下太平了。」

【時析】

孟子這麼說，跟他的人性本善說有關。既然人的天性是善的，那麼順着它好好發展就可以了，也容易。善最初表現的地方當然是跟父母的關係，在傳統社會，也是跟族人和鄰里的關係。孝悌忠信，在鄉里生活中都能實踐，並不需要講甚麼大道理。孟子的話體現了儒家的一個特點，那就是哲學是生活中來，也要到生活中去，是實踐的哲學，而且是平易的哲學。這跟西方哲學有很大的區別。

西方哲學是要追求超越性的真理，其論點有時會遠離常識（如笛卡爾「我思故我在」是純粹抽象的「思想我」，恰恰要打破日常生活的我的常識）。但是儒家的這種性格，也常常使它局限在人際關係中，難以走向高遠，去發現世界和宇宙中難以想象的奧秘，因此，如馮友蘭所說，儒家並沒有發展科學的必要性。

Three

Translation:

Mencius said, "The Way is close at hand, yet people seek it afar; the task can be handled easily, yet people make it difficult. If only all men loved their parents and respected their elders, the world would be at peace." (Chapter 7.11)

Contemporary interpretation:

Mencius saw that man has the ability to do good, so he considered man's most straightforward path in life was to cultivate himself in line with this skill. The starting point is for sure one's relationship with one's parents. In the context of a traditional society, the next would be the relationship with relatives and fellow villagers. It is therefore useful to practice the virtues of filial piety, fraternal respect, conscientiousness and trustworthiness. Mencius's ideas embody a uniqueness seen in Confucianism as a philosophy that both originates from and constantly returns to daily life. Unlike Western philosophy, it is a practical philosophy that everyone can understand. In contrast, Western philosophy pursues the transcendental truth, and its theories often appear to be rather detached from the common sense of daily life. (Such as the Cartesian claim "I think therefore I am" refers to a purely abstract "thinking I," with an intention to break away from

四

孟子曰：「居下位而不獲於上，民不可得而治也。獲於上有道，不信於友，弗獲於上矣。信於友有道，事親弗悅，弗信於友矣。悅親有道，反身不誠，不悅於親矣。誠身有道，不明乎善，不誠其身矣。是故誠者，天之道也。思誠者，人之道也。至誠而不動者，未之有也。不誠，未有能動者也。」（卷七 離婁章句上·十二）

【今譯】

孟子說：「處在低的職位上卻不被上級信任，就治理不好自己管轄的百姓。要獲得上級的信任是有方法的，（要獲得朋友的信任），得不到朋友的信任，就得不到上級的信任。得到朋友的信任是有方法的，（要獲得父母的信任），侍奉父母而不能使他們高興，也就不能獲得朋友的信任。令父母高興是有方法的，（要自己做到誠心誠意），如果反省自己沒有做到誠心誠意，那就不能令父母高興。要使自己誠心誠意是有方法的，（要懂得甚麼是善），如果不懂得甚麼是善，那就做不到讓自己誠心誠意。所以，誠是天道，想做到誠是人道。完全達到誠的境界還不能使人

the common sense about "I.") The Confucian way of thinking, however, confines itself to human relationships, making it difficult to discover mysteries about the world and the universe. This may explain why Feng You-lan said that there is no need for Confucianism to develop scientific knowledge.

Four

Translation:

Mencius said, "If a man in a subordinate position cannot gain the confidence of his superior, he will not be able to govern the people. There is a way to gain the confidence of his superior: if he is not trusted by his friends, he will not gain the confidence of his superior. There is a way to gain the trust of his friends: if in serving his parents he is unable to please them, he will not be trusted by his friends. There is a way to please his parents: if he looks inward and finds that he is not true to himself, he will not please his parents. There is a way to become true to himself: if he does not understand what is good, he will not be true to himself. Hence, truthfulness is the Way of heaven and to become true to oneself is the way of man. A man who is true to himself never fails to touch the heart of others, while a man who is untrue to himself never succeeds in touching the heart of anyone." (Chapter 7.12)

感動，這種情況是不會有的。自己做不到誠，是
不能感動別人的。」

【時析】

孟子這段話是經驗之談，一個人的誠信是從
自身開始，由身邊的人驗證的。一個欺騙身邊人
的人，很難想象他到了外面的花花世界不會做出
更大的欺騙行為。這裏孟子說，要得到上級的信
任，便要獲得朋友的信任，而得到朋友的信任，
需獲得父母的信任，把上級、朋友與父母的關係
連結起來考慮。

不過，這也容易陷入「由身邊人決定命運」
的陷阱。比如，在大陸文革期間，一個人當兵、
上大學，都要原單位、機構開介紹，以瞭解這個
人的道德、信用、出身、思想等情況，而這又是
由身邊個別人（如領導）做出的，就難免產生抑
制人才的現象。在九十年代初，連考研究生都需
要單位開證明，因此，往往是「身邊人」決定你
的終生命運，這不知造成多少悲劇。

一個人跟家庭成員相處得不好，可能不是他
自身的原因（如遇上待自己不好的繼母之類），他
到了外面，可能會跟志同道合的朋友相處得很好。

Contemporary interpretation:

Whether a person is truthful or not, people around him can tell. If a person is dishonest with people close to him, it is unlikely that he can stop himself from cheating others in an outer world full of temptations. In this passage, Mencius pointed out that in order for someone to gain the trust of his superiors, he must first gain the trust of his friends; in order to gain the trust of his friends, he must first gain the trust of his parents, thus linking the relationship between superiors, friends and parents. We should take Mencius's advice with caution, since our relationship with our associates is not the only thing that we should count on. For example, during the Cultural Revolution in China, someone wanting to enroll in the army or a university would have to submit a reference written by his work unit or institution. The unit was expected to know everything about this person, including his conduct, his credibility, his social origins, as well as his personal views. Yet very often the reference would represent only the view of one person (mostly in authority) and the practice resulted in squandering many talents. Even in the 1990s, one would have to get a permit from one's unit in order to apply for graduate school. A policy such as this that relied heavily on the comments of one's associates resulted in many tragedies in China. It is a fact that even if one cannot get along well

耶穌說，先知在家鄉是不受歡迎的，這可能跟「僕人眼中無偉人」一樣，身邊人看到你的也許總是你的缺點，但這並不意味着你在遠方就不能成為先知，闖出一片天地。

對於從政的人物，品德的要求當然要嚴格一點，因為他公權力大，可能會對公眾利益造成損害。但即使是從政人物，也要區分私德和公德。不妨礙公德（公共利益）的私德問題，不必斤斤計較。克林頓和萊溫斯基的緋聞，沒有影響到他對美國管治的決定，也不足以使他下台。

西方對政治人物從來不會以「聖王」那樣的道德完人理想去要求。相反，從聖經舊約裏的經常犯罪、犯錯的大衛王開始，國王之類大人物在道德上都是靠不住的，跟百姓一樣都是罪人，因此，西方只是比較單純地從政治功能的角度着眼，國王或官員起到行政的功能就可以了，不必在道德上吹毛求疵。

相比之下，中國自古以來就有「聖王」傳統，對統治者的治理能力和道德都有很高的要求。因此，不僅歷代統治者都要把自己打扮成道德楷模，普通的讀書人也都以「修齊治平」來要求自

with one's family (such as with a difficult stepmother), one may be able to get along well with friends who share similar ambitions in life. Jesus once said, "No prophet is accepted in his hometown." This is like the saying, "No servants consider their master a great man." Sometimes those whose relationship is close can too easily find fault in each other and find it hard to appreciate the goodness in the other. This does not mean, however, that one will never get the recognition one deserves from other people.

Politicians have a duty to set strict moral standards for themselves because they have great public powers in their hands which, if exercised with bad intentions, can harm public interests. It is important, however, for us to be able to distinguish between personal morals and public morals; and those personal moral issues that are not relevant to public interests (thus public duty), we should let pass. The Clinton-Lewinsky case offers a good example. Clinton's moral fault in having an affair did not affect his governmental decisions and therefore did not cost him the presidency. In the West, political leaders have never been treated as "sage kings," such as the erring King David we see in the Old Testament; he was as sinful as the average person, and therefore he was not expected to be morally faultless. We can see that when appraising their

己。在這種情況下，如果帝王有錯，或有道德瑕疵，就容易把過錯推諉到宰相，或者下級官員身上。對於下層來說，也有「只反貪官不反皇帝」的心理，即認為皇帝是好的，只是皇帝身邊出了壞人，把皇帝的好政策弄壞了，因此即使造反，也只是為了「清君側」。

修齊治平的理想當然是沒有錯的，統治者最好是德才兼備的人，但是歷史上常常出現有才無德，或者有德無才的情況，考慮到這種情況，不如從分工的角度，將治理之才跟道德品質區分開來，對統治者的職能加以明確，權力加以制衡，起到維護社會的正確運轉的功能就可以了。這樣萬一統治者道德品質差，若不是貪腐，也不會把國家折騰到哪裏去。

五

孟子曰：「君子所以異於人者，以其存心也。君子以仁存心，以禮存心。仁者愛人，有禮者敬人。愛人者，人恆愛之；敬人者，人恆敬之。有人於此，其待我以橫逆，則君子必

political leaders, people in the West tend to focus on their political merits and demerits, rather than finding fault in their moral conduct.

In contrast, since ancient times there has been a tradition of "sage kings" in China, and the Chinese have always had high expectations of their political leaders in their governing competence as well as their moral conduct. The rulers were obliged to play the role of moral exemplar. What is more, it is common even for the average educated man to adhere to the demanding moral principles of "edifying oneself, harmonizing the family, serving the country, and bringing peace to the world." Yet when the ruler erred or had moral faults, he might conveniently shift the blame to his officials. In the same way, when people suffered from bad governance, it was common for the people to insist on the innocence of the ruler and pass the blame onto his ministers who would instead become the targets of revolt. It is of course a noble goal for one to edify oneself, harmonize the family, serve the country, and bring peace to the world; and it is as desirable for the ruler to be complete with virtues and talents. However, it is rare that we find someone with such a combination of qualities. This being so, it would be better if we separated governing competence from moral conduct, and clearly defined the duty and

自反也：『我必不仁也，必無禮也，此物奚宜至哉？』其自反而仁矣，自反而有禮矣。其橫逆由是也，君子必自反也：『我必不忠。』自反而忠矣。其橫逆由是也，君子曰：『此亦妄人也已矣。如此則與禽獸奚擇哉？於禽獸又何難焉！』是故君子有終身之憂，無一朝之患也。乃若所憂則有之。舜人也，我亦人也；舜為法於天下，可傳於後世，我由未免為鄉人也，是則可憂也。憂之如何？如舜而已矣。若夫君子所患則亡矣。非仁無為也，非禮無行也。如有一朝之患，則君子不患矣。」（卷八　離婁章句下・二十八）

【今譯】

孟子說：「君子不同於常人的地方，在於他保存了本心。君子把仁保存在心裏，把禮保存在心裏。仁人會關愛別人，有禮的人會尊敬他人。關愛別人的人，別人也會關愛他。尊敬別人的人，別人也會尊敬他。如果這裏有個人，他對我的態度很粗暴蠻橫，那我作為一個君子一定會反省：『我一定對他有甚麼不仁的地方，一定對他有無

authority of governance expected of our political leader so that any abuse of public power can be checked. The sole function of the political leader should be to necessitate the smooth functioning of society. Whether or not he is morally blameworthy for his personal conduct should be irrelevant to leadership, as long as it doesn't involve corruption.

Five

Translation:

Mencius said, "A gentleman differs from others in what he preserves in his heart. The gentleman preserves benevolence and propriety in his heart. A benevolent man loves others and a proper-mannered man respects others. He who loves others is always loved by others; he who respects others is always respected by others. Suppose a man acts rudely and unreasonably towards me. A gentleman will always reflect upon himself, 'I must have failed in benevolence and propriety, otherwise why has he treated me like this?' If, upon reflection, the gentleman finds that he has already treated the man with benevolence and propriety and the rude and unreasonable acts continue, then he will reflect further, 'I cannot have been truthful enough to him.' If, upon reflection, the gentleman finds that he has been truthful enough and the

禮的地方，不然，事情怎麼會弄成這個樣子呢？』反省的結果是我確實做到了仁，反省的結果是我確實做到了有禮。可是這個人對我的粗暴蠻橫還是老樣子，我作為君子一定要反省：『我對他一定還不誠實吧？』自我反省的結果是我對他是誠實的。可是這個人對我粗暴蠻橫的態度仍舊不變。君子就說：『這個人不過是個虛妄自大之徒罷了。他這樣，跟禽獸又有甚麼區別呢？我對於禽獸，又有甚麼好責備的呢？』所以，君子有終身憂慮的事情，沒有一時憂慮的事情。至於他終身憂慮的事情，包括：舜是人，我也是人；舜給天下人樹立了榜樣，影響可以流傳到後世，我卻仍然是個普通凡人。這才是值得我憂慮的事情。憂慮了又怎麼辦呢？像舜那樣去做就好了。至於君子一時所害怕的事，那是沒有的。不仁的事不去做，不合禮的事不去幹。即使有一時的擔憂，君子也不認為真正值得憂慮。」

【時析】

這段話講君子為人處世的道理。一是遇到問題要多從自己身上找原因；二是以希聖成賢為人生志向。

說到人生之憂，古今說「內憂外患」的詩文

rude and unreasonable acts keep coming, then the gentleman will say, 'He is not an arrogant man. He acts in such a beast-like manner. How could a man consider a beast blameworthy?' Hence, while a gentleman has life-long worries, he is not bothered by short-term nuisances. And his worries are like this: Shun was a man, and I am a man, too. Shun set a good example for generations to follow; what am I other than an ordinary villager? This is truly something worth worrying about! And since I am worried about this, what should I do? I should strive to become like Shun. That's all. In this way there would be nothing else that could bother the gentleman. If he never does anything lacking in benevolence or propriety, but he sometimes faces short-term nuisances, he will never be bothered by them." (Chapter 8.28)

Contemporary interpretation:

In this passage Mencius talks about how one should conduct oneself in worldly affairs. On the one hand, if one gets into trouble, one should reflect upon oneself for the cause; on the other hand, one should emulate the sages and aspire to become as virtuous as they were. While the different worries we face in life are often written about, such as in: "One needs not live to the age of a hundred to have a thousand years of worries to bear." In the eyes of Mencius, however, most of

不少，比如「生年不滿百，常懷千歲憂」之類的句子。但一般人的生活之憂，在孟子看來，都只是一時之憂，是暫時的，總能應付，或者能過去的。對於君子來說，最大的憂，則在於能否達到聖賢那樣的境界，像曾子那樣「吾日三省吾身」。如果滿懷仁心，達到堯舜那樣的為人，對於外患，就不會看成甚麼大不了的事。若是外來橫禍呢？那跟道德修養沒有關係，因此也不必為此苦惱。

其實，君子也是普通人，能夠達到孟子所說的理想只在少數，現實點說，君子也要面對生活上的種種問題，他們憂的恐怕還主要是小民之憂，一味追求達致堯舜境界是遠水解不了近火的。所以，就算作為君子，還是要先自救，在生活、經濟方面能夠獨立，才能具備向聖賢看齊的基礎。

六

孟子曰：「養心莫善於寡欲。其為人也寡欲，雖有不存焉者，寡矣。其為人也多欲，雖有存焉者，寡矣。」（卷十四 盡心章句下‧三十五）

these worries are merely short-lived troubles that can either be solved or just ignored. For a gentleman, his deepest worry rests on how he can become as virtuous as the sages. Zeng Zi's famous saying "I reflect on what I have done three times a day" may illustrate a state of mind pretty close to this ideal. If one could become as genuinely benevolent as Yao and Shun, one would not be bothered by troubles other than that of one's own self-edification. Similarly, one would not be bothered by unexpected misfortunes either. It is known that even gentlemen share the limitations of human beings, and few can live out the Confucian ideal without the need to worry about issues in life. What gentlemen worry about would mainly be trivial in Mencius's eyes, but the grand examples of Yao and Shun can't help them remove the worries just like that. Hence, realistically speaking, on his way to becoming a sage, man must first be able to sustain his own livelihood, since self-sufficiency is the ground upon which he can achieve his aspirations to become wise.

Six

Translation:

Mencius said, "In nurturing the heart, there is no better way than to reduce one's desires. When a man has but few desires,

【今譯】

　　孟子說：「修養心性，沒有比減少欲望更好的辦法了。如果做人能做到欲望很少，那麼他的善性雖然會有所失，也不會失去太多。如果他做人欲望多多，那麼他的善性雖然會有所保留，但保留下來的也不會太多。」

【時析】

　　這裏的「欲」是指甚麼欲呢？人有沒有求美、求義的欲望？孟子這裏應當是指物質欲望。寡欲，不是禁欲，因此與後來佛教禁欲有所不同。寡欲，估計是只讓人滿足基本的物質需求。將欲與善性對立起來，可能導致後來宋明理學的「存天理，滅人欲」。陳義過高就容易導致道德理想主義，走到了極端就要求人人做聖人，節制欲望。

　　不過，在別處，孟子又說君主要與百姓同樂，音色之類一同分享，似乎他並不鼓勵君民寡欲。那麼，這裏可能是針對君子說的話，只是作為一種養心的辦法，就跟今天有人打坐吃素、練瑜伽一樣，作為調整心態的一種手段。

　　在對待「欲」的態度上，荀子的主張比較開明。荀子從現實的人是甚麼樣子講起，人都有欲

even if the goodness in his heart lessens, it cannot be by much. Whereas for a man of many desires, though he does preserve goodness in his heart, it cannot be much." (Chapter 14.35)

Contemporary interpretation:

One may wonder what kind of "desires" is referred to in this passage. Could Mencius be referring to aesthetic or moral desires? To read within context, the term "desires" here is almost certainly referring to material desires. Mencius's advice on reducing material desires is different from Buddhism's rejection of desires. Mencius might find it acceptable to desire the satisfaction of our basic needs. This idea was later taken up by Neo-Confucian scholars of the Sung and Ming dynasties and was pushed to the extreme. They advocated "preserving the Principle of Heaven through eradicating human desires." Thus the heavenly human goodness was seen as antithetical to material desires, the latter of which had to be eradicated in order for man to attain the moral ideal of the sage. Yet such a high-sounding moral imperative might turn out to be too unsympathetic to human nature and in the end fail to serve its cause.

In other parts of *Mencius*, however, Mencius encouraged the ruler to share his interest in music with the people, and it

求，有欲求就難免產生爭奪，因此要「群」，聖王發明禮儀，就是為了讓大家不爭，依照秩序滿足大家的欲求，「群」是為了合適地順從個人欲望而講禮讓。荀子，可以作為孟子陳義過高的一個有力矯正和補充。

七

　　孟子曰：「舜發於畎畝之中，傅說舉於版築之間，膠鬲舉於魚鹽之中，管夷吾舉於士，孫叔敖舉於海，百里奚舉於市。故天將降大任於是人也，必先苦其心志，勞其筋骨，餓其體膚，空乏其身，行拂亂其所為；所以動心忍性，曾益其所不能。人恆過，然後能改。困於心，衡於慮，而後作。徵於色，發於聲，而後喻。入則無法家拂士，出則無敵國外患者，國恆亡。然後知生於憂患，而死於安樂也。」（卷十二　告子章句下・十五）

【今譯】

　　孟子說：「舜發跡於農田之中，傅說是從築牆工提拔起來的，膠鬲原是個賣魚和鹽的小販，

actually sounded as if he thought that the ruler and the people did not substantially have to restrict their desires. Perhaps the idea of reducing desires as presented here was meant to be a self-cultivation exercise for the gentleman, rather like the exercises we put into our spiritual practice nowadays, such as meditation, a vegetarian diet and yoga. In comparison, Xun Zi adopted a more liberal view on his approach towards human "desires." He acknowledged the existence of human desires which lead to fights. He then inferred that fights among men over their desires were inevitable. In order to avoid fights, "the community" should be informed and under the governance of the sage king, rites and manners would be established so that the desires of every member of the community were satisfied in an orderly way. To achieve proper satisfaction of everyone's desires, emphasis should be placed on the moral virtue of courtesy. Xun Zi's claims served to amend and supplement what Mencius's high-sounding views might have overlooked.

Seven

Translation:

Mencius said, "Shun hailed from the fields; Fu Yue was raised from the construction site; Jiao Ge was brought up from the fish and salt market; Guan Yi Wu was raised from the prison;

管仲是從監獄裏舉薦出來的，孫叔敖是從海邊提拔起來的，百里奚原來是被出售的奴隸。可見，天如果要把重大任務交給某個人，就總會先讓他心裏受苦，筋骨勞累，腸胃挨餓，身無分文，事事不順，倒楣透頂；如此才能讓他心有所動，性格堅韌，增加他自身欠缺的才能。一個人，總是會犯各種錯誤，需要他不斷地改正。他心裏總會有困惑，需要反復琢磨，然後才有所作為。（他的才能在）臉上有表現，言語有吐露，然後為人所知曉。一個國家，如果國內沒有掌控法度的大臣和輔佐的人才，國外沒有敵國和外患，那這個國家總會滅亡的。這樣，我們就可以知道，危險和禍患使人生存，安逸和享樂使人滅亡。」

【時析】

如何看待生活和工作中的苦難、挫折、不如意？是消極應付，甚或「破罐子破摔」，還是積極應對，化「危」為「機」，逆流而上，逆襲成功？孟子這段話是千古名文，千百年來激勵着有志之士，把生活的困苦當作磨煉，用來鍛煉自己的意志和精神，堅忍不拔地達到理想。

一個人只有在困難中，才能調整自己的態度，虛心認真地學習，吃常人吃不了的苦，增加

Sun Shu Ao was raised from the sea; and Bo Li Xi was raised from the slave market. This is how heaven tests a man before entrusting him with important tasks: his determination will be shaken, his will suffer physical hardship and starvation, he will be broken, and his efforts will be in vain. These experiences will inspire him, toughen up his nature and build up his strength. Man always commits mistakes and then corrects himself. It is only when someone is in distress and cannot find a way out that he will contemplate at length; and then he will act. It is only when someone's intentions and ideas are expressed through his acts that others can truly understand him. In any state, if there are no law-abiding families nor thoughtful advisors on the one hand, and no foreign enemies and external threats on the other, the state will for sure fall to pieces. The lesson for us to learn here is that we live on in adversity and we perish in ease and comfort." (Chapter 12.15)

Contemporary interpretation:

How should we respond to the sufferings and frustrations in our personal as well as our professional lives? Should we ignore them or even become heedless? Or should we confront them and try to seek a way out? This classical passage from *Mencius* has been the maxim for generations of aspiring gentlemen, motivating them to endure the hardships of life

對人性、社會和國家的瞭解，加強自己的本事，從體魄到精神，都獲得處在順境中的人難以獲得的寶貴的人生經驗。

在有的宗教中，在處理「為甚麼上帝創造的世界中會有苦難」這個神正論問題時（如基督教），發展出了「靈魂塑造說」（soul making），認為這是上帝為了考驗人的自由意志，使人們通過生活的磨煉而使靈魂得到淨化，達到自由地愛上帝的地步。

在有的宗教派別中，甚至以肉體的苦行來加強精神的淨化，如鞭笞派（以鞭抽身）、苦修派（基督教沙漠教父）。

佛陀在早期也曾苦修六年，後來意識到苦修無法到達究竟，才放棄苦修。

二戰以後，東亞經濟快速發展。如果翻開企業家們的傳記，會發現很多人都是幾起幾伏，從低處、從基層做起的。香港、台灣經濟起飛時代，企業家的打拼精神很重要。

中國大陸改革開放後，尤其在八十年代，湧

and see these adversities as necessary ways to toughen up their mind and willpower to attain their ideals. Generally speaking, man learns the most from adverse experience. As man adjusts and humbles himself to learn in the face of extraordinary difficulties, he also deepens his understanding of humanity, society and his country, thus strengthening not only his ability and body but also his mind. These are valuable lessons that can never be learned without any adverse experience.

In some religions of the world, people are perplexed by the question: "Why does God permit the existence of suffering in the world he created?" In Christianity, the problem was solved by a theory of soul making: God has gifted man with the freedom of will, and He exposed him to hardships in life as the way to cleanse his soul, in the hope of loving God on his own. Some denominations or sects within Christianity have used bodily hardship as a means of soul making, such as the self-flagellation seen in pre-Revolution Russia and the ascetism practiced by the desert fathers. Buddha also practiced severe ascetism for six years before he rejected it as a futile exercise.

After the Second World War, rapid economic development was evident in the East Asia region. As is well known, many of the famous entrepreneurs of this time achieved their

現的第一批企業家很多都來自草根階層，他們吃過很多苦，受過很多挫折，對於社會和經濟的基本情況相當瞭解，知道哪裏有需求、客戶的愛好等，因此能夠成功。

即使在今天，在互聯網等領域也仍舊存在激烈的競爭，成功和失敗常常是幾年甚至幾月之間的事，因此，創業者要有對試錯和失敗的心理準備，成功固然可喜，失敗也不要一挫即喪敗，一蹶不振，而要潛心學習，做好自己，看準時機，東山再起。

現在的學生一般家境都很好，比起他們的父母，生活水準提高了很多，嬌生慣養的較多，從小在順境裏長大，生活磨煉很少，有的稍一碰到考試不好、失戀、人際關係失調等，就受不了，甚至自殺。這都需要老師和家長予以正確的教育。

挫折教育就是一種培養學生正確面對失敗、挫折的教育。讓學生做好準備迎接失敗、不如意，增加心理上的抗壓能力，使意志力得到鍛煉，在艱難的環境下也不輕言放棄，為以後人生的風浪準備足夠的「暈船藥」，是會有預防功效的。

success only after years of hard toil, working their way up from poverty. Their perseverance was the key to success in the economic boom witnessed in Hong Kong and Taiwan. On mainland China, the first generation of entrepreneurs who emerged after the reformative policies in the 1980s were mostly from the grass-roots level. They underwent many hardships and setbacks and had intimate knowledge of the social and economic situation. Their understanding of the needs and wants of the majority was crucial to their success in the economic market. Even today, among internet businesses competition is still intense; success or failure is a matter of several months or years. Entrepreneurs should be prepared for trial and error and failure. They have to have the stamina to commit themselves to learning, to perfect themselves, seize opportunities and try again if they fail.

In contrast, today's younger generation has been raised in relative affluence with a lot of care and attention given to them. They have experienced few hardships or setbacks in their over-protective environments. Hence, they tend to be more weak-willed and emotionally vulnerable, and are susceptible to mental instability in the face of minor frustrations like failing an exam, a broken romance, or troubled personal relationships. This trend poses a new challenge for parents as

八

景春曰：「公孫衍、張儀豈不誠大丈夫哉？一怒而諸侯懼，安居而天下熄。」孟子曰：「是焉得為大丈夫乎？子未學禮乎？丈夫之冠也，父命之；女子之嫁也，母命之，往送之門，戒之曰：『往之女家，必敬必戒，無違夫子。』以順為正者，妾婦之道也。居天下之廣居，立天下之正位，行天下之大道；得志與民由之，不得志，獨行其道；富貴不能淫，貧賤不能移，威武不能屈——此之謂大丈夫。」（卷六 滕文公章句下·二）

【今譯】

景春說：「公孫衍、張儀難道不是真正的大丈夫嗎？他們一發怒，諸侯就害怕，他們一安靜，天下的戰爭就停止了。」

孟子說：「這怎麼能稱得上大丈夫呢？你沒有學過禮嗎？男子舉行加冠禮的時候，有父親訓導他。女子出嫁的時候，有母親訓導她，要把她送到門口，告誡她說：『到了你自己的家後，一定要恭敬警惕，不要違逆丈夫。』把順服當作原

well as educators about how to nurture our youth to become resolute and resilient adults. Adversity education is important in empowering students with resilience and resolution so that they are able to stand up to failures and setbacks that are a part of life.

Eight

Translation:

Jing Chun said, "Are not Gongsun Yan and Zhang Yi truly great men? When they are enraged, the vassal state rulers tremble with fear; when they are at ease, the world can make peace."

Mencius said, "How can you say such men are great? Have you never studied rites? When a young man comes to age, he receives advice from his father. When a young woman gets married, she receives advice from her mother; the mother always accompanies the bride to the door and cautions her with these words: 'When you reach your new home, be respectful, be alert, and never disobey your husband.' For submissiveness is the proper way of a woman. A man, on the other hand, resides in the spacious dwelling (propriety), puts himself in the proper position (propriety), walks on the great path of the

則，這是婦女的行為規範。男子漢居住在天下最大的住宅（禮）裏，站在天下最正確的位置（禮）上，走在天下最廣闊的道路（義）上；自己的主張能夠推行，就和百姓一起前行；不能推行，就獨自前行。富貴不能亂我的心，貧賤不能變我的志，威武不能屈我的節，這才叫大丈夫。」

【時析】

這段話中最後「大丈夫」一句，是名言，對後世影響巨大。超脫個人私利，不為富貴、貧賤、威武所擺佈，只為追求真理、實現天下正義而奮鬥，為鼓舞中國知識份子精神獨立，保持氣節起了一定的作用。

當然，如果具體分析，公孫衍、張儀、蘇秦這樣的縱橫家 —— 相當於今天的國際戰略家 —— 所起的作用未必像孟子說的這麼不堪，未必沒有原則，其個人動機也未必像孟子所說的只是為了個人的私欲。

即使有私欲（如做國師必然帶來的個人名望和好處），也不能因為有私欲便認為是錯誤的，還是要看其縱橫策略給所在國家、天下帶來的總體利益。

world (righteousness). If he gains support, he shares it with the people; if he doesn't, he walks his path alone. Neither riches nor honors can corrupt him, neither poverty nor wretchedness can frustrate him, neither threats nor force can beat him — this is what I would call a 'great man.'" (Chapter 6.2)

Contemporary interpretation:

According to Mencius, the great man is the one who acts above his own interests and will not deviate from the proper path from either fortune, poverty or threats of force; his only goal is to pursue truth and fight for realization of world justice. This saying has inspired an independent spirit and integrity in generations of Chinese intellectuals.

At the same time, we should not follow Mencius in belittling the contribution of diplomatic strategists like Gongsun Yan, Zhang Yu and Su Qin. These men may not have adopted these strategies out of their personal desires. But even if they did (such as the ruler's advisor bringing them prestige and benefits) we can't conclude that they were wrong. We should also consider the overall effects their strategies brought to the states and the world. In likening their acts as "the ways of women," Mencius not only belittled his political counterparts' actions but also exposed his own prejudice (which was widely

　　孟子將縱橫家所做的事視為「妾婦之道」，一方面貶低了競爭對手，另方面也貶低了女性，不自覺地反映了當時歧視婦女的心態。

　　孟子是個道德主義者，認為只要搞仁政，以道德治國，就能在激烈的國際競爭中快速勝出，他的觀點實在有點陳義過高，不切實際，因此他的主張並不為諸侯採納。

　　把道德力量強調到極點，就容易產生道德超人的幻覺，以為政治、經濟、社會的病症光靠道德就能救好，他很可能是開錯了藥方。

　　歷史上，真正做到孟子所說「大丈夫」境界的知識份子，雖然不多，但還是有的。比如文天祥，就寧可被砍腦袋也要保持對宋君的忠，不向元朝投降。

　　再比如現代史上傳奇人物陳獨秀，為了他所認識到的真理，而成為胡適所說的「終生反對派」，不怕跟所有黨派（包括北洋軍閥、國民黨、共產黨）鬧翻，也不怕坐牢，一生起起落落，過着顛沛流離的生活，最後潦倒死去。

accepted at that time by those who knew him) against women.

Mencius as a moralist believed that by practicing benevolent governance and moral principles, vassal states could prevail in intense competition. His views sounded too lofty and impractical to the rulers, who declared them unacceptable. In emphasizing the importance of moral ability, Mencius might have gone too far and misled people into believing the existence of some sort of a "moral superman" who could save the world from its social, economic and political illnesses solely by his outstanding moral qualities. One may reasonably doubt that this was a valid prescription.

In history, while there were only a few "great men" as described by Mencius, there were still some. For example, Wen Tian-xiang, an official who was deeply loyal to the Song dynasty forsook his life resisting the invasion of the Yuan and didn't yield. Another example is the legendary figure in modern Chinese history Chen Du-xiu, who antagonized all the political parties (including the northern warlords, the Nationalist Party and the Communist Party) in his time because of his insistence on what he believed to be the truth. He fell out with all the parties and was jailed, leading a rather unsettled and destitute life until his death.

九

孟子曰：「魚，我所欲也；熊掌，亦我所欲也。二者不可得兼，舍魚而取熊掌者也。生，亦我所欲也；義，亦我所欲也。二者不可得兼，捨生而取義者也。生亦我所欲，所欲有甚於生者，故不為苟得也。死亦我所惡，所惡有甚於死者，故患有所不辟也。如使人之所欲莫甚於生，則凡可以得生者，何不用也？使人之所惡莫甚於死者，則凡可以辟患者，何不為也？由是則生而有不用也，由是則可以辟患而有不為也。是故所欲有甚於生者，所惡有甚於死者，非獨賢者有是心也，人皆有之，賢者能勿喪耳。一簞食，一豆羹，得之則生，弗得則死。呼爾而與之，行道之人弗受；蹴爾而與之，乞人不屑也。萬鍾則不辨禮義而受之。萬鍾於我何加焉？為宮室之美、妻妾之奉、所識窮乏者得我與？鄉為身死而不受，今為宮室之美為之；鄉為身死而不受，今為妻妾之奉為之；鄉為身死而不受，今為所識窮乏者得我而為之——是亦不可以已

Nine

Translation:

Mencius said, "I like fish; I also like bear paws. If I cannot have both, I would give up the fish and take the bear paws. My life is also what I want; righteousness is also what I want. If I cannot have both, I would sacrifice my life for the sake of righteousness. While my life is what I want, when there is something more desirable than my life, I will not cling to my life at all costs. While I hate the prospect of my death, when faced with something more hateful than my death, I will not evade misfortune. If there is nothing more desirable than one's life, then why does one still scruple about exhausting any means to stay alive? If there is nothing more hateful than death, then why does one still hesitate to take all means to evade misfortune? Indeed, there are ways of survival that we decline, and there is misfortune that we choose to face. These attitudes show the ability of our heart — all human beings, not just the noble men, possess the ability to cherish things more than their own life and hate things more than their own death. The noble man simply never loses his heart.

"Now there is a basket of rice and a bowl of soup, and getting them is a matter of life and death for a dying man. When the food is offered in an insulting way, even a wanderer will not

乎？此之謂失其本心。」（卷十一 告子
章句上・十）

【今譯】

孟子說：「魚，是我想得到的；熊掌，也是
我想得到的。在兩者不可同時得到的情況下，我
願意捨棄魚而選擇熊掌。生命，是我想得到的，
正義，也是我想得到的。在二者不能同時得到的
情況下，我寧可捨棄生命而選擇正義。生命也是
我想要得到的，但我想得到的東西中有比生命更
寶貴的，所以我不會選擇苟且偷生。死亡是我所
厭惡的，但還有比死亡更令我厭惡的，所以有的
災禍我不會逃避。假如人最想要的不過是活命，
那麼凡是可以活命的手段，有甚麼不能用的呢？
假如人最厭惡的不過是死亡，那麼凡是可以逃避
災禍的手段，有甚麼不能用的呢？但是，有些人
本來可以採取這樣的手段活命，卻不採取，本來
可以採取這樣的手段逃避災禍，卻不採取，因此
可知，他們所想要的東西比生命還重要，他們所
厭惡的東西比死亡還可惡。不只是賢者有這種心
理，普通人也有這種心理，只不過賢者能夠不讓
它喪失罷了。一籃子食物，一盤子菜肴，吃得到
就活命，吃不到就餓死。可是，如果你喝叱着給
他，就是過路的人也不會接受的。如果你踏上一

accept it. When the food is trampled on before being handed out, even a beggar will refuse it. But when ten thousand bushels of grain are offered as a stipend, people accept it right away without asking whether it is proper or right for them to do so. What does one gain from accepting the payment? A beautiful residence? Pampering wives and concubines? Or appreciation from poor friends who seek help? In the past a man would not accept such bounty even if it would cost him his life; he now accepts it for a beautiful residence. In the past he would not accept it even if it would cost him his life; he now accepts it for pampering wives and concubines. In the past he would not accept it even if it would cost him his life; he now accepts it for getting appreciation from poor friends who seek help. Can a man ever abandon righteousness to receive his bounty? Such a way is called losing one's intrinsic heart." (Chapter 11.10)

Contemporary interpretation:

When we offer food to a starving dog, it will instinctively seize it from us. Yet for a starving man, he will think twice before he reacts. Am I depriving others of a fair chance to get the food? What if I had to betray my friends to accept the offer? Should I take the food even if I was treated in the most insulting way? In Mencius's view, moral considerations such as these

腳後給他，乞丐也不屑於接受的。然而對於一萬的俸祿，有人卻不問合乎禮義與否就欣然地接受了。一萬的俸祿對我有甚麼好處呢？是為了住宅的豪華、妻妾的服侍、寒酸的故舊感激我嗎？以前寧願去死也不接受的，今天卻為了住宅的豪華而去接受；以前寧願去死也不接受的，今天卻為着妻妾的服侍而去接受；以前寧願去死也不接受的，今天卻為了寒酸的故舊而接受 —— 這些難道不可以收手嗎？這就叫做丟失了本心。」

【時析】

孟子認為，人跟動物的不同在於人有道德意識，能進行道德反思，這樣，人在饑餓時，面對食物，他不會像一隻狗那樣毫不猶豫地撲上去，而是會有理性的、道德的考慮：我吃了這食物，會不會把別的人餓死？或者，我吃了這食物，但要答應給我食物的人，出賣我的朋友？或者，我吃了這食物，但要接受這個人對我的侮辱？所以，人會考慮到自己的尊嚴，會在接受不接受中進行選擇。換句話說，人有自由意志，狗不會有自由意志，它只聽從本能的召喚。

當把道德原則強調到無以復加地步的時候，就可能導致宋明理學家那樣的主張：餓死事小，

differentiate human beings from other animals. Man is capable of moral thinking and moral action; in other words, man can act out of his own free will and be morally responsible, whereas a dog can only act on its instinct.

Yet when moral principles are too steadfastly held, there is a danger of becoming a harsh moralist like the Neo-Confucians of the Sung and Ming dynasties who claimed that dying from starvation was of no importance while chastity was a woman's most solemn commitment. They reasoned that since chastity should be preserved at all costs, it would be wise for a woman to kill herself if she was robbed of her chastity. The underlying logic is the same as "to sacrifice one's life for the sake of benevolence."

There was a tragic case some years ago in China of a lady foot masseuse who jumped from a building and killed herself in order to escape sexual assault by a customer. Was the lady justified in killing herself in such circumstances? If she had lived in the Sung or Ming dynasty, hers would have been regarded as a noble act and probably a chastity memorial erected in her name.

Yet nowadays, few of us believe that chastity has an

失節事大。對於一個女人來說，貞操是最重要的，如果被人侵犯了貞節，那還不如一死了之，保全名節最為重要。因此，貞節比生命重要，這是「殺身成仁」在女性觀上的一個變體。

大陸曾發生過這樣的事：一名足浴城的女服務員受到性侵，為了保全貞節，她從高樓視窗跳下身亡。她這樣死值不值得？如果是在宋代或明代，也許政府還會給她立一個貞節牌坊，但現在，相信不會有太多人認為，貞節比生命還要重要。在貞節和生命不可兩全的情況下，當然是生命重要。沒有生命哪來的其他？何況這種道德觀念對於女性並不公平。

即使是孟子，面對這樣的討論，可能也不會站到理學家那一邊，而說該名女子遇到這種情況，不如「權變」，以保全生命為先，再保留侵害者的罪證以送其入獄。

十

　　孟子謂宋勾踐曰：「子好游乎？吾語子游：人知之亦囂囂，人不知亦囂囂。」曰：「何如斯可以囂囂矣？」

incomparably higher value than life. If one had to choose between the two, life should definitely be chosen because it is the necessary condition for any values to be realized. In fact, the emphasis on chastity as the virtue for women represents just one of the inequalities faced by Chinese women that needs to be corrected. Mencius's response to a case like the above would, unlike the Neo-Confucians of the Sung and Ming dynasties, probably be to point out the importance of exercising discretion and to advise the victim to hold dear to her life so as to seek justice and send the criminal to jail.

Ten

Translation:

Mencius said to Song Gou Jian, "Do you enjoy traveling around the states and offering counsel to the vassal state rulers? I will teach you the way to do it: no matter whether the others recognize your worth or not, always be content." "How can one be content at all times?" "If one honors virtue and delights in righteousness, then you can be content. This is why a gentleman never forsakes righteousness in hardship, and never abandons the Way in success. He stays true to himself for not forsaking righteousness in hardship; he will not disappoint the people for not abandoning the Way in success.

曰：「尊德樂義，則可以囂囂矣。故士窮不失義，達不離道。窮不失義，故士得己焉。達不離道，故民不失望焉。古之人，得志，澤加於民；不得志，修身見於世。窮則獨善其身；達則兼善天下。」（卷十三 盡心章句上·九）

【今譯】

孟子對宋勾踐說：「你喜歡游說諸侯嗎？我告訴你游說時的態度：別人理解你時，要安然自得，別人不理解你時，也要安然自得。」宋勾踐說：「怎麼做才能安然自得呢？」孟子說：「崇尚德，喜愛義，就可以安然自得。所以，士人在窮困時不要放棄義，在發達時不要背離道。窮困時不放棄義，所以能保持自我。發達時不背棄道，所以百姓不會失望。古時候的人，如果得志，就可以把恩惠普施於百姓；如果不得志，就完善自己，為世人做一個表率。窮困時就做好自己；發達時就提高天下。」

【時析】

「窮不失義，達不離道」，當然是一種理想的境界，但現實生存環境有時比較複雜也緊迫。比如，在華夏遭受異族統治的情況下，是獨善其

In the past, when his aspirations were realized, a gentleman sought to benefit the people; and when he failed to achieve his aims, he edified himself to set an example for others.

During hardship, he focused on betterment of himself; upon success, he endeavored to bring betterment to the world." (Chapter 13.9)

Contemporary interpretation:

In principle, the exhortation to "never forsake righteousness in hardship and never abandon the Way in success" offers a lofty ideal for self-edification. In practice, however, one might find the perplexities of life make adhering to this daunting. For example, when in ancient China the people of Huaxia were subject to foreign rule, was it better for the gentleman to serve in public office or not? How should one judge what was best to do in such a circumstance? During the turbulent period of the Five Dynasties and Ten Kingdoms, Feng Dao (882-954) served as chancellor for four dynasties and ten emperors. Even though intellectuals from later generations like Ouyang Xiu and Zhu Xi criticized him as a despicable and dishonest man, he was widely acclaimed by his contemporaries for his role in stabilizing the situation and securing people's

身好，還是出來當官好？在那時的處境中，應該
如何去評價？馮道（882-954）在五代十國那樣
動盪的時代，為四個朝代十個皇帝做過臣相，被
後來的歐陽修、朱熹罵為「不知廉恥」的「無節
操」小人。

但馮道受到同時代人很高的評價，認為他在
當時起到維持穩定、有利民生的作用。

再如大儒吳澄（1249-1333），在元朝蒙
古人統治時，入國子監任職講學，這跟另一些儒
士退隱山林是不同的。在面對異族入侵時，有的
選擇抵抗或不合作，有的選擇合作或妥協，如面
對德國入侵，維希政權選擇合作，戴高樂選擇抵
抗；蔣介石選擇抵抗，汪精衛選擇合作。孟子有
較強的「華夷之辯」情結，估計他可能是選擇「獨
善其身」，在這樣的亂世退隱。那麼天下誰來救
呢？或者在異族統治下，誰來減緩百姓的痛苦呢
（兼善天下）？恐怕他也會有很多的心理矛盾。

十一

孟子曰：「君子之於物也，愛之
而弗仁；於民也，仁之而弗親。親親

livelihoods. Another example is the great Confucian Wu Cheng (1249-1333). He served in the Directorate of Education under Mongolian rule during the Yuan dynasty and made a significant contribution in education, while other Confucians chose instead to lead a hermit life. There were also cases of opposing stances towards foreign invasion, such as the supportive Vichy regime during the Nazi occupation of France versus the de Gaulle resistance government, the anti-Japanese Chiang Kai-shek camp versus the pro-Japanese Wang Ching-wei camp during the Japanese occupation of China. We may wonder what Mencius would choose to do if faced with such a predicament. As an outspoken proponent for distinguishing between Hua (Chinese) and Yi (barbarian), he might rather choose to distance himself from the foreign-ruled regime. However, in so doing, he would be forsaking the people who lived in an abyss of suffering. One can imagine that Mencius would not find such a moral dilemma easy.

Eleven

Translation:

Mencius said, "A gentleman cherishes all things but shows no benevolence towards them. He treats the people with benevolence but show no familial affection towards them. He

而仁民，仁民而愛物。」（卷十三 盡心章句上・四十五）

【今譯】

孟子說：「君子對於萬物，是愛惜它們，但不是仁愛它們；對於百姓，是仁愛他們，而不是親愛他們。君子由親愛親人，而仁愛百姓，由仁愛百姓，而愛惜萬物。」

【時析】

孟子在這裏說愛有等差，由近及遠，符合人之常情。但作為行為規範，是否容易導致裙帶關係？

現在大家庭瓦解，大都變成小家庭，有的還是丁克和單身，養寵物不養孩子，對寵物之「愛」超過對民之「仁」，甚至超過對親之「親」。

有人養狗，花的錢比人要多，狗獲得的照料比親戚要多。反而親子關係，因為離婚率高而來不及照顧或不管不顧。這些早已顛倒了孟子的「外推」的秩序。

孟子說這個等差之愛針對墨子的博愛，提供

loves his relatives with affection while he loves the people with benevolence; he loves the people with benevolence while he cherishes all things." (Chapter 13.45)

Contemporary interpretation:

In this passage, Mencius differentiates the degree of love and regard between recipients in different relationships, which was a fair depiction of human psychology. However, when it became a norm for all to follow, it eventually resulted in nepotism.

In modern society, the traditional extended family has become fragmented into nuclear families or occasionally childless families. Some even choose to stay single for their whole lives. Many people now keep pets instead of having children, and their affection towards their animals already exceeds their benevolence towards people or even affection towards their relatives. People tend to spend more money on their dogs than they do on their relatives; they also often take better care of their dogs than of other people. In contrast, the parent-child relationship seems to have taken a downturn since the rise in the divorce rate. These social phenomena all serve to undermine the family-prioritized model of love put forward by Mencius.

了施愛的支撐點。但在現今社會，等差之愛作為規範，就會有問題，因為後面還涉及法律問題。

若父母受子女虐待嫌棄，父母不想將遺產交給子女，而交給照顧他們的外人，是否便沒有遵守道德規範（要優先交給親人）？

十二

孟子曰：「萬物皆備於我矣，反身而誠，樂莫大焉。強恕而行，求仁莫近焉。」（卷十三　盡心章句上・四）

【今譯】

孟子說：「一切我都具備了。反躬自問，自己是誠實的，快樂沒有比這更大的。努力地以推己及人的恕道做事，追求達到仁的境界，沒有比這更直捷的。」

【時析】

恕是對待別人的態度，《論語》說「己所不欲，勿施於人」，「己欲立而立人，己欲達而達人」，都說到推己及人，考慮別人的需要和感受，

Still, we must appreciate Mencius's acknowledgment of human love as naturally differential in character; his view offered a more humanly possible starting point compared with the universal love of Mozi. At the same time, we must be wary of the underlying legal implications if differentiation of love is taken as the moral norm for subsequent action. For example, would it be morally wrong for parents to deny their abusive or negligent children as heirs, and grant the inheritance right instead to an unrelated yet conscientious caretaker?

Twelve

Translation:

Mencius said, "All things are complete in me. If upon self-reflection I find that I am true to myself, there will be no greater joy than that. If I exert all my effort in treating others the way I wish to be treated, I will find the shortest way to benevolence." (Chapter 13.4)

Contemporary interpretation:

Confucius said, "What you do not want must not be imposed upon others; when you want to stand up, you need to help others to stand up as well; and when you want to understand, you need to help others also to understand."

視人如己。它是正義的一個基礎。

「強恕」中的強字用得很好，有強推、強使的意思，強迫自己做到視人如己，愛人如己，這樣一來，當然就離「仁」（愛人，掌權者推廣則為仁政）近，堪稱捷徑。

「萬物皆備於我」這句話歷來難解，有人認為指「萬理」，有人認為指一種與物同體、萬物一體的神秘體驗。

從文中來看，很可能是指我對萬物、他人都有一種同情體驗，對它們（他們）是誠心誠意的，沒有辜負、傷害它們（他們），並且對它們（他們）一視同仁，而不是將它們（他們）看作可以宰割的物品、客體。這種解釋跟孟子一貫的仁愛、仁政思想是相通的。

十三

孟子曰：「君子有三樂，而王天下不與存焉。父母俱存，兄弟無故，一樂也。仰不愧於天，俯不怍於人，二樂也。得天下英才而教育之，三樂

In order to become benevolent, one must put oneself into others' shoes and try to consider their needs and feelings as one's own. In other words, empathetic understanding is very important in being just to others. Mencius talked a lot about "compelling oneself" to treat and love others the way one wishes to be treated and loved oneself. If a person is doing this, he must already be practicing benevolence to a great extent (by loving others, a ruler practices benevolent governance).

This is why Mencius said consideration of others is the shortest way to benevolence.

"All things are complete in me" is a statement that has puzzled many scholars. Some take "all things" as referring to "all principles"; others claim that it describes a mysterious experience of becoming one with all things.

In its context, this statement can be interpreted as pointing to an empathetic experience in which the person values the existence of all things, and treats them the same but not as something at their disposal.

Such an interpretation is congruent with Mencius's philosophy of benevolence.

也。君子有三樂，而王天下不與存
焉。」（卷十三 盡心章句上・二十）

【今譯】

孟子說：「君子有三種樂事，而當天下的帝王並不在其中。父母都還在世，兄弟也不缺少一人，這是第一個樂事。抬頭無愧於天，低頭無愧於人，這是第二個樂事。得到天下優秀的人才而培養他們，這是第三個樂事。君子有三大樂事，當天下的帝王並不在這三大樂事當中。」

【時析】

儒家很重視教育，在科舉時代，通過教育來塑造社會，是儒家思想發揮作用的一個重要管道。「得天下英才而教育之」，堪稱古代的精英教育。不管是民主社會還是傳統社會，能夠管理、影響社會的都只能是一小部份精英，「關鍵少數」。

通過影響這「關鍵少數」，就能對社會風氣、精神面貌發揮作用。如果這些英才本身發生了畸變，只顧自己的利益，像錢理群教授批判的北大那樣，培養出來的人多數是「精緻的利己主義者」，那麼，整個社會的導向就會出問題。孟子

Thirteen

Translation:

Mencius said, "The gentleman takes joy in three things, and to rule over the world is not among them. To have both of his parents alive and his brothers in good health, this is the first of his joys. To have nothing to be ashamed of before heaven or people, this is the second of his joys. To be able to gather the most talented students and educate them, this is the third of his joys. The gentleman takes joy in three things, and to rule over the world is not among them." (Chapter 13.20)

Contemporary interpretation:

Education has always been central to Confucian thought. The implementation of the imperial examination system offered an important channel for Confucian thinking, through intellectuals, to make great social impact. "To gather the most talented students and educate them" may be regarded as an ancient account of what we today call elite education. In fact, from traditional societies to modern democratic nations, the educated elite, the so-called "critical minority," has always played an important role in shaping and reforming social ethos and moral standards. Therefore, if the elite class became corrupted, society as a whole would suffer. A notable example of this is Professor Qian Liqun's attack on Beijing

將教育視為人生「三樂」之一，實際上也跟他的
仁政理想、王道思想一致，只不過跟游說國王實
行仁政和王道比較起來，教育的功效更加長遠，
沒有那麼急切而已。

為甚麼要把「王天下」排除在「三樂」之外
呢？一個主要原因，是「王天下」乃是聖王之樂，
普天之下只有極少數的幾個人能夠達到，因此，
普通君子就不要奢望能享有此樂了。而進行教育
是平民也能做的。

孔子樂意教書育人，他甚至不像孟子這樣
「精英主義」（想教英才），學生只要願意讀書，
交幾條「束修」（乾肉脯）就行了。

另外兩樂，第一條家庭和睦，親人俱健在，
看似平凡，但提醒人們，不要「身在福中不知
福」，趁親人在世時好好相處，不然，出現「樹
欲靜而風不止，子欲養而親不在」的遺憾就不好
了。

第二條是很高的道德要求，要求人做到無愧
於天地人神，心中沒有因為種種原因導致的愧
疚。

University for nurturing so many "sophisticated egoists." In order to protect society from the bad influence of corrupted intellectuals, it is the duty of any ruler to place strong emphasis on education as a part of his benevolent governance or the kingly way. This is why Mencius took educational success as one of his three joys in life.

One may wonder why "to become the king of the world" was not among Mencius's ultimate joys in life. The main reason rests on his view that the joy of the king can only be attained by a handful of sage kings, and thus is out of reach for ordinary gentlemen. In contrast, becoming an educator is an attainable mission for everyone and therefore can be seen as one of the ultimate joys of a gentleman. Confucius was as enthusiastic as Mencius in teaching, yet he was not an elitist like Mencius (who wanted to teach the most talented students). Confucius would welcome anyone as his student; all he wanted in the way of payment for his tuition was just a few pieces of preserved meat.

The first joy cited is about harmonious family relationships. It sounds uninspiring, yet it might well be the one joy that is most overlooked while it is still in our hands. Mencius reminds us to love our family the best we can so that we will have no

十四

孟子曰：「事孰為大？事親為大。守孰為大？守身為大。不失其身而能事其親者，吾聞之矣；失其身而能事其親者，吾未之聞也。孰不為事？事親，事之本也。孰不為守？守身，守之本也。曾子養曾晢，必有酒肉；將徹，必請所與；問有餘，必曰『有』。曾晢死，曾元養曾子，必有酒肉；將徹，不請所與；問有餘，曰『亡矣』，將以復進也，此所謂養口體者也。若曾子，則可謂養志也。事親若曾子者，可也。」（卷七 離婁章句上·十九）

【今譯】

孟子說：「侍奉誰最重要？侍奉父母最重要。守護誰最重要？守護自己最重要。自己的操守沒有過失而能侍奉父母的，我聽說過；自己沒有操守而能侍奉父母的，我沒有聽說過。誰不應該被侍奉呢？但是侍奉父母，是侍奉的根本。誰不應該被守護呢？守護自己，（保持節操），是守護的根本。曾子供養曾晢，每頓飯都一定有酒肉；吃完要撤除了，一定要問，剩下的給誰；如果曾

regrets when death parts us, forever. The second joy represents a high moral call on oneself to become true not only to one's conscience but also to the whole universe.

Fourteen

Translation:

Mencius said, "What is the most important duty? One's duty to serve one's parents. What is the most important thing to keep? One's integrity. I have heard of a man who has never lost his integrity and is able to serve his parents, but I have never heard of one who lost his integrity and is still able to serve his parents. There are indeed many duties one has to serve; yet the duty to serve one's parents is the most essential. There are indeed many things for one to keep; yet one's integrity is the most essential for one to hold on to.

"When Zeng Zi looked after Zeng Xi, he always served him wine and meat; and when clearing away the dishes, he always asked to whom the leftover portion should be given. When his father asked if there was any food left, Zeng Zi always said, 'Yes, there is.' After Zeng Xi died, Zeng Yuan looked after Zeng Zi, and he always served him wine and meat. But when clearing away the dishes, Zeng Yuan did not ask to whom

皙問他還有沒有多餘的，一定會答『有』。曾皙
死後，曾元供養曾子，每頓飯也是一定有酒肉；
吃完要撤席時，曾元不問曾子剩下的東西給誰
吃。曾子問還有沒有多餘的，曾元說『沒了』。
他要將多餘的酒肉再給他父親吃。這就叫做口體
之養。至於曾子對父親的做法，可以叫作『養
志』——滿足父母內心的想法。侍奉父母能像曾
子那樣，就可以了。」

【時析】

曾子養父親，為讓老人不擔心，說家裏食物
足夠，讓老人安享晚年，精神愉快。

曾元養父親，則讓老人憂慮家境不好，家人
吃不飽。——我們不知道曾子是否為了讓父親開
心而說謊，比如家裏食物本來不夠了，但他要說
夠，如是，則是「善意的謊言」了。

後來儒家有所謂對比父母的「三養」，即養
體、養色（使高興）、養志（實現父母對自己的
寄託）。

照這個標準，曾子對父親也只是盡到了「養
色」一級。至於「養志」，雖然天下的父母都「望

the leftover portion should be given. When his father asked if there was any food left, he always said 'No, there is none.' For he wanted to serve the leftovers to his father again. This can only be described as looking after the mouth and the body. In contrast, what Zeng Zi did was to look after his parent's wishes. It would be good for one to emulate how Zeng Zi looked after his parent." (Chapter 7.19)

Contemporary interpretation:

Zeng Zi always made sure that his father did not need to worry about food and enjoyed his old age in peace and happiness. Zeng Yuan, however, in his turn, suggested to his father that they might not have enough food for the next meal and thus made his father worried. Did Zeng Zi really have plenty of food at home or did he lie to his father in order not to worry him? If the latter was true, then he was lying to his father with good intentions.

Later Confucians identified three kinds of care someone could give to his parents, that is, to look after his parents physically, to look after his parents' mood (to make them happy) and to look after the wishes of his parents (to gratify them through one's achievements in life). With these criteria in mind, we see that even Zeng Zi succeeded only in giving the second kind of

子成龍」，但「子」真正能夠成「龍」的卻寥寥
無幾，因此恐怕大部份人都做不到「養志」。

十五

萬章問曰：「敢問友。」孟子
曰：「不挾長，不挾貴，不挾兄弟而
友。友也者，友其德也，不可以有挾
也。」（卷十 萬章章句下・三）

【今譯】

萬章問孟子說：「請問如何交友。」孟子說：
「交朋友，不應該考慮年齡大小，地位高低，關
係親疏。交朋友，交的是朋友的品德，不可以倚
仗別的東西。」

【時析】

孟子泛道德化的毛病在交友一事上表現出
來。他着重朋友德的方面。孔子說，「三人行，
必有我師」，不講只友其德，還有其他方面。孔
子交朋友，有的是德友，有的是「多聞」的朋友。

孟子的朋友都是有德而且是特別純粹的人，
我們相信這樣的朋友是有的，但是恐怕也是極少

care to his father, that is, to make him happy. The last kind of care is probably the most challenging task for all of us because it requires time, effort and often luck for anyone to become as successful and outstanding in life as our parents themselves might wish us to be.

Fifteen

Translation:

Wan Zhang asked, "May I ask about friendship?"

Mencius said, "Do not make friends reckoning on what advantage to take from the other's seniority, standing, or relations. To befriend someone is to befriend his virtue, one should not reckon on anything else." (Chapter 10.3)

Contemporary interpretation:

In discussing friendship, Mencius exposed the narrow-mindedness of his overstated moralistic stance. Confucius said, "Whenever three people walk together, one of them will be my teacher." Confucius considered that we can have different types of friends. While some of them may be "righteous," others can be "well informed"; therefore we can learn different things from different friends. Yet Mencius asked us to befriend

的。不知孟子當時交上沒有？

十六

孟子曰：「子路，人告之以有過則喜。禹聞善言則拜。大舜有大焉，善與人同，舍己從人，樂取於人以為善。自耕、稼、陶、漁，以至為帝，無非取於人者。取諸人以為善，是與人為善者也。故君子莫大乎與人為善。」（卷三 公孫丑章句上·八）

【今譯】

孟子說：「子路這個人，別人指出他的錯誤，他聽了就高興。禹這個人，聽到好的建議就給人敬禮。大舜更偉大，他善於跟別人一致，拋棄自己的不是，接受別人的是，喜歡博采眾長，把事情做好。從耕種莊稼，到製陶、打魚，到當帝王，沒有一樣不是博采眾長的。博采眾長來做好事，這就促使大家一起做好事。所以君子最大的長處就促使大家一起做好事。」

【時析】

聽從其他人的意見，就能集思廣益，從善如

only those who were virtuous people. Wouldn't this greatly narrow our social circle?

Sixteen

Translation:

Mencius said, "Whenever anyone told Zi Lu that he had made a mistake, he was pleased. Whenever Yu heard a fine speech, he bowed before the speaker. The great Shun was even greater. He was good at achieving consistency with others, and gave up his ideas and followed others, and he was willing to learn from others how best to do things. From the time he was a farmer, a potter, as well as a fisherman, to the time he became a king, he learned all sorts of things from others. To learn from others what is good is to join hands with others to do good. The greatest thing a gentleman can do is to join hands with others to do good." (Chapter 3.8)

Contemporary interpretation:

If a person is willing to take advice from others, then he can pool their combined [wisdom] and talents and together try and put these to good use. One must be able to let go of one's ego in order to collaborate with others. As the saying goes, two heads are better than one. The ability to pool wisdom

流。不拘己見，才能同大家一起為善。所謂三個
臭皮匠，賽過諸葛亮。無論普通人還是國君，誰
能集思廣益，誰就能發家致富，發國致強。一個
人學習他人之善，又會促使他人積極行善，最後
互相激勵，善善與共，形成良性循環的社會氛圍。

is essential for any success, whether it is an ordinary person running a business or a ruler running a country. What is more, if one is willing to learn from the good deeds of others, those others will be motivated to do even better. Gradually, progress will be seen on both sides and in this way society as a whole will benefit from a cycle of shared virtuousness.

性善及
存養

The Nature and
Cultivation of
Human Goodness

一

孟子曰：「人之所不學而能者，其良能也。所不慮而知者，其良知也。孩提之童，無不知愛其親者，及其長也，無不知敬其兄也。親親，仁也。敬長，義也。無他，達之天下也。」（卷十三 盡心章句上・十五）

【今譯】

孟子說：「人不用學習就會做到的，是良能。人不用思考就會知道的，是良知。兩三歲的小孩子，沒有不愛他的父母的，等他長大後，沒有不敬他的兄長的。親愛父母就是仁，尊敬兄長就是義。沒有別的，把良能良知推到天下就天下大治了。

【時析】

人有所謂自私基因，也有利他基因。在一些社會生物如蜂群、蟻群中，有些成員為了保全群體是可以作出自我犧牲的。人作為動物，當然有他的本能，如孩子生下來就會吃奶，依賴父母，但有意識的愛恐怕小時是沒有的。一般來說，孩子長大後會愛父母，但這只是一般來說，不一定必然會。父母愛孩子，孩子卻不一定必然會愛父

One

Translation:

Mencius said, "What a man can do without having to learn it, is his innate ability; what he knows right away, is his innate understanding. Even toddlers know their love for their parents; and when they grow older, they all know their respect for their elder brothers. Loving one's parents is benevolence, respecting one's elders is righteousness. All one needs to do then is to make use of them to take care of the whole world." (Chapter 13.15)

Contemporary interpretation:

Human beings are born with so-called selfish genes as well as altruistic genes. Social animals such as bees and ants may sacrifice themselves for the group's sake. Humans, like other animals, are also born with natural instincts, such as those of babies suckling or relying on their parents. But it is doubtful if babies recognize their love for their parents. In general, as children grow up they come to love their parents, but this is not always the case. While parents love their children, the children may not repay this love, suggesting a biological mechanism might be at work. Respect for elders is even less evident. Mencius may have seen the positive side of man, but he failed to admit to the dark side and thus came to his biased conclusions.

母。這裏面可能是有些生物規則在起作用。至於敬長更不一定了。孟子只看到好的一面，光明的一面，而沒有看到另外一面，是有偏頗的。

照孟子的邏輯，既然性善，有良知良能，那麼把它發揚光大即可成就善人善社會，由親親敬長一路推到天下，仿佛一個直線演繹。

可惜，世界並非這麼簡單，否則早已天下大治太平了。有時世界上的衝突，不一定是善惡之間的衝突，而是善與善之間的衝突，是價值 A 跟價值 B 之間的衝突，或者同一價值鏈上位次不同者之間的衝突。

良知良能說在傳統簡單的熟人鄉村社會，可能是足以解釋善惡判斷的，但在今日複雜的城市社會、陌生人社會中，分工細化，組織機構眾多，人際關係多樣，法律規條千絲萬縷，交往瞬息萬變，道德與法律的灰色地帶多不可數，有的新領域甚至人類也所知不多（如 DNA、AI、轉基因等高科技），單靠良知良能，哪能下判斷？再比如對於人性的理解，今天可能跟二千年前大為不同，如再造人、機器人、人工智能涉及一系列哲學、倫理與法律問題，需要艱深的討論和論證，

Mencius's reasoning is rather straightforward: since man is endowed with goodness, inborn ability and inborn knowledge, he is capable of loving his parents and respecting his elders. Once he can extend his virtuous acts further, society will become humane and filled with good people.

Unfortunately, we do not live in a world as simple as this, otherwise the world would be at peace. Conflicts in values may not just be between good or bad, but between good choices, or having to prioritize between two things of similar values.

The doctrine of intrinsic goodness may be useful to explain what is good or bad in the context of the traditional community of fellow villagers. If we take into consideration the current complex metropolitan or so-called strangers society — with its intricate organizational structures, delicate human relationships and sophisticated rules and regulations, we are faced not just with endless gray-area problems in law and morality but also overwhelming information from newly created disciplines (such as DNA analysis, AI, genetic engineering, etc.). How can a simple assertion on human goodness offer ground for all of our judgments? What is more, the modern understanding of humanity has evolved

單靠良知良能，無法對這些領域作出有效判斷。哲學，包括倫理，必須跟着時代向前步伐，而有所更新、發展。

二

孟子曰：「仁，人心也。義，人路也。舍其路而弗由，放其心而不知求，哀哉！人有雞犬放，則知求之，有放心，而不知求。學問之道無他，求其放心而已矣。」（卷十一 告子章句上‧十一）

【今譯】

孟子說：「仁，是人的心。義，是人的路。放棄正路而不走，喪失人心而不曉得尋找，真是可悲啊！人們把雞和狗丟失了，還曉得要去找，把心丟了，卻不曉得去尋找。學問的宗旨沒有別的，只是把丟失的心找回來而已。」

【時析】

對於蘇格拉底來說，學習就是把前世知道的東西「回憶」出來。對於孟子來說，學問就是把丟掉的心重新找回來，就跟把丟失的雞狗重新找

into a state that could not have been imagined by people two thousand years ago. Concepts such as human cloning, robots, AI, etc. involve complicated philosophical as well as moral and legal issues and call for in-depth discussions and arguments. The doctrine of intrinsic goodness seems inadequate as a ground for any valid judgments. We must now regenerate and develop our philosophy, ethics included, to keep up with the times.

Two

Translation:

Mencius said, "Benevolence is the heart of man, and righteousness his path. How sorrowful it is for a man to walk away from his path and be unguided and let his heart wander and not go after it! When a man finds his chickens and dogs missing, he knows he will go after them, yet he knows not what to do when his heart has gone missing. The proper way for the quest of learning is none other than this: to go after one's missing heart." (Chapter 11.11)

Contemporary interpretation:

Socrates considered that learning was simply a recollection of what one already knew in a previous life. For Mencius,

回來一樣。

孟子認為人天生就有善性，就有四端，學習
的任務不過是把這四端重新找出來發揚罷了，因
此，學問在孟子這裏並非向外部世界去探求，而
是向已有的內在世界去重新發現，這樣，學問就
成了一種狹窄的倫理學科。這種「心學」使人注
重內省，而缺乏向外求索的動力，不能指望它發
展出自然科學來。從方法上說，孟子對於如何在
真實的人性基礎上進行道德和政治規勸，都缺乏
細緻的認識和考察，更遑論對實際的治國理政進
行經驗主義的探討。

三

孟子曰：「無或乎王之不智也。
雖有天下易生之物也，一日暴之，十
日寒之，未有能生者也。吾見亦罕
矣，吾退而寒之者至矣，吾如有萌焉
何哉？今夫弈之為數，小數也；不專
心致志，則不得也。弈秋，通國之善
弈者也。使弈秋誨二人弈，其一人專
心致志，惟弈秋之為聽。一人雖聽

learning is to recover one's missing heart, in the same way we go after a missing chicken or dog.

Mencius believed that man was endowed with intrinsic goodness — the four nascent virtues, or senses, of benevolence, righteousness, wisdom and propriety, and that the task of learning was to recover these senses and develop them to the fullest extent. In this way, learning became a narrow ethical pursuit focusing on discovery in the inner world, instead of an inquiry towards the outer unknown word. As a result of this emphasis on self-reflection, the quest for an understanding of the external world was discouraged and so was the development of scientific inquiry. Methodologically speaking, Mencius did not support his moral and political claims with any thorough investigations into human nature at work.

Three

Translation:

Mencius said, "No wonder the king is not wise. Even a tough plant cannot survive if one exposes it to the sun for one day and then to the cold for ten days. I rarely meet with the king, but every time when I leave, those who chill him [numb his senses] come to him. How can I help the sprouts [of

之，一心以為有鴻鵠將至，思援弓繳
而射之，雖與之俱學，弗若之矣。為
是其智弗若與？曰：非然也。」（卷
十一 告子章句上・九）

【今譯】

孟子說：「齊王糊塗，這沒甚麼奇怪的。天
下雖然有很容易生長的植物，但曬它一天，再凍
它十天，它也沒法活。我見齊王的機會太少了，
我退居在家，那些諂媚的人就圍到他身邊，我怎
麼能夠幫他萌發他的仁心呢？比如下棋，那只是
一門雕蟲小技，但如果不專心致志地學，也下不
好。弈秋是全國最好的棋手。如果讓弈秋來教兩
人下棋，其中一人專心致志地學習，只聽弈秋講
課。另外一人雖然也在聽，卻一心以為一隻天鵝
要飛來，想要拿起弓箭去射天鵝。他雖然是跟人
在一起學習，卻不如人家。是他的智力不如人家
嗎？只能說並非如此。」

【時析】

仁只是人心裏的一個嫩芽，雖然很容易生
長，也需要持續的陽光雨露。如果一曝十寒，常
年處於嚴冬，那它怎麼能生長發育成一棵大樹
呢？齊王的仁心為甚麼長不大？雖然孟子如陽光

benevolence] in him to grow? Now think of the game of chess: it is indeed an easy game, yet without focus and devotion, one cannot become good at it. Qiu is the best chess player in the state. If we ask him to teach two men to play chess, one of whom is focused and devoted, and listens to Qiu's teachings attentively, while the other, though he listens, daydreams about seeing a swan and wishes to shoot it down, even though this man takes the same lessons with the other, he will never be as good. Is this because he is not as intelligent? I would say, no, it isn't." (Chapter 11.9)

Contemporary interpretation:

Benevolence is like a little sprout in our heart, it grows only when there is abundant sunshine and precipitation. If we expose it to heat for a while and then to the freezing cold, it is hardly likely to flourish into a big tree. So why was King Qi unable to become benevolent? Mencius tried to shine on him like the sun as best as he could, but when Mencius was not around, he was mostly surrounded by the "freezing cold" (his crooked counselors). So even though King Qi had the potential to become a benevolent king, in practice he was like the daydreaming student of chess and therefore his chances of success were slim. It seems that here Mencius tried to explain why King Qi failed his class on "benevolent governance."

那樣能夠照到他，但也只是照一照，大部份時間他都被嚴寒包圍（佞臣）。他的智力雖然足以把仁政這門課修好，但他就像那個分心的學棋者一樣，時時走神，怎麼能畢業呢？

看來，孟子這是在向外人解釋，為甚麼他向齊王講了「仁政」這門課，齊王卻經常缺課，上課時還不專心，心猿意馬，因此學業不佳，畢不了業。

仁政相當於今天的道德課和政治課，要學得好，看來還得實踐。在這裏，孟子沒有提到實踐可能是因為他的這個學生根本就沒想實踐，而且一聽課頭就大了。

四

孟子曰：「人之所以異於禽獸者幾希，庶民去之，君子存之。舜明於庶物，察於人倫；由仁義行，非行仁義也。」（卷八 離婁章句下・十九）

【今譯】

孟子說：「人區別於禽獸的地方就那麼一點

Either he skipped classes, or he paid no attention when there. No wonder he got bad grades and didn't achieve a pass.

The classes on benevolent governance were like contemporary courses in ethics and politics. Putting what one has learned into practice is essential for any achievement in these disciplines. In this passage, however, Mencius said nothing about practice. The reason, most probably, is that his student had no interest in the topic from the start, and no desire to put it into practice.

Four

Translation:

Mencius said, "The difference between man and the beasts is very slight. The commoner misplaces it; the gentleman retains it. Shun was knowledgeable about a variety of things and was perceptive about human relationships. He acted out of benevolence and righteousness; he did not act in order to look benevolent and righteous." (Chapter 8.9)

Contemporary interpretation:

Mencius's view of the intrinsic goodness of human nature regarded good behavior as stemming from our inner sense

點，百姓丟棄了它，君子保存了它。舜懂得事物的道理，瞭解人際的倫常；他秉性仁義，順着本性做仁義的事，而不是刻意地做仁義的事。」

【時析】

孟子認為人性善，只要保留這點善並發揚，那麼做起善事就如順水行舟，自然而然，是自主自動的，而不是外在強加的，所以說「由仁義行，非行仁義」。

不過，這種對性善和道德良知良能的肯定，要面對道德本能、道德直覺可能出錯的問題。在傳統的農耕、熟人社會，道德判斷是比較簡單的。在現代複雜的陌生人社會、流動性社會，以及複雜的政治、經濟、法律環境中，道德判斷有時很難憑本能作出，而要經過複雜的思考和判斷，否則不會有那麼多難解的現象了。比如，路上老人摔倒了你要不要扶？這麼簡單的事情，在傳統社會根本不用思索，但現在由於信用關係的缺乏，可能扶他你會陷入陷阱。（因為時時有老人訛詐的新聞傳出。）即便在親情上，中國現代家庭也發生了巨大變化，比如再生家庭增多，核心家庭增多，獨生子女多，常常除了父母外，談不上有多少「尊老」的機會，相應這方面的「道

of goodness. It should be spontaneous and self-initiated, instead of being imposed from external sources. This is why he said, "He acted out of benevolent and righteous concerns; he did not just act in order to look benevolent and righteous." However, such an assertion about the intrinsic goodness of human nature has to deal with the problem arising from the fallibility of our moral instincts and moral intuitions.

In the traditional acquaintance-based rural community, moral judgments were relatively simple and straightforward. In our modern complicated, fluid society populated by strangers and characterized by a variety of political, economic and legal conflicts, it seems impossible to reach a moral judgment solely on one's moral instinct. If this were not the case, there would be many fewer unsettled moral disputes. As a simple case example, if an elderly person fell on the street, would you help him? In a traditional society, there would be no question: one would not hesitate for a second about what to do. Yet in our modern distrustful society, giving a hand to a stranger might result in the benefactor being tricked. (Reports of elderly people participating in scams are not uncommon.) Similarly, on the issue of filial piety, family structure in China has undergone tremendous change resulting in a great increase in the number of one-child families. The only adults the children

德直覺」估計也萎縮了。而對街上遇到的陌生人，在沒有信任關係的前提下，很難做出「敬長」的舉動。

另外，孟子似乎將人的道德情感視為高於其他動物。其實，禽獸未必沒有親情、敬長的本能或直覺，甚至還可能更符合孟子的標準。因為人的理性思考常常會出錯，而動物憑本能可以更直接地達到「道德」行為。比如，動物失去伴侶會有感情，有親子情和伴侶情，大象、天鵝都有這些行為表現。猴子在同類遇難時也會幫助救援的。說到長幼秩序、情感表達，群居動物內部似乎也不缺乏，如猴子群體內就有猴王后妃之類的分層，一定的權力等級關係，服從與被服從的關係，亦有地盤之分，這是否類似於人類群落、國家的分界，統治階級的權力及倫理規範？如果猴子有語言，很可能也發展出仁義禮智之類的道德話語。所以，孟子以「道德」來區分人禽可能有問題。相對來說，則有以「理性」來區分人禽，但也有爭議。單純以「理性」來區分人獸，有可能將人對動物的「同情心」遮罩在外。比如，在笛福的《魯濱遜漂流記》中，魯濱遜在思考自己要不要殺死當地「食人生番」時，想到這樣一個問題，當地野蠻人之所以會把敵對部落的俘虜殺

now interact with daily are their parents, and it may not be as "instinctual" for the children to act morally and properly to other older people, not to mention those whom they have never met. Hence, it may indeed be unnatural for them to be able to treat the elderly with due traditional respect in a society where public trust is lacking.

Also, it seems that Mencius regarded the moral attachment of humans as stronger than that of other animals. However, it is known that wild animals can have caring instincts towards parents and spontaneous respect for elders. In fact, wild animals may better fulfill Mencius's obligations since, unlike man whose judgment might become muddled by his reasoning, their instinctual "moral" behavior is far more straightforward. For example, animals like elephants and swans will grieve over the loss of a family member; others like monkeys will offer rescue to fellow monkeys. What is more, social animals do have some sort of order based upon seniority. In monkey communities there are alpha males and females with hierarchical power relationships and assigned territories. Aren't these very much like human society — with delineation of national borders, the power of the sovereign and ethical norms? If monkeys were able to speak a language, it might be possible for them to develop a moral discourse with

死吃掉，可能是因為他們不再把俘虜看作「人」，因此可以「心安理得」地吃掉戰俘，這就跟人類將家畜視為低人一等的動物，從而「心安理得」地屠宰牠們一樣。曾流行過一個法國拍的生豬屠宰場的視頻，上千上萬的豬被屠宰，去毛，掛在鐵桿上被切割，真是一副「人間地獄」的場景。人之屠殺動物真是毫無同情心，這跟他們把動物視為低人一等的「異類」的理性判斷有關。相形之下，佛教認識到人對動物等「有情眾生」是有慈悲心的，佛教的「戒殺」，跟孟子所說的對動物（如牛）的惻隱之心，有點近似。從孟子的角度說，宰殺動物堪稱合理而不合情。合理而且合情時，人才不會把有情眾生當成異類，納粹才不會把猶太人妖魔化，當成另類，從而在屠殺猶太人時心安理得。

五

告子曰：「性，猶杞柳也；義，猶桮棬也。以人性為仁義，猶以杞柳為桮棬。」孟子曰：「子能順杞柳之性而以為桮棬乎？將戕賊杞柳而後以為桮棬也？如將戕賊杞柳而以為桮

moral vocabularies like ours. Hence, Mencius's distinction between human and other animals based upon "morality" might not be as valid as it seems.

Similarly, the distinction based upon "rationality" sounds as doubtful because it overlooks how humans can treat animals with "compassion." If we examine Daniel Defoe's *The Life and Adventures of Robinson Crusoe*, when Crusoe deliberated on whether he should kill the cannibals on the island, he thought the reason the cannibals were able to kill and eat the prisoners with "no qualms of conscience" was because they didn't consider the prisoners as "humans." The same is true of humans regarding livestock. They view these animals as an inferior class and slaughter them with no moral compunction.

A widely shared video showing thousands of pigs about to be slaughtered and butchered was truly a portrayal of hell on earth. The rationale for such brutal slaughter of other beings in the world is grounded in our rational categorization of animals as the inferior "other." In contrast, according to Buddhism, man should show loving kindness to other "sentient beings" and refrain from taking their lives. The Buddhist stance is close to what Mencius called "the heart of compassion" towards animals (e.g. cattle). For Mencius, it would be "reasonable"

捲，則亦將戕賊人以為仁義與？率天
下之人而禍仁義者，必子之言夫！」
（卷十一　告子章句上・一）

【今譯】

告子說：「人的天性，正如杞柳；義，正如
杯盤；認為人的天性是仁義的，正如把杞柳看成
杯盤。」孟子說：「您能順着杞柳的天性把它做
成杯盤嗎？還是要毀壞杞柳而後才把它做成杯
盤？如果要毀壞杞柳才能把它做成杯盤，那您也
要毀壞人性才能實行仁義嗎？率領天下的人來損
害仁義的，一定是您的這些話！」

【時析】

告子，一般認為是墨子的弟子。孟子和告子
關於人性論發生過爭論，這場爭論的地點是在齊
國，其時孟子剛到那裏，而告子在齊國的稷下已
有年頭。當時孟子是四十歲出頭，告子則差不多
八十歲了。

杞柳是一種枝條柔韌的柳樹，桮棬是木製飲
器。告子反對孟子將人性等同於仁義。告子認為
人性只是原始材料，需要加工才有仁義，就好比

but against our "heart" to willfully slaughter animals. Only when man is able to reason with his heart, will he then not thoughtlessly deny the value of other beings.

Had the Nazis been able to do this they would not have demonized the Jews as "the other," and would not have attempted to exterminate the entire Jewish people with "no qualms of conscience."

Five

Translation:

Gaozi said, "Human nature is like the Qi willow. Righteousness is like cups and bowls. Drawing benevolence and righteousness from human nature is like making cups and bowls out of Qi willow wood."

Mencius said, "Can you follow the nature of the Qi willow in order to make cups and bowls? Or must you hack the tree to fashion them? If you have to hack the tree to make cups and bowls, then in the same manner you have to hack a man in order to make him benevolent and righteous? These words of yours will surely lead the world to cripple benevolence and righteousness!" (Chapter 11.1)

杞柳需要加工才能做成杯盤。孟子的關注則是，從本性到仁義固然要加工，但是你能把人性加工成仁義，那也得是因為人性本來就具有可以加工成仁義的條件呀！

正如你用杞柳做成杯盤，其前提條件是杞柳有可以成為杯盤的本性，你不過是順着它的本性才能做出杯盤，否則，你就得破壞杞柳的本性去做杯盤。人性之所以能做到仁義，是因為人性中本來就有仁義的萌芽。只有「順」着本性裏仁義的萌芽，才能在後天培養並發展出仁義。

如果像告子那樣，認為人性中本來沒有仁義，仁義是從外面對原材料加工的結果，是把原材料破壞、毀壞後造出來的，那就等於承認仁義是違背人性的，這就會否定仁義，這種主張會禍害天下。

其實，兩人的辯論中，在對「性」的定義上是有差異的。孟子的「性」，不是純粹被動的、無善無惡中性的、只待被加工的原材料，而是有主體性、主動性和正面性的。人的選擇都是自主的，選善選惡都可能。善性容易丟失，故要涵養，培養發揚「四端」，不走失陷溺。

Contemporary interpretation:

It is generally believed that Gaozi was a disciple of Mozi. There was a heated debate at one time between Mencius and Gaozi on human nature in the state of Qi. Mencius was then a newcomer to Qi, while Gaozi had lived there for many years; Mencius was in his forties, while Gaozi was almost eighty years old.

The Qi willow is a type of willow tree with flexible branches. The cups and bowls mentioned above were wooden drinkware. Gaozi opposed Mencius's view in regarding human nature as benevolent and righteous. He held that human nature was a raw material for making benevolence and righteousness, just as the willow wood was to make drinkware. Mencius, however, insisted that there must be some qualities inherent in human nature enabling man to become benevolent and righteous. In the case of the willow, one can make drinkware out of its wood because its nature makes this possible. Similarly, man is endowed with budding senses of compassion, which enable him to become benevolent — provided that he nurtures these senses properly.

Gaozi argued that morality was alien to human nature; therefore, in order for man to become moral, his nature must

　　如果從基督教人論來看孟子會比較有意思。基督教說人是上帝「形象」，上帝把自然法刻在人心裏，人如果能順着上帝賦予的自然法去行善，就能符合上帝安排的本來的秩序。但是，由於罪的出現，人不能順性而行善，只能逆性而行惡，因此需要上帝的說明（恩典）。這跟孟子認為人的天性純善，但在後天遭到破壞和喪失相似，只不過孟子並不承認人格神的上帝的拯救。

六

　　告子曰：「性，猶湍水也，決諸東方則東流，決諸西方則西流。人性之無分於善不善也，猶水之無分於東西也。」孟子曰：「水信無分於東西，無分於上下乎？人性之善也，猶水之就下也。人無有不善，水無有不下。今夫水搏而躍之，可使過顙，激而行之，可使在山，是豈水之性哉？其勢則然也。人之可使為不善，其性亦猶是也。」（卷十一　告子章句上・二）

【今譯】

　　告子說：「人的天性就跟湍急的水一樣，從

be mutilated. Such a stance implies a denial of the moral capability of human beings, which in Mencius's view would bring calamity to the world.

It must be noted, however, that Mencius and Gaozi had differences in their definition of human nature. Mencius saw human nature not as a passive and neutral raw material, but as an autonomous, active and positive capability that could like wood be molded. Hence, man was free to choose between the good and the evil. But as it was not an easy task for a person always to remain good, Mencius emphasized self-edification to develop our budding senses through constantly nurturing them in our practice of virtues so that they wouldn't get ensnared by our vices.

The Christian view of human nature may enrich our understanding of Mencius's thought. According to Christian doctrines, God made man in His own "image" and imparted the natural law to the human mind. If man acts according to the law of God, then he will be able to realize God's divine order. However, after the fall of man and his commitment of sin, he turned away from his good self and sought evil — and he therefore needed God's grace. As such, the Christian view is similar to Mencius's claim about the intrinsic goodness

東邊開了口子就向東邊流去，從西邊開了口子就向西邊流去。人的天性不分善和不善，正如水沒有向東或向西的定向一樣。」

孟子說：「水確實沒有向東或向西的定向，但沒有向上或向下的定向嗎？人的天性趨向於善，正如水總是往下流一樣。人沒有不善的，水沒有不往下流的。當然，你可以把水拍得跳起來，高過額頭，施加壓力讓它倒流，可以引上山。這難道是水的天性嗎？是人為造成的形勢使它這樣的。人可以被脅迫做壞事，人的天性也是這樣被扭曲的。」

【時析】

告子認為人性不分善惡，正如流水不分東西，水流的方向，都是偶然出現的，並沒有所謂的定向。孟子則認為，水流固無東西，卻有上下，水的定向就是向下流動。人性也跟水一樣，有向善的傾向。那麼，不善是怎麼來的呢？孟子認為是由外部環境、形勢造成的。

基督教哲學家奧古斯丁認為，人心的定向是上帝，人心是有「重量」（傾向）的，它傾向於上帝正如石頭要落地，火焰要往上飄一樣。在《懺

of human nature, but it was sabotaged and lost. Mencius, nevertheless, did not acknowledge the possibility of salvation from a personal god.

Six

Translation:

Gaozi said, "Nature is like swirling water; make an opening at the east then it will flow east, make an opening at the west then it will flow west. Human nature is disposed towards neither good nor bad, just as water does not flow inevitably towards east or west."

Mencius said, "It is true that water does not flow inevitably towards east or west, but does it not inevitably flow downwards instead of up? Man is inherently good, just as water keeps flowing downwards. There is no man who is by nature not good; there is no water that by nature does not flow downwards. Now, by splashing one can make it shoot up over the forehead, and by blocking its way one can lead it uphill. But how can that be the nature of water? It merely bows to the force of circumstance. For man, it is also possible for him to be led astray, when he bows to the force of circumstance." (Chapter 11.2)

悔錄》第一章，他有一句名言：「我們的心若不依偎在你（上帝）懷裏，就不能得到安息。」

　　歐洲中世紀經院派哲學家和神學家湯瑪斯的自然法理論認為，人心中天然地刻有自由法，內容有趨善避惡、生養後代、樂群、追求真理等，如果人能完整地保全自然法，依法而行，則天下太平。但是，由於罪的污染，以及壞風俗等環境因素的影響，人達不到自然法的要求，就需要恩典拯救了。這種解釋，跟孟子有異曲同工之處。

七

　　公都子曰：「告子曰：『性無善無不善也。』或曰：『性可以為善，可以為不善，是故文武興則民好善，幽厲興則民好暴。』或曰：『有性善，有性不善，是故以堯為君而有象，以瞽瞍為父而有舜，以紂為兄之子且以為君，而有微子啟、王子比干。』今曰『性善』，然則彼皆非與？」

　　孟子曰：「乃若其情則可以為善矣，乃所謂善也。若夫為不善，非才

Contemporary interpretation:

Gaozi saw human nature as neither good nor bad, just as water can flow either east or west. Both are taken as contingent upon the situation prevailing at the time. Mencius, however, pointed out that even though water does not flow in any fixed direction, it always flows from the upland to the lowland; likewise, human nature is always disposed to the good. What then has caused the depravity of man? According to Mencius, it is due to external influences and circumstances that ensnare man's judgments. Christian philosopher Saint Augustine held that man's mind was inclined to God: the mind gravitates to God, just as the rock falls down or the flame shoots up. A famous quote from chapter 1 of his *Confessions* states: "O Lord, and our heart is restless until it rests in thee." Such a view is comparable to Mencius's doctrine. Thomas Aquinas's theory of natural law tells us that the human mind is imprinted with the freedom to choose good and avoid evil, to procreate and nurture our offspring, to live harmoniously together, to pursue the truth, etc. If all men can abide by the natural law, then the world will be at peace. However, man is often contaminated by sin and corrupted by evil customs, and subsequently fails to abide by the natural law. This is when God's grace shall save us from our sins. Thomas's and Mencius's accounts, despite their differing approaches, share the same faith in human nature.

之罪也。惻隱之心，人皆有之；羞惡
之心，人皆有之；恭敬之心，人皆有
之；是非之心，人皆有之。惻隱之心，
仁也；羞惡之心，義也；恭敬之心，
禮也；是非之心，智也。仁義禮智，
非由外鑠我也，我固有之也，弗思耳
矣。故曰：『求則得之，舍則失之。』
或相倍蓰而無算者，不能盡其才者
也。《詩》曰：『天生蒸民，有物有
則。民之秉彝，好是懿德。』孔子曰：
『為此詩者，其知道乎！故有物必有
則，民之秉彝也，故好是懿德。』」
（卷十一 告子章句上 · 六）

【今譯】

公都子說：「告子說：『本性中沒有善，也
沒有不善。』有人說：『本性可以是善的，也可
以是不善的，所以周文王、周武王興起時，百姓
就喜歡善，周幽王、周厲王在位時，百姓就喜歡
兇暴。』也有人說：『有的人本性善，有的人本
性不善，所以在堯做君主的社會，卻有象這樣的
壞百姓，在瞽瞍做父親的家庭裏，卻有舜這樣的
孝子，在紂做侄兒並且做君主的時代，卻有微子

Seven

Translation:

Gong Du Zi said, "Gaozi says that human nature is neither good nor bad. Others say, 'Human nature can become good or it can become bad. That is why when King Wen and King Wu came to power, the people behaved with kindness; when King You and King Li came to power, the people were cruel.' Still others say, 'Some people are good-natured while others are not. That is why even under King Yao's rule, there was the evil man Xiang; why Shun could have a bad father like Gu Sou; and why also good people like Viscount Qi of Wei and Prince Bi Gan ended up with their tyrant nephew Zhou as ruler.' Now you say human nature is good. Does that mean all the others are mistaken?"

Mencius said, "Rely on what one is endowed with, and one can become good; this is what I mean by intrinsically good. If a man becomes bad, it will not be the fault of his natural self. The heart of compassion is possessed by all men alike; the heart of shame is possessed by all mean alike; the heart of respect is possessed by all men alike; the heart of right and wrong is possessed by all men alike. In the heart of compassion lies benevolence; in the heart of shame lies righteousness; in the heart of respect lies propriety; in the heart of right and

啟、王子比干這樣的賢人。』現在老師說『本性善』，那麼他們都錯了嗎？」

孟子說：「從人性這種實際的情況看，是可以行善的，這就是我所說的性本善。如果做壞事，那不是沒有不做的能力的罪過。同情憐憫之心，人人都有；羞恥之心，人人都有；恭敬之心，人人都有；是非之心，人人都有。同情憐憫之心，是仁；羞恥之心，是義；恭敬之心，是禮；是非之心，是智。仁義禮智，並非別人從外面給予我的，而是我本來就有的，只不過我沒有反思過罷了。所以說：尋找它，就能得到，捨棄它，就會失去。人與人之間的差距，有一倍、五倍、乃至無數倍的，就是因為不能充分發揮他們的才。《詩經》說：『天降生了百姓，讓事物都有規則。百姓只要堅持規則，就是喜歡這些美德。』孔子說：『寫這首詩的人，真是懂得大道啊！所以有事物便有規則，百姓只要堅持常規，就會因此喜歡這些美德。』」

【時析】

公都子介紹了當時三種人性論，一是告子的「性無善無不善」論，一是「性可以為善可以為

wrong lies wisdom. Benevolence, righteousness, propriety and wisdom are not affixed to me from outside, they are inherently mine; I have merely been unaware of them. Therefore, it is said, 'Seek and you will get it, let go and you will lose it.' Indeed, there are some people who are twice, five times or even countless times better than others, but this is only because the others have not yet exerted what they've been endowed with to the fullest extent. The *Book of Poetry* says:

'Heaven produces numerous people,

And where there is a thing there is a norm,

If the people held on to their endowed nature,

They would be attracted to the most admirable virtue.'

"Confucius has commented, 'The author of this poem must have realized the Way! Hence, where there is a thing there is a norm; if the people held on to their endowed nature, then they would become attracted to the most admirable virtue.' "

(Chapter 11.6)

Contemporary interpretation:

In this passage, Gung Du Zi summarizes three popular accounts of human nature of the time. First, the neither-good-nor-bad thesis of Gaozi. Second, the possibly-good-or-bad thesis. And third, the some-are-good-some-are-bad thesis.

不善」說，一是「有性善有性不善」說。這只是一種經驗的概括，無助於道德主體的挺立。

孟子說「乃若其情，則可以為善矣，乃所謂善也。」表明他所謂性善，是說根據人性有仁義禮智四端這樣的實情，就可以做出具體的善的行為，人是有這個能力（潛能，「可以」）的，他就是在這個意義上說人性的善。倘若由於某些原因這種行善的可能沒有實現出來，仍舊不影響人性內在的為善稟賦。

孟子一路講的並非事實上的善，而是說人有善的可能，有天生的好善懿德的傾向。那麼可不可以反駁說，人難道不也有天生的惡的傾向嗎？孟子對此的回答是，人性善的潛能是一個正面的、肯定的東西，惡只是這個肯定的東西的缺乏。這就跟新柏拉圖主義奠基人柏羅丁將惡說成是善的缺乏一樣。善是一個正面的、肯定的東西，是存在。惡不存在，惡是虛無。基督教哲學中也有類似的辯護，比如湯瑪斯對自然法為何在某些人身上、在某些群體身上缺乏或者被扭曲的解釋。

基督教的自然法說，道德「應當」的標準由神刻在人心裏。人沒做到會覺得良心不安，因沒

Yet these accounts seemed to be just partial descriptions from experience and could not offer any support for the development of the moral self.

Mencius said, "Rely only on what one is endowed with, and one can become good; this is what I mean by intrinsically good." He made it clear that the possibility for any human acts of goodness are based on the fact that all human beings possess four nascent senses that may grow into the virtues of benevolence, righteousness, propriety and wisdom. He put the emphasis on the inherent ability (i.e., potentiality, "can") of human beings to do good and sought to define human nature as such. Hence, if it happens that any potential to do good is blocked by unfavorable circumstances, the endowed goodness remains intact.

One must be reminded that the goodness which Mencius repeatedly talked about is not the actual goodness that man has achieved, but his potential goodness. That is, the inherent human disposition towards doing good. One might query, whether man can also have evil dispositions? Mencius's answer would be that the potential to become good is a positive and affirmed capability, whereas any evil act merely demonstrates a lack of this affirmed capability. In this, Mencius

達到理想「應當」。湯瑪斯說，上帝代表善，但他要面對宗教和文化多元的問題，因為別的宗教和文化，也可以說我的神即代表善，那如何判斷真善，或者說公共的善？

八

孟子曰：「牛山之木嘗美矣。以其郊於大國也，斧斤伐之，可以為美乎？是其日夜之所息，雨露之所潤，非無萌蘗之生焉，牛羊又從而牧之，是以若彼濯濯也。人見其濯濯也，以為未嘗有材焉，此豈山之性也哉？雖存乎人者，豈無仁義之心哉？其所以放其良心者，亦猶斧斤之於木也。旦旦而伐之，可以為美乎？其日夜之所息，平旦之氣，其好惡與人相近也者幾希，則其旦晝之所為，有梏亡之矣。梏之反覆，則其夜氣不足以存。夜氣不足以存，則其違禽獸不遠矣。人見其禽獸也，而以為未嘗有才焉者，是豈人之情也哉？故苟得其養，無物不長；苟失其養，無物不消。孔

predates the influential philosopher Plotinus (third century AD) in regarding evil as the absence of goodness: there exists only goodness, evil is not a real existence, it is merely a negation of goodness. There are similar arguments in the Christian philosophical tradition in defense of this view, such as that of Thomas Aquinas about why the natural law applies to some people, but not to others.

The Christian natural law theory states that God has imprinted the moral standards into human minds. If man fails to abide by them, his conscience will be disturbed because he hasn't lived up to the norm. Thomas said that God is the symbol of goodness. This stance, however, has to deal with a methodological issue brought forth by religious and cultural pluralism because every religion or culture can proclaim: "My God is the symbol of goodness." How, then, can we decide whose God represents the genuine good, or let's say, the common good?

Eight

Translation:

Mencius said, "The trees of Ox Mountain once flourished, but since the mountain is on the outskirts of a great city, the

子曰：『操則存，舍則亡。出入無時，莫知其鄉。』惟心之謂與！」（卷十一 告子章句上・八）

【今譯】

孟子說：「牛山的樹木曾經長得很茂密，但由於它位於大都市（齊都臨淄）的近郊，在斧頭的砍伐下，怎麼能保持茂密呢？當然了，它日日夜夜都在生長，雨露也滋潤着它，因此並非沒有新的嫩芽長出來，只是人們又來這裏放牛牧羊，就搞得像現在這樣光禿禿的。大家看它那光禿禿的樣子，以為它從來沒有長過樹木，這難道是山的本性嗎？在人的身上，怎能會沒有仁義之心呢？人之所以拋棄了良心，就跟斧頭把樹木砍光了一樣。天天都砍伐它，還能長得茂密嗎？一個人在日裏夜裏所長出來的善心，在天剛亮時接觸到的清明之氣，使得他的好惡跟別人總是有一點點相近的。但是一到白天，所作所為又把這善心丟掉了。反復再三地丟失，那麼，他在夜裏發出的善心就不足以存在，便和禽獸相差不遠了。人們只看到他是禽獸時的樣子，還以為他從來不曾有過善心，這哪裏是人本來的情形呢？所以，假如能夠得到保養，沒有事物是不能生長的；假如失去了保養，沒有甚麼是不能消滅的。孔子說：

trees were soon cut with axes. How then could they flourish anymore? They might recover slowly after days and nights nourished by rain and dew, when they would start to sprout and produce green shoots. But then cattle and sheep come to graze on the mountain, turning it into a barren land. Now when people see the barren land, they assume that trees never flourished here, but how does that match with the nature of a mountain side? As for man, how could he possibly have no heart of benevolence and righteousness? That a man lets go of his true heart is like repeatedly cutting a tree with axes, day after day. How can it flourish? His heart, if left to recover after days and nights, and re-freshened by the cleansing morning energy, would allow his better nature to get closer to those of others. But it is what he does repeatedly during the day that loses his heart, and if such loss continues daily, the night air would not be enough to preserve his heart — and when that happens, he is close to becoming a beast. Now when people see his beastly deeds, they assume that there has never been any goodness in him. But how could it possibly be the case? Hence, given proper nourishment, anything will grow; deprived of it, anything will wither. Confucius said, 'Hold onto it and it will remain; let go of it, then it will vanish; when it comes and where it goes, nobody knows.' Was he not talking about the heart?" (Chapter 11.8)

『把握它，它就存在；捨棄它，它就消亡。該出的時候不出，該入的時候不入，人們就不知道它到底去了哪裏。』這說的就是人的心吧？」

【時析】

孟子這段話是很經典的，它要解釋性善說的一個問題，就是既然性善，開始一切都好，後來為甚麼出現問題呢？原因是砍伐太多，被牛羊啃食丟失的太多。四端作為萌芽，是需要保養維護的。四端可以視為潛在狀態，現實狀態可能是不堪的。四端能否被徹底消滅呢？從牛山這個比喻來看，也有可能會變得一毛不剩的。不過放心，只要它是本性中有的，它就還是會像鬍子一樣長出來。這是孟子性善說的必然結論。

孟子這裏談到的「平旦之氣」和「夜氣」，後來也有一些儒家小教派（如四川的劉門）將之與孟子在另一處說的養「浩然之氣」結合起來，進而發展為一種修煉工夫。孟子認為，人皆有惻隱之心，雖然白天忙碌，與物交接，受到誘惑，迷失本心，昧着良心，喪失惻隱，專幹壞事，但是，一到晚上或者清晨，本性就會神奇地恢復。這就像前一天刮鬍子，第二天還會長出來一樣。有人認為，人在白天開始活動，與人糾纏，與物

Contemporary interpretation:

This passage offers a classic example of Mencius's rhetorical style. Mencius attempted to solve a dilemma faced by his doctrine of intrinsic goodness, namely, if the human heart is endowed with goodness from the start, how come in many cases it turns out to be evil? The damage, Mencius says, was caused by our repeated cutting away of our heart. The four budding senses are fragile seedlings that need protection and nurture, otherwise, they will soon wither. Will our nascent virtues be all gone one day?

As seen from the Ox Mountain analogy, it is indeed possible this will happen. Nevertheless, since the human potential to do good is inherent in us, these seedlings will soon shoot up again. This is the logical conclusion we draw from Mencius's doctrine of intrinsic goodness.

What Mencius spoke of here as "the cleansing morning energy" and the healing "night energy" were later linked by some Confucian schools (such as the School of Liu in Sichuan) with what Mencius mentioned elsewhere, "the boundless vital energy," and further developed into a form of spiritual practice. Mencius claims that every man is endowed with a humane heart; and even if one is subject to temptations and

交接，處處誘惑，處處陷阱，時時要計算，刻刻
會迷失，很容易就忘卻本心，丟掉原則，做出見
利忘義的事情，也容易生氣，情緒不穩定，不夠
理性。只有到了晚上，精神不受干擾，擺脫了欲
望，能夠自身反顧，知道哪裏出錯了，從而回到
良心狀態。四端就在這時重新顯露出來，不受外
界砍伐。睡覺時思想停止，當時更無計算誘惑。
清晨道理相同，基本上等於說，睡一覺道德感就
強了。（有人睡一覺後，再大的情緒都平復了。
當然，有的人則越想越生氣。）總體說來，孟子
所謂「平旦之氣」和「夜氣」，是指在精神不受
擾動和刺激，因而也缺少誘惑，不易迷失的情況
下，對自身的一種反顧，在這時，它較易恢復到
善的狀態。

　　在某些宗教的人性論當中，也有相似的說
法。比如佛教說人處在「無明」中（對應於孟子
的「放失」），但佛性始終是有的，佛性的根是
不可消滅的。基督教雖然說人在「原罪」中，但
人當初受造的時候是被賦予了上帝的「形象」的，
這個形象是怎麼都不會毀滅的，因此人有得救的
基礎。

　　後世的「正氣」觀念，「理直氣壯」這樣的

closes his ears to the voice of his conscience and does evil during the day, his true heart will be revitalized at night and be refreshed in the morning. This is just like a beard that regrows after shaving. Some may agree that one's heart is easily clouded by the many confusing relationships and contriving temptations of the day, when one might become morally corrupt as well as emotionally agitated; and only when night falls, does one find it easier to return to one's true heart undisturbed and free from desires, so that the call of the conscience becomes apparent again.

The nights and the mornings are beneficial to the nurture of our four budding senses because they are also the best times for a good rest. A good sleep is the key to revitalizing the disturbed heart. While some find a good night's sleep calming, other might not, so in brief, "the cleansing morning energy" and the healing "night energy" refer to the state where the human mind is free from agitation and temptation, so that one can tune in to one's senses and return to the state of true goodness more easily.

Similar discussions on human nature occur in other religions. For example, according to Buddhist doctrines, man is in the state of "ignorance" (c.f. "lost" in Mencius), but is endowed

詞彙，可能跟孟子所說「浩然之氣」有關係。

九

孟子曰：「堯舜，性之也；湯武，身之也；五霸，假之也。久假而不歸，惡知其非有也？」（卷十三 盡心章句上‧三十）

【今譯】

孟子說：「（仁義）在堯、舜那裏是出自本性；在商湯、周武王那裏是身體力行；在春秋五霸那裏不過是假藉的名義罷了。假藉久了，回不到本性那裏，但你怎麼知道他本性中就沒有善呢？」

【時析】

這裏是退化史觀。「仁義」從古到今，一步步減少蛻變，但仍舊是有的，因為它就在人性當中。這對應於「牛山濯濯」，不能否定其本有。無論怎麼假，善之端都仍舊是有一點的。五霸即使「虛偽」，扯來的仁義旗號像面具一樣長在臉上，好像撕不下來，但他們的本心裏面，也還是保留着本有的善性的。

with the perpetual nature of Buddha and cannot be eliminated. The Christian point of view is that despite the existence of "original sin," man was created at the very beginning in "the image" of God; and this image is eternally imprinted in human nature and cannot be destroyed. It is this which makes it possible for man to be redeemed through the grace of God.

Certain common terms used in later times such as "the righteous energy" or "upright and energized" can be traced back to "the boundless vital energy" coined by Mencius.

Nine

Translation:
Mencius said, "It was inherent in Yao and Shun; Tang and King Wu exemplified it; the Five Hegemons used it as a pretext. If a man uses it as a pretext for too long, how can one be sure that he doesn't have it?" (Chapter 13.30)

Contemporary interpretation:
This passage articulates a degenerative view of history. Benevolence and righteousness have gradually degenerated from ancient times till the present, yet they still exist because they are inherent in human nature. This passage echoes

這段話最後一句話的翻譯素有爭議。我們這裏，根據孟子哲學的基本前提性善說，譯為現在這樣。

十

孟子曰：「人之於身也，兼所愛；兼所愛，則兼所養也。無尺寸之膚不愛焉，則無尺寸之膚不養也。所以考其善不善者，豈有他哉？於己取之而已矣。體有貴賤，有小大。無以小害大，無以賤害貴。養其小者為小人，養其大者為大人。今有場師，舍其梧檟，養其樲棘，則為賤場師焉。養其一指，而失其肩背，而不知也，則為狼疾人也。飲食之人，則人賤之矣，為其養小以失大也。飲食之人，無有失也，則口腹豈適為尺寸之膚哉？」
（卷十一 告子章句上·十四）

【今譯】

孟子說：人對於自己的身體，哪一部份都珍愛。哪一部份都珍愛，就哪一部份都保養。沒有一丁點皮膚是不珍愛的，因此沒有一丁點的皮膚

Mencius's story about "the barren land in Ox Mountain" (c.f. Chapter 11.8). Despite its barren appearance, one cannot refute its original lushness. Likewise, no matter how false the Five Hegemons are, there exists, however meager, a sense of goodness in their hearts. Mencius suggests that despite being hypocrites, the Five Hegemons might in the end take the mask that purports to be benevolent and righteous as their true face, and then it cannot be removed. This means that human goodness must still linger inside their hearts.

There has been dispute over the interpretation of the last sentence of the passage. The translation presented here is based upon Mencius's philosophical doctrine on intrinsic goodness.

Ten

Translation:

Mencius said, "A man loves all parts of his body, therefore he nurtures them all. If there is not an inch of his skin that he does not love, then there is not an inch of his skin that he does not nurture. So we can tell if one is good at nurturing his body or not by observing how he chooses to nurture it. Some parts of the body are precious, while the others are not; some parts are

是不保養的。考察他愛護得好不好，還能有別的方法嗎？只是看他所注重的是身體哪一部份罷了。身體各個器官，有高貴有卑賤，有重要有次要。不要用次要的來損害重要的，不要用卑賤的損害高貴的。保養次要器官的是小人，保養重要器官的是大人。如果有一位園藝師，放下他的梧桐樹和楸樹，而去保養他的酸棗樹和荊棘，他就是個不稱職的園藝師。如果有一個人，為了保養自己的一根手指而損失了肩膀和脊背，對此還不知錯，那他就是一個糊塗蟲。只知道吃吃喝喝的人，人們都鄙視他，因為他只顧着保養次要部份卻丟失了重要部份。如果只知吃吃喝喝的人算不上錯，那麼，吃吃喝喝難道只是為了長好身體嗎？」

【時析】

　　人是身心合一的事物，身體各個器官所佔位置不同，有本末輕重的區別。人貴在有心，有理性，有思想，有意志，能控制自己的身體和感性欲望。作為完整的人，當然希望身心都得到發展，需要都能得到滿足，但是，在不能事事都如意的情況下，要優先照顧心靈對道德的要求，節制自己的欲望，達到一種內心的幸福與平衡。如果放縱感性欲望，甚至倒過來，讓理性為欲望作謀士，

important, while the others are not. One should not harm an important part for the sake of a trivial one, or a precious part for the sake of an inferior one. He who nurtures his trivial parts becomes a petty-minded man; he who nurtures his important parts becomes a great man. Now consider a gardener who gave up Chinese parasol and Manchurian catalpa [fine trees] in order to grow hog plum and thorn [common ones]; we would say he was an inferior gardener. A man, who keeps his finger at the expense of his shoulder and his back and is ignorant of this, is a muddled man. A gluttonous man is despised by others because he nurtures his trivial parts and neglects the important parts. If one says the gluttonous man has not done anything wrong, then should we say eating and drinking are just for keeping the body fed?" (Chapter 11.14-11.15)

Contemporary interpretation:

A human being is a unity of body and mind. Different organs are in different parts of the body, with some more important than others. Human beings are precious because of their heart, rationality, thoughts and will, and their ability to control their body and desires. As a complete human being, we all hope for a well-rounded development of body and mind and satisfaction of our needs. But if we have to choose between the two, we should always give priority to the mind/morality

就會顛倒存在的本來秩序，導致不好的後果。現代人往往因小失大，如金錢本是為人服務的，是手段不是目的，但現在人往往把追求金錢本身視為目標，把金錢當作幸福本身，結果或損害健康，英年早逝，或貪贓枉法鋃鐺入獄。這就是孟子所說的不識大體，捨本逐末。

十一

公都子問曰：「鈞是人也，或為大人，或為小人，何也？」孟子曰：「從其大體為大人，從其小體為小人。」曰：「鈞是人也，或從其大體，或從其小體，何也？」曰：「耳目之官不思，而蔽於物。物交物，則引之而已矣。心之官則思；思則得之，不思則不得也。此天之所與我者，先立乎其大者，則其小者不能奪也。此為大人而已矣。」（卷十一 告子章句上·十五）

【今譯】

公都子問：「同樣是人，有的是君子，有的是小人，為甚麼呢？」

and learn to regulate our bodily desires so that happiness and balance can be achieved. If we indulge ourselves with bodily desires and even use rationality to justify desires, we will jeopardize the intrinsic order and produce deeds that are opposed to our nature and have undesirable outcomes. In the modern world, we often see people doing the same sort of wrong things, such as those people who spend their whole life craving monetary wealth and in the end die early from overwork or get jailed for fraud or bribery. The root of their problem, according to Mencius, is that they attend to trifles at the expense of the essentials.

Eleven

Translation:

Gung Du Zi asked, "If all of us are equally human, why then is it the case that there are great men as well as small men?"

Mencius said, "Man guided by his great self is a great man; man guided by his small self is a small man."

Gung Du Zi then asked Mencius, "If all of us are equally human, why are some guided by their great selves while others are guided by their small selves?"

孟子說：「聽從身體中重要器官（心）的是大人，聽從身體中不重要的器官（五官）的是小人。」

公都子說：「同樣是人，有的聽從大體，有的聽從小體，為甚麼呢？」

孟子說：「耳朵和眼睛這類器官不會思考，會被事物的表象所蒙蔽。（耳目不過是物罷了。）耳目這類事物，一跟外物相交，就跟着外物跑了，迷惑了。心這個器官卻可以思考，它如果思考，就會得到知識，不思考就得不到。這是老天賜與我的。如果能先把重要器官確立起來，那麼次要器官就不會佔據首位，這樣就可以成為君子。」

【時析】

奧古斯丁說「認識你自己」，認識存在等級，神比心高，心比物高，要先愛神，再愛人如己，再愛物。如果先後輕重不分，比如以己為物，則會陷溺於物，將自己等同如物。倘若愛己甚於愛神，那就更顛倒悖逆，不識大體了。

孟子說人因有心，故能思考，要面對感官快樂和道德原則時，人能受道德原則的支配，而不

Mencius said, "The ears and eyes are organs that cannot think and are thus muddled by things [they hear and see]. When ears and eyes are in contact with things [stimuli] they can be led astray [unable to reason]. The heart is an organ that thinks. If it thinks, it will be enlightened, and if it doesn't think, it will receive no enlightenment. This is an ability that heaven gives me. So if a man puts priority on establishing his great self, then his small self will not be able to take over. This is how a great man comes to be." (Chapter 11.15)

Contemporary interpretation:

Saint Augustine said, "Know thyself." But there are levels of understanding involved. God is higher than the heart, the heart is higher than things; therefore we should love God in the first place, then love others as oneself, and then pursue material objects. If one gets muddled with the priorities and treats oneself as an object, then one will indulge with the object. And if a man's love for himself overrides his love of God, then he must be utterly out of his mind.

Mencius said a man thinks with his heart, so that when he has to choose between physical pleasure and moral principles, he knowingly chooses to abide by moral principles. For example, when a dog is offered a bun it will jump at it, while

一味地追求快樂原則。比如面對一個包子，狗會不假思索地撲上去，人卻可能不食嗟來之食，因為人會考慮到尊嚴，人有道德原則。心之官思考，比感官重要，感官受心之官的支配，故應先立其大者。但孟子未否定小者，故儒家不禁欲，不視之為惡，而是主張疏導和引導，將欲放在道德原則之下，禮的範圍之內。

十二

孟子曰：「大人者，不失其赤子之心者也。」（卷八 離婁章句下・十二）

【今譯】

孟子說：「大人，就是不丟失他嬰兒時善良天性的人。」

【時析】

這跟孟子的性善說有關係。既然人性就是善的，所以保留並發揚這天性，人就能成為大善人了。

這跟基督教原罪說相映成趣。奧古斯丁在《懺悔錄》中說，嬰兒有原罪，是非常自私的。

a man will think twice out of moral consideration. In order to become great men, we should master thinking with our heart so that our sensations can be properly guided. However, it should be noted that Mencius did not despise "the small self" (sensations). Confucians (like Mencius) don't forbid bodily desires and don't consider them evil; instead they seek to place desires under the guidance of moral principles and the restraints of proprieties.

Twelve

Translation:

Mencius said, "A great man is one who has not lost the heart of a newborn baby." (Chapter 8.12)

Contemporary interpretation:

This passage is again in line with Mencius's doctrine on intrinsic goodness. Since human nature is endowed with intrinsic goodness, all someone has to do is to retain it and develop it to the fullest extent so that he will become a great man.

We can see an interesting contrast here with the doctrine of original sin as espoused by Christianity. In his *Confessions,*

比如，如果嬰兒在吃奶，這時如果另外有一個嬰
兒也要來吃奶，他一定會惡狠狠地把這個跟他搶
奶的嬰兒打走的。所以「赤子之心」到底是不是
天然就善，跟我們的經驗是不是符合，是不是完
全符合，也仍舊是值得爭論的。

十三

孟子曰：「有天爵者，有人爵者。
仁義忠信，樂善不倦，此天爵也。公
卿大夫，此人爵也。古之人，修其天
爵而人爵從之。今之人，修其天爵以
要人爵。既得人爵而棄其天爵，則惑
之甚者也，終亦必亡而已矣。」（卷
十一 告子章句上 · 十六）

【今譯】

孟子說：「爵有兩種，有天然的爵位，有人
間的爵位。天然的爵位，是仁、義、忠、信，喜
歡善而不停止這一類品德。人間的爵位，是公、
卿、大夫這一類等級。古代的人，修的是天然的
爵位，修好後人間的爵位自然也就跟來了。今天
的人，修天然爵位的目的是為了得到人間的爵
位。這樣，他就在得到人間的爵位後，拋棄天然

Saint Augustine described babies as extremely selfish because they were born with original sin — as could be demonstrated by one hungry baby fiercely snatching the milk from another competitive baby. Hence, drawing from our experience, we may wonder, whether the heart of a newborn is really as pure as Mencius thought.

Thirteen

Translation:

Mencius said, "There are honors bestowed by heaven and honors bestowed by men. Benevolence, righteousness, conscientiousness, trustworthiness and the untiring pursuit of the good, these are honors bestowed by heaven. Positions such as Duke, Minister, and Counselor, these are honors bestowed by men. Men of the past acquired heavenly honors and the human-bestowed honors followed. Men today pursue heavenly honors in order to win human-bestowed honors; but once the latter are won, they discard the heavenly honors. How foolish these people are; in the end their earthly honors will be lost." (Chapter 11.16)

Contemporary interpretation:

Mencius imagined a golden age in ancient times when people

的爵位，真是很愚蠢，最終一定連人間的爵位也
會丟掉的。」

【時析】

　　孟子設想了一個古代的黃金時期，人人道德
高尚，幸福自然而來。後來人類墮落，人人自私
自利，即使講求道德，也只是以之為手段，謀取
私利，可稱「偽善」。是否存在過那樣的黃金時
代？

　　孟子對於德與福的關係的認識，與孔子相
似。無論有無從政的機會（得志與否），我都自
己做好自己，修好德性。福是外在的東西，得之
是幸運，不得亦無妨；德是內在的東西，操之在
我，修之則有，不修則不存。德本身亦是一種得，
可令人有滿足感和幸福感，就算身陷貧賤，也無
損這種感覺。

were virtuous and thus blessed. Later on, people became corrupted and selfish, and they regarded the virtues merely as a means to their selfish ends — they were the so-called hypocrites. Did such a golden age of humanity actually exist?

Mencius and Confucius shared similar views on the relationship between virtue and fortune. No matter whether I have the opportunity to play a part in politics, I should edify myself and nurture my virtues. Fortune was seen as something external: if I can have it, I feel blessed; if I can't, it's just as well. On the other hand, virtues were considered as something internal and within their control: whether I can attain them or not depends solely on my effort in self-edification. What is more, the attainment of virtues is itself an achievement that brings forth fulfillment and happiness. They dwell in us even when we are penniless.

命 Destiny

一

孟子曰：「盡其心者，知其性也。知其性，則知天矣。存其心，養其性，所以事天也。夭壽不貳，修身以俟之，所以立命也。」（卷十三　盡心章句上·一）

【今譯】

孟子說：「充分擴展本心的人，是懂得其本性的人。懂得自己的本性，就懂得天了。保存自己的本心，培養自己的本性，這就是事奉天的方式。無論壽命長短，都專一不變，修煉好自己，以等待天命，這就是安身立命的方式。」

【時析】

《中庸》說：「天命之謂性，率性之謂道，修道之謂教。」湖北郭店楚墓出土的儒家文獻竹簡記載的「性自命出，命自天降」是由上而下，此處孟子是由下而上（下學而上達），由本心出發，上達知天立命。

孟子這裏所謂的盡心存心，指的是將四端之心擴充至其極（盡）並加以操存（存），能盡能存，就能通過實踐，體認到四端所對應的四

One

Translation:

Mencius said, "When a man exerts his heart, he realizes his intrinsic nature. When a man realizes his intrinsic nature, he knows heaven. In order to serve heaven, he should retain his heart and nurture his intrinsic nature. Regardless of whether he may die young or live long, he steadfastly edifies his intrinsic nature awaiting whatever to befall him; this is how he stands firm in his proper destiny." (Chapter 13.1)

Contemporary interpretation:

The *Zhong Yong* states, "What heaven ordains is called 'intrinsic nature,' the actualization of the intrinsic nature is called 'the Way,' the embodiment of the Way through self-edification is called 'nurturance.' Texts in the Confucian work from the Guo Dian Chu Slips [bamboo] tell us, "Nature derives from destiny," and "Destiny is ordained by heaven." Both texts referred to heaven above as the origin of man's intrinsic nature. In contrast, Mencius emphasized how man could reach up to heaven through self-edification. According to Mencius, in order to cultivate his heart, man should develop his four budding, or nascent, senses, i.e., to realize in practice the virtues of benevolence, righteousness, propriety and wisdom to the fullest extent, and keep them. Since these senses

種德目，即仁義禮智，乃是我之本性（知性），由於這本性並非外加於我，所以是我所本有，亦可以說是上天給予我的。上天能給予我這些德目，上天本身當然也一定包含這些德目，這不是讓我瞭解天的意義（知天）嗎？這就是孟子「盡心 —— 知性 —— 知天」的思路。能「盡心 —— 知性 —— 知天」，看到三者的價值和互為因果的關係，自然就會繼續「存心」、「養性」以回報天（事天）。從上可見，孟子所指的天，顯然不是今日自然意義的天，而是通過道德實踐（盡心知性、存心養性）體證的，是充滿道德意義的天。

由於每個個體都可以通過道德實踐體證這個天，所以這個天是既內在（於每個個體）又超越（於個人的成見）的。盡心、存心和養性，完全操之在我，並不受限於任何外在條文或規定，因此，是完全自主自律的。這是儒家自律道德的核心概念。

人活在自然世界，總要面對各種順逆禍福，這是命，是我們無法改變的，但不管怎樣，這些所謂命卻無法限制我們盡心、存心、養性的實踐。人在定律支配的自然世界中並沒有自主權，但操

emerge from within rather than from outside our heart, we can therefore say that they belong to our intrinsic nature as endowed by heaven. In the same way, we can come to know heaven through self-understanding, since our endowed virtues all originated from heaven. Mencius attempted to link the important triadic relationship between "heart," "intrinsic nature" and "heaven," namely, to exert our heart — to realize our intrinsic nature — to know heaven. In the same manner, once we know how to "retain our heart," we know how to "nurture our intrinsic nature," then we will know how to "serve heaven."

It must be noted, however, the heaven that Mencius refers to is rich in moral implications that can only be grasped through self-edification gained by practice, and we should be careful not to read "heaven" merely in its cognitive sense. Since anyone of us can embody heaven through our own moral practice, we can say heaven is at the same time immanent (in individual hearts) and transcendent (beyond personal biases). Moreover, Mencius pinpointed the core Confucian concept of moral autonomy: man is free to exert his heart, retain his heart and nurture his intrinsic nature, and as such his conduct is not predetermined by external rules or regulations. As a mortal being living in a natural world full of contingencies, it is true

之在我的盡心、存心、養性等實踐活動，卻是人的自由王國，孟子說立命，就是在這個自由王國中安身立命。

二

孟子曰：「求則得之，舍則失之，是求有益於得也，求在我者也。求之有道，得之有命，是求無益於得也，求在外者也。」（卷十三 盡心章句上・三）

【今譯】

孟子說：「追求它，就能得到它，放棄它，就會失去它，這樣的追求有益於獲得，是追求自己固有的東西。追求有一定的方法，能不能獲得卻要看天命，那這樣的追求無益於獲得，是追求我自身之外的東西。」

【時析】

這裏前半段指求德，後半段指求祿。德是我人性中本來有的，是本性，祿則是在我之外的，能不能得到是命。

命具有偶然因素，出於天意，與我自己的道

that man cannot be in control of whatever is happening to him, yet he is still free to exert his heart in his practice. So even though man is not free to change the course of happenings around him, he is still free to determine his own way of practice in the realm of human autonomy — in Mencius's words, self-edification is the way to attain heaven's destiny in this realm of human autonomy.

Two
Translation:

Mencius said, "Seek and you will get it, let go and you will lose it — in such a case, the seeking itself contributes to what will be attained, and what is sought after lies within myself. But if there is a way to seek it, and only fate can tell whether I can get it, then the seeking itself does not contribute to what may be attained, and what is sought after lies beyond myself." (Chapter 13.3)

Contemporary interpretation:

The first half of the passage refers to the pursuit of morality, while the second half refers to the pursuit of wealth. Moral goodness resides in our heart, it is our intrinsic nature, whereas wealth is external to our heart and there is no guarantee that

德努力無關。在不能保證福必然隨德而至的情況下，還是專注於以德為樂吧。

三

孟子曰：「口之於味也，目之於色也，耳之於聲也，鼻之於臭也，四肢之於安佚也；性也，有命焉，君子不謂性也。仁之於父子也，義之於君臣也，禮之於賓主也，知之於賢者也，聖人之於天道也；命也，有性焉，君子不謂命也。」（卷十四　盡心章句下・二十四）

【今譯】

孟子說：「口對於美味，眼睛對於好色彩，耳朵對於好音樂，鼻子對於好氣味，四肢對於安逸舒適，都是喜歡的，這是本性。但能否得到它們，卻是天命，因此，君子不把它們看作本性，（不認為必然能得到。）仁對於父子，義對於君臣，禮對於賓主，知對於賢者，聖對於天道，（雖然能否實現）受到天命的影響，但（仍然取決於你自己的求與不求）這裏面有本性的作用，所以君子不把這說成是命運。」

we can get it, however hard we try. Since wealth does not necessarily come with moral goodness, it may be wise for us to focus on our moral pursuits and seek the contentment that lies within this.

Three

Translation:

Mencius said, "The mouth prefers good taste, the eyes prefer nice colors, the ears prefer good sounds, the nose prefers good scents, and the four limbs prefer comfort. This is our innate nature. Since our preferences are predestined by nature, the gentleman does not regard them as our intrinsic nature [not in one's control]. Benevolence is the way to act between fathers and sons, righteousness is the way to act between rulers and officials, propriety is the way to act between guests and hosts, wisdom is the way to act for the noble ones, sagacity is the embodiment of heaven's way; whether a man can flourish through his virtues depends on situational factors, yet the gentleman does not regard them as predestined because they are initiated by his intrinsic nature." (Chapter 14.24)

Contemporary interpretation:

Professor Mou Zong-san has offered an insightful explication

【時析】

關於這段，牟宗三先生在《圓善論》（第151頁）「性命對揚」一節裏有精闢的分析：口目之怡人都喜歡，但能否得到要看命，但君子不說因為有命，就要放縱此方面欲望。仁義禮智是我的性，我必須做，但由於父母不好、君主壞等環境影響，我做不成功，但我不能因此找藉口說這不是我的性，這是我的命，我仍要盡力擴充我的性。

孟子在這裏仍舊是在清楚區分內在外在、固有與偶然，以界定清楚人的道德責任的範圍。感性欲望的滿足，能否實現要看外部條件，並非你想得就能得到，因此有「命」的因素，對此要承認。那不是你求就能得到的。

因此，對於這些外在的「福」要看輕。至於仁義禮智這些品德，雖有可能遇不到好的事物、環境、機遇，但你只要求就能得到，不求就得不到，這完全操之在你，因此，想不想具備這些品德是你人性份內的事，你要負起道德責任，失德時無可推諉。這類似於界定清楚法律上的權責利，出了道德事故就要追責，是一種道德追責制。

of this passage in a section titled "Fate vs. Intrinsic Nature" in his book *Yuan Shan Lun* (p.151):

...we all enjoy good food and beautiful things, yet we can never be sure if we can get hold of them. For a gentleman, even when he enjoys good food or beautiful things, he will not indulge himself in these things just because he is blessed with them. Every one of us is endowed with the virtues of benevolence, righteousness, propriety and wisdom for which one is responsible. Even though my efforts might be partly ruined by bad parents or wicked rulers, saying that one has failed due to fated bad influence is no excuse for not exerting oneself in self-edification.

In order to clearly mark the scope of our moral responsibility, Mencius sharply distinguished between "within" and "beyond," "endowed" and "by chance." Whether or not we can have our natural desires satisfied depends on circumstantial factors that are out of our control, therefore we should admit that they are contingent on our "fate" and thus take these external "fortunes" lightly. On the contrary, whether or not our virtues of benevolence, righteousness, propriety and wisdom can be actualized depends solely on

　　跟孔子相比，孟子似乎把仁義禮智單向化了。孔子「以直報怨」，君對臣不好，臣也沒必要對君好，君臣關係是雙向的、對等的。孟子則把臣對君的義務單向化，臣無論遇不遇，都要做好。這樣就把孔子的對等關係的思想狹窄化、極端化了。

　　孟子把士人的道德標準提高了，一味向內求，產生了臣對君的心理上的不對等和義務上的不對等，可以說是一種「自我強加的枷鎖」。臣子再難以「他不仁我不義」，發展下去就成了董仲舒的「正其誼不謀其利」，面對暴君，臣子只能一味高尚地盡義務，乖乖聽話。從這裏可以看出，雖然唐以後孔孟並稱，但實際上，孔子很瀟灑，孟子很拘束。孟子講恆產，講私有財產，那是對小民、對普通百姓來說，對士人來說，則因為他們背負道德，因此有恆心，也就無需私產。

　　這裏面暗含着「有產」是一種道德標準不高的生活，是小民的生活，真正的君子或士，是無需私產的。中國的知識份子在後世一直恥言私利和報酬，講究自尊，跟孟子這種小民有「恆產」才有「恆心」，君子無恆產也要有恆心的觀點應該是有關係的。這導致了他們在利益面前的一種

our own choice of action for which we are strictly liable. Of course, there are chances that we cannot accomplish our good intentions because of circumstantial factors, yet the will to take up our own moral responsibility is in our own hands and we cannot be excused for not trying to do so. With the above demarcation, Mencius set down clearly the scope of our moral accountability.

In comparison with Confucius, Mencius might have curtailed the implied reciprocity of the virtues. Confucius sought to "repay grudges with justice" — what is right for me to do depends on how my counterpart treats me; for example, in the ruler-official relationship, the official is not obliged to be good to the ruler if the latter is not good to him. Mencius, however, took it for granted that the official should be obliged to the ruler, even when the ruler did not treat him with due respect. In consequence, Mencius twisted Confucius's idea of a more egalitarian ruler-official relationship and went to the extreme. By boosting the officials' moral demands upon themselves, Mencius turned their responsibility to the rulers into a kind of "self-imposed yoke" so that the officials were obliged loyally to serve whomever they served, as similarly echoed in the Han scholar Dong Zhongshu's words: "to properly follow the righteous way instead of seeking to take advantage out of it."

虛偽，心裏想要得到利益，但是口頭還是要裝着
清高。孟子指責縱橫家的一個理由，就是他們的
「道德低」，認為他們是為了私利才到處游說，
合縱連橫的，沒有解決當時的經濟社會狀況和可
能的國家長遠利益問題。

So even when it was a tyrant that one served, it would still be one's duty to be loyal and submissive.

From this passage, it may be easy to spot the difference between Mencius and Confucius, who since the Tang dynasty have often been lumped together: Confucius was self-directive while Mencius was rather self-constraining.

When Mencius talked about the benefits of privatization of property, he only had the common people on his mind; it would be needless for gentlemen and learned people to own any property because their hearts had already found a safe haven in virtues. Mencius expected them to be dedicated to their moral pursuits instead of worldly pursuits. Such a view implies belittling the moral status of property owners (the common people) as well as the value of profits and rewards. This might have encouraged a tradition of hypocrisy among the Chinese intelligentsia who tried to conceal their selfishness under moral aloofness. Moreover, in the same manner, Mencius criticized the strategic diplomats at the time for having low moral standards because he thought that they ran around persuading different states to form allies just for the sake of self-interest, but at the same time failed to address the socio-economic problems and the possible long-term interest of all states.

教養 Teaching and
Learning

一

孟子曰：「君子之所以敎者五：有如時雨化之者，有成德者，有達財者，有答問者，有私淑艾者。此五者，君子之所以敎也。」（卷十三　盡心章句上・四十）

【今譯】

孟子說：「君子敎育人的方式有五種：有像及時雨那樣澆灌人心的，有成全人品德的，有使人才能通達的，有解答疑問的，有作為榜樣被人私下裏學習的。這五點，就是君子敎育人的方法。」

【時析】

君子直接敎育的人始終是有限的，但他一旦成為榜樣，就可以超時空地成為別人的導師。一些宗敎之所謂「敎主」，就是這樣的。如佛作為後人學佛時獲得「覺悟」的榜樣，基督的言行作為基督徒效法的榜樣，都體現這種巨大的影響力。

二

孟子曰：「中也養不中，才也

One

Translation:

Mencius said, "A gentleman teaches in five ways: first, he nurtures people's hearts like timely rain; second, he helps people realize their virtues; third, he helps people excel in their talents; fourth, he answers people's questions; and fifth, he sets an example for people to follow. These five are the ways in which a gentleman teaches." (Chapter 13.40)

Contemporary interpretation:

Only a few people can receive direct education from a gentleman. Nevertheless, if the gentleman becomes a role model, people across time and place can learn from him. Some religious founders are examples of this, such as the Buddha being the role model for those who want to be "enlightened" and Jesus the role model for Christians to follow.

Two

Translation:

Mencius said, "Those who show moderation nurture those who don't; those who are talented nurture those who are not. That is why people are glad to have good fathers and elder brothers. If those who show moderation abandon those who

養不才，故人樂有賢父兄也。如中也
棄不中，才也棄不才，則賢不肖之相
去，其間不能以寸。」（卷八　離婁章句
下・七）

【今譯】

孟子說：「辦事不失分寸的人應該教導辦事
偏頗的人，有才能的人應該教導沒有才能的人，
這樣人都會喜歡有賢明的父兄。如果辦事不失分
寸的人不去教有偏頗的人，有才能的人不去教沒
有才能的人，那麼，賢明的人和不賢的人之間，
也就沒有甚麼差距了。」

【時析】

子張和曾子曾討論對不如己者要否幫助。孟
子大概是繼續這個討論。如果聰明的人不去教
不聰明的人，有品的人不去教無品的人，那整
個社會就不會有進步。如果賢能的人不去教不
賢的人，有道德的人不去教沒道德的人，那賢
能有道德的人本身也有了缺陷，跟不賢不道德
的人也就沒甚麼區別。整個社會呈現低道德化
的趨勢。

任何社會要保持基本的道德水準，都要提倡

don't, and those who are talented abandon those who aren't, then we will not be able to see any difference between the virtuous and the depraved." (Chapter 8.7)

Contemporary interpretation:

There had been a discussion between Zi Zhang and Zeng Zi on whether it was appropriate to offer help to those less capable than oneself. This passage may be Mencius's follow-up on the topic. If those who are intelligent do not teach those who are not, and those who are virtuous do not teach those who are not, then society as a whole will not progress.

If good people refrain from teaching those who are not as good, then those so-called good people are in fact not as good, and we will then see no difference between the good person and the bad. As a result, society as a whole will suffer moral decline.

In order to maintain the social moral standard, we need to advocate morality, set role models and be critical of bad conduct. Apart from the government's advocacy, various social bodies such as religious organizations, educational institutions as well as social media all bear responsibility for promoting a healthy moral culture.

道德，樹立道德楷模，批判失德現象。除了官方的提倡外，一般的社會組織，如宗教系統、學校系統、報紙輿論，也都有這個義務。

三

孟子曰：「君子深造之以道，欲其自得之也。自得之則居之安，居之安則資之深，資之深則取之左右逢其原。故君子欲其自得之也。」（卷八離婁章句下·十四）

【今譯】

孟子說：「君子用正確的方法深入探討，是想使自己有所收穫。自己獲得的道理，堅持它才會心安理得，堅持起來心安理得，才會積累深厚，積累深厚，使用起來才會左右逢源。所以君子希望通過自己有所收穫。」

【時析】

孟子這是向學生講為學之道，有他自己的研究心得。學習的「自得」非常重要，只有自己親身體驗、獲得了，有了主動性，並且持續下去，才能在學問、道德上有所發展。

Three

Translation:

Mencius said, "A gentleman investigates with a proper approach because he wishes to obtain knowledge by himself. When he obtains knowledge by himself, he will be at ease by holding onto it. When he is at ease by holding onto it, he will have profound knowledge. When he has profound knowledge, it will be at his disposal. That is why a gentleman wishes to obtain knowledge by himself." (Chapter 8.14)

Contemporary interpretation:

In this passage Mencius talked to his students about the way to learn by sharing with them what he had learned from his own studies. In the pursuit of knowledge as well as of virtues, it is important for the learner to be self-driven — to gain first-hand experience, to obtain understanding, to persevere in learning and to seek further comprehension. It is only through such efforts that he can gradually become a knowledgeable or moral person.

In his study of the concept of "justice," American philosopher John Rawls spent nearly twenty years before writing the masterpiece, *A Theory of Justice*. In this book, he offered a detailed analysis of the concept of "justice" and those deeply

美國哲學家羅爾斯（John Rawls）花了一二十年的功夫，在「正義」這個概念上挖掘，寫出名著《正義論》。越往下挖，就發現「正義」跟其它概念有着深度的聯繫，從而形成一個深層的概念網絡。做哲學、科學研究的都有同樣的現象。愛因斯坦通過對「同時性」、「時間」等人們習以為常的概念的突破，發現了相對論。孟子在仁、仁政這樣的概念上也花了幾十年的時間認真研究，越挖越深，終於建立自己的仁政和人性論體系，發展了孔子的思想。

四

孟子曰：「博學而詳說之，將以反說約也。」（卷八 離婁章句下·十五）

【今譯】

孟子說：「廣泛地學習，詳細地解說，是要以這種方法回到簡略地懂得大旨。」

【時析】

讀一本書，大致可分兩步：第一步是把書讀厚，第二步是把書讀薄。第一步要細讀，在字裏行間讀出「字外行上」的內容，在講原理原則的

connected to it, thereby developing a complex conceptual system supporting his political claims. Likewise, in the realm of science, Albert Einstein took a similar path when he incessantly dug into the mostly assumed concepts of "time" and "simultaneity," and consequently founded the theory of relativity. As for Mencius, it had taken him several decades of study of the Confucian concepts of "benevolence" and "benevolent governance" till he finally succeeded in incorporating Confucius's ethical thoughts into his own political views and philosophical stance on human nature.

Four

Translation:

Mencius said, "Learn extensively and explain in detail what you have learned so that you can sum it up succinctly." (Chapter 8.15)

Contemporary interpretation:

There are two steps in reading a book: first, read it as if to lengthen it; and secondly, read it as if to shorten it. "To lengthen it" means one should read a book carefully and read between the lines of the text, and try to grasp the ideas and principles with cases familiar to oneself; and when any difficult

地方用自己所知道的實例加以充實和理解，在有問題的地方加以析疑，不明白的地方要結合自己以前的知識加以理解弄明白；第二步是要把書讀薄，做減法，提煉出書的基本綱要、宗旨、原理。這時所理解的綱要，不是乾巴巴的綱要，是要通讀原書、並且加以自己經驗去理解的綱要，因此它既有豐富的內容，也具有提綱挈領的抽象概念，是具體和抽象的統一。比如，新儒家錢穆先生圍繞中國歷史和文化傳統一輩子寫了數百萬言，晚年用一篇小文章總結說，中國思想的根本旨趣就是四個字，「天人合一」。再比如，毛澤東活了 84 歲，他一生做了許多事，他自己在晚年的總結是，他一生只做了兩件事：一件是趕走蔣介石，統一了中國；另一件事是搞「文革」，有很大爭議。這就是提綱挈領的總結。

把書讀薄不是一件容易的事，需要在通讀全書後對全書有一個準確的把握，並且用簡潔的語文表達出來，這考驗讀書人總結抽象的能力。在上世紀 80 年代，內地曾經流行一種文風，寫得越長越繞越好，越晦澀讓人看不懂越顯得有水準，有時看完後讀者莫名其妙，作者自己恐怕也是在說胡話。這不僅不是把書讀薄，而是存心欺騙讀者。

questions arise, one should try to solve them with the best knowledge available. "To shorten it" means to extract from the text the gist, the themes and the theories. The gist, however, is not just an outline of a work, it should be the product of a thorough understanding of the whole book which brings out the essential points in a concise yet elaborate way. Neo-Confucian Qian Mu offered us a good example. His works on Chinese history and culture were voluminous, yet in his later years he wrote a small article summarizing the basic themes in four words, "Heaven–human–bond–united." Another example can be found with Mao Zedong, who died at the age of eighty-four and was engaged in many historical events. In his later years he summarized his life as doing just two things: the one was to drive off Chiang Kai-shek and unify China; the other was to initiate the Cultural Revolution, which led to many controversies.

To "read a book as if to shorten it" is not an easy task and poses a real challenge to scholars. On the one hand, it requires a reader to have a thorough understanding of a book; on the other, it requires him to put his understanding into a succinct summary. In the 1980s, it was popular among writers in China to write in such a wordy and abstruse style that even the authors themselves probably did not understand what they

五

公孫丑曰：「道則高矣、美矣，宜若登天然，似不可及也。何不使彼為可幾及而日孳孳也？」

孟子曰：「大匠不為拙工改廢繩墨；羿不為拙射變其彀率。君子引而不發，躍如也。中道而立，能者從之。」（卷十三 盡心章句上・四十一）

【今譯】

公孫丑說：「道是很高很美，但好像登天一樣，似乎夠不着。為甚麼不讓它成為差不多夠得着的，從而可以一天天地努力呢？」

孟子說：「高明的工匠不會因為笨木工就把繩墨規矩改了，神射手羿不會因為笨射手就把拉開弓和射中靶心的標準改了。君子（教導別人，正如射手）拉開弓卻不輕易射箭，只是作出躍躍欲試的樣子。他站在正確的道路上，有能力的人便能跟上來。」

【時析】

公孫丑認為，孟子教的課程目標太高了，學

wrote. In such cases, the writers not only failed "to shorten" their books, but also cheated their readers deliberately.

Five

Translation:

Gong Sun Chou said, "The Way is so lofty and beautiful that it seems as unapproachable as the sky. Why not make it more approachable so that people are willing to learn a little more each day?" Mencius said, "A great carpenter does not put aside the plumb-line because of the unskilled craftsmen; Yi would not lower his standards of archery in order to accommodate the unskilled archers. A gentleman stands poised with his bow drawn to the full, as if he were about to shoot. He stands firm in the proper way, and those who are capable will follow suit." (Chapter 13.41)

Contemporary interpretation:

Gong Sun Chou thought that Mencius was setting too high a standard of curriculum for students to achieve and he advised him to lower it so that students could learn with ease. Mencius, however, saw no reason to do this, even though he recognized that he might not be able to achieve the required height himself. For in his view, the standard was set not in

力夠不上，他想讓孟子調低標準，降低要求，也好畢業。孟子則強調，標桿不能降。他不射，但確立了標桿。就算他做不到，也要擺出這個姿態。這就好比老師對學生說：「雖然這個很難，但你一定要做到。」學生說：「你先做。」老師說：「我做不到也要擺出這個樣子，讓你們知道是怎麼做的。」這會不會是虛偽呢？老師是不是成了偽君子？

我們可以這樣來理解：教練把田徑或球類的規則教給學生，給他們示範做樣子，但他自己不能達到運動員那樣的水準；再如導演，他可以把每個人的角色安排好，做好說明，但他自己不一定能演好，他只是把遊戲規則和行業標準教給演員。「師父領進門，修行靠個人」，還是要靠學生在實踐中達到目標。可見，孟子所說的教育標準還是比較有道理的。否則，今天這個老師降低標準，明天那個老師降低標準，門檻越來越低，教育就會毫無成效和必要了。

六

孟子曰：「天下之言性也，則故而已矣。故者，以利為本。所惡於智

order to guarantee success, but instead as a target at which all students should aim. So even when there are times that the teacher himself might not meet the standard, he should insist on asking his students to try to reach it. This may be better illustrated using the case of the sports coach or the film director. When a coach demonstrates techniques to athletes, he may not have the performance skills of the athletes themselves, but he remains the key person who can give them advice on how to succeed well. When a film director asks actors to play their roles as told, his own acting skills may not be as good as theirs, but his role is crucial in guiding them to perform at their best. We can see from these examples that the most important role for the teacher is not to showcase the best performance but to set a high standard and motivate students to strive for it. This is timely advice for us since the modern approach to teaching is prone to lowering the standard rather than encouraging the students to take on the challenge.

Six

Translation:

Mencius said, "All our discussions on the nature of things aim at explaining how they work. Any explanations should be in compliance with the reality. Some smart people are

者，為其鑿也。如智者，若禹之行水也，則無惡於智矣。禹之行水也，行其所無事也。如智者亦行其所無事，則智亦大矣。天之高也，星辰之遠也，苟求其故，千歲之日至，可坐而致也。」（卷八　離婁章句下・二十六）

【今譯】

孟子說：「天下人談論事物的本性，只是為找出其原因罷了。找出原因，以順應事實為根本。人們討厭那些自作聰明的人，是因為他們穿鑿附會，違背事實。如果聰明人都像禹順着水性把水引導，人們也就不會討厭他們的聰明了。禹把水引導，就是順勢而為。如果聰明人也能順勢而為，他們的智慧就算很大了。天那樣高，星辰那樣遠，如果能找出它們的原因，那麼，一千年後的夏至和冬至，也是坐着就能推算出來的。」

【時析】

孟子這段話跟道家有點相似，只不過道家更徹底，講「無為而無不為」，「治未病」。大禹疏導而不堵，也還是有為，只不過是「順勢而為」，就省力多了。

despised because the explanations they offer distort the reality. If they could learn from Yu how he guided the flood waters, they would not be despised. In guiding the flood waters, Yu exploited the most natural way according to the circumstances. If those smart people could act in the most natural way according to the circumstances, then they would be as wise, too. Despite the sky being so high and the stars so distant, if one can explain how they work, then one will be able to predict the solstices of the next thousand years without even leaving one's seat." (Chapter 8.26)

Contemporary interpretation:

What Mencius said in this passage is similar to Taoism, but the latter explains it more thoroughly. When Yu guided the flooded rivers, he attempted to make the least intervention by following the natural course of the rivers. In this way, he did make an effort, but it was already the most efficient way. Taoism would, however, push the reasoning even further and advocate "action through non-action," and "to heal before falling ill."

In our continuous interactions with nature and things, we get familiar with their patterns and laws, as well as the causal relationship of happenings; we can then use such

在長期跟事物打交道的過程中，人們會逐漸增加對事物發展規律的認識，知道一件事物發生的原因及結果，把握其來龍去脈，從而利用它來造福人類。

至於一些玩弄小聰明的人，則是只見現象不找原因，穿鑿附會，不看大規律，最終或會違背自然去妄為，造成損害。大智慧則可看到物性、根本規律。掌握規律，人類就可以推算出事物將來會怎麼演發，可以怎麼利用其規律為自己造福。

七

孟子曰：「羿之敎人射，必志於彀；學者亦必志於彀。大匠誨人，必以規矩；學者亦必以規矩。」（卷十一告子章句上・二十）

【今譯】

孟子說：「羿教人射箭，一定要以拉滿弓為目標；學習（道）的人也一定要把（仁的）弓拉滿。高明的木匠教人，一定要用圓規和曲尺；學習（道）的人也一定要有圓規和曲尺。」

knowledge gained from experience to benefit humanity. However, there are those people with petty cleverness who look no further than the phenomenon and offer conjectures instead of convincing arguments. Their reckless actions can be detrimental to humanity. Only those who are wise can see the nature of things and the law of nature, and thereby make proper projections of the natural course of development and devise the best plans for human action.

Seven

Translation:

Mencius said, "When Yi taught people archery, he always aimed at drawing the bow to the full, so those who learned from him also always aimed at drawing the bow to the full. The master carpenter always teaches carpentry by means of the compass and the try square, so those who learn from him always learn by means of the compass and the try square." (Chapter 11.20)

Contemporary interpretation:

Goal setting and methodology are both essential for any kind of learning. Without goals, any organization — be it a company, an association, a political party or a country,

【時析】

學習要有目標（志），也要有方法。一個公司、一個組織、一個政黨、一個國家，如果沒有目標，就不成其有機團體，而只是人群的沙聚罷了。有了目標，還要有規矩，不然就亂了。對於國家來說，所謂規矩就是法律，依法治國是非常重要的。傳統國家是統治者憑法作為治國手段，統治者自己卻可以犯了法不受懲罰；現代國家多強調法律面前人人平等，統治者也要服從法的統治，並且建立一套互相制衡、監督的制度，使得統治者犯法後，有司法系統對之進行懲罰。

八

孟子曰：「梓匠輪輿，能與人規矩，不能使人巧。」（卷十四　盡心章句下·五）

【今譯】

孟子說：「造器具的木匠，搞建築的木匠、造車輪的木匠，造車箱的木匠，他們可以教人怎麼用圓規和曲尺，卻不能夠使人用得靈巧，（那是需要個人在實踐中自己去領會的。）」

would become an aimless mass of people and thus could not function well as a unit. Apart from having goals, there should be regulations for the sake of order. For running a country, adherence to the rule of law is very important. In some traditional societies, the rulers rule according to the law, but they themselves are exempted from any punishment for breaking it. In modern societies, however, everyone is equal before the law and there is no exemption for their rulers. In view of this, a system of checks and balances has to be set up in order to supervise the ruler and put him under trial in case of him violating the law.

Eight

Translation:

Mencius said, "A tool carpenter, a building carpenter, a wheel maker or a carriage chamber maker can teach people how to use the compass and the try square, but he cannot teach them to become masterly." (Chapter 14.5)

Contemporary interpretation:

Theoretical knowledge offers us a general account of the principles, whereas mastery of any skill needs practice, and practice requires hands-on experience and the power of

【時析】

「巧」跟實踐密切相關。理論只能說明原理大概，具體操作還要靠個人的經驗和悟性。西方哲學重視理論，比如亞里斯多德的《形而上學》就講普遍原理，而對具體實踐中獲得的技巧是不太重視的。

中國哲學則重視人手操作中一些難以言傳的技巧，默會之知。比如莊子就認為，聖人留下的書籍不過是糟粕而已，後人難以回到古人的處境，理解時就會出現偏差。北京人所謂「寸勁」，就是指木匠、演出中一些只能意會難以言傳的技巧，非得悟性高的在長期的實踐中才能體會出來。

有人說，中醫是一門藝術，西醫是一門技術；中餐是一門藝術，西餐是一門技術。西醫、西餐用硬性的製定和器械，能達到基本一致的結果，而中醫、中餐就靠操作者個人的經驗和悟性了。

在智商差不多的情況下，從同一個學校、專業、班級畢業的學生，「巧」勁不一定一樣。因此，要加強實踐操作，最好有師父在旁邊個別指導，這樣才能造就大國巧匠。

understanding. Western philosophies attach importance to theories, such as Aristotle's *Metaphysics*, emphasizing general principles and downplaying the significance of practical skills. In contrast, Chinese philosophies often stress tacit knowledge acquired from physical practice. For example, Zhuang Zi believed that the writings of ancient sages were trash because they made no sense to those who lived in a totally different time in history. Another example can be taken from the so-called "one-inch knack" in Beijing dialect that refers to the ineffable mastery of craftsmanship and performance that can only be acquired through long-term practice by those with a high power of understanding. Some say that Chinese medicine and Chinese cuisine emphasize artistry, while Western medicine and Western cuisine emphasize technique. While Western practitioners rely on the use of standardized procedures and advanced technology for consistent results, Chinese practitioners put their trust in personal experience and the power of understanding.

Students of similar intelligence, receiving the same training and graduating from the same schools may still differ in their "skillfulness." To facilitate learning in practical skills and raise the craftsmanship of students to the masterly level, it may be best in practice to have the individual guidance of a master.

九

孟子自范之齊，望見齊王之子，喟然歎曰：「居移氣，養移體，大哉居乎！夫非盡人之子與？」孟子曰：「王子宮室、車馬、衣服多與人同，而王子若彼者，其居使之然也。況居天下之廣居者乎？魯君之宋，呼於垤澤之門。守者曰：『此非吾君也，何其聲之似我君也？』此無他，居相似也。」（卷十三　盡心章句上・三十六）

【今譯】

孟子從齊國的范邑來到齊都，遠遠地望見了齊王的兒子，長歎一聲說：「位置改變氣度，飲食改變身體，位置的作用真是大啊！他難道不也是人的兒子嗎？」

孟子說：「王子的房屋、車馬、衣服大都和別人一樣，可是王子的氣質卻與別人不一樣，是他的位置使他這樣子的。何況把天下當作大位置的人呢？魯國的君主到了宋國，在宋都東南門外叫喊開門，守門的人說：『這個人不是我國國君，他的聲音卻怎麼像我國國君呢？』這沒有別的原因，是因為他們的位置相似啊。」

Nine

Translation:

Mencius travelled from Fan to Qi. When he saw the son of the king of Qi from a distance, he sighed, "The environment a man dwells in transforms his bearing just as the diet he takes changes his body. How important the environment is! Isn't the prince the son of someone just like the rest of us?

"The house, the carriage as well as the wardrobe of the prince are similar to those of the others, yet the prince is so different. The reason lies in the environment. How much more different would one be if one lived in the grandest environment of the world? The ruler of Lu went to Song and called at the gate of Die Ze. The gatekeeper said, 'This is not my ruler, how come his voice sounds so much like my ruler?' The answer is simply that they both dwell in similar environments." (Chapter 13.36)

Contemporary interpretation:

"Environment" in this passage refers to the social position and status of a person. The privileged position of the king or the prince enables him to be surrounded by talented people of the state. While on the one hand, these officials serve to offer constructive advice so as to broaden the king or the prince's mind, on the other, they are deferential to their masters and

【時析】

這裏的「居」指環境，主要跟位置、地位有關。王子或國王的位置，使得在他周圍的人都是較有才華的人，這些人建言獻策，使他開闊視野，同時這些人對他的態度都是俯首帖耳，都要他來決斷，長久以往，就培養了王子和國王一種比較自信、頤指氣使凌駕於別人的特別的氣質。宋王和魯王雖然國家不同，但在這一點上倒是相同的。所以說，甚麼樣的位置決定了甚麼樣的人生。

近些年，大陸流行「民國範兒」，像梁啟超、梁思成、林徽音、梁漱溟、陳寅恪等，這些「精神貴族」傳為佳話，這跟民國時期社會上尚存一些自由是有關係的，因此當時的人還能保存一些獨特的性格和為人處世的風格。當時中國古典教養和西方教養齊進，古今中西融為一爐，因此造就獨特的「民國範兒」。又有人說中國有「紅色貴族」，比如某某元老的後裔成為名媛、名公子等。其實，三代出一個貴族，精緻文化的形成不是一代兩代人就能形成的，往往要經過數代才能形成。眾所周知，民國以後，江山易主，翻身農奴把歌唱，從農民到貴族，哪能那麼容易？況且，現在的大氣候也未到能培養出精神貴族的時代，現在更多處於多數人求生存和暴發戶掙錢的

submissive to their orders. Living in such an environment helps to cultivate a kind of self-assurance and grandeur in the prince or the king that set him apart from the common people. So, despite their coming from different states, the king of Song and the king of Qi both shared the same demeanor. This is how social position determines a person's personality.

In recent years, "Republic (of China) role models" have become a hit in China, like Liang Qi-chao, Liang Si-cheng, Lin Hui-yin, Liang Shu-ming, Chen Yin-ke, etc. These were so-called "noble minds." The rise of these legendary names may have resulted from the social freedom of a period which helped to promote individuality and a variety of personal outlooks. When Chinese classical culture joined hands with Western culture in nurturing and shaping the minds of Chinese scholars of the time, many became role models for the common people. Others talked about "the red aristocrats" — descendants of communist leaders becoming public icons. In fact, as the proverb says, "It takes three generations to bring up a nobleman"; the development of any refined culture takes more than three generations to get into shape. As we all know, republican China gave way to communist rule, and the peasantry have their day. But it may take ages for the peasantry to rise to nobility.

時代，培養出貪婪的官員和不擇手段掙錢的企業家是有可能的。至於貴族，還是等兩三代後再說吧。孟子是道德主義者，認為只要你有道德，你就相當於「天下之廣居」了，你的談吐氣質，要遠勝於甚麼齊王宋公。這跟他的身心一體論結合起來，當會得出非常有趣的結論。那就是，一個居在天下的「仁」「廣居」中的人（居仁由義），心中充滿浩然之氣，貫通周身，流露於四周，尤其眸子中，整個人都會顯得道貌岸然，成為一看即可辨識的道德君子。

十

公孫丑曰：「君子之不敎子，何也？」孟子曰：「勢不行也。敎者必以正；以正不行，繼之以怒；繼之以怒，則反夷矣。『夫子敎我以正；夫子未出於正也。』則是父子相夷也。父子相夷則惡矣。古者易子而敎之，父子之間不責善，責善則離，離則不祥莫大焉。」（卷七 離婁章句上·十八）

【今譯】

公孫丑說：「君子不親自教自己的孩子，為

Furthermore, if we look at the current social atmosphere, it is hard to nurture noble minds. We are living at a time when the majority of people still struggle for survival, while the nouveau riche continue to struggle to make more money, giving rise to corrupt officials and unscrupulous entrepreneurs. As for "nobility," that may require two or three generations to nurture properly.

Mencius was a moralist who believed that a moral mind would put a man into "the grandest environment of the world," where he would acquire a more decent demeanor than the rulers of Qi and Song. If we follow Mencius's integration of the body–mind and see them as one, we may arrive at a very interesting conclusion: the moral person who dwells in the grandest environment of benevolence is so thoroughly filled with righteousness and dignity that his whole body will look solemn and dignified. When you look into his eyes you will find an especial glow of dignity in them.

Ten

Translation:
Gong Sun Chou said, "Why does a gentleman not teach his own son?"

甚麼呢？」孟子說：「情理上行不通。教育一定
要用正確的道理去教；用正確的道理去教卻沒有
效果，就會發怒；一發怒，就會造成傷害。（兒
子會這樣想：）『你拿正確的道理教我，自己卻
不遵守正確的道理。』這就是父子互相傷害了。
父子互相傷害就不好了。古時候互相交換孩子來
教育，父子之間就不會因為求好而互相責難。如
果為了求好而互相責難，父子之間就會有隔閡，
有隔閡就是最糟糕的事。」

【時析】

　　西方有所謂「牧師的兒子」，即叛逆的一代，
因為天天聽父親說教，但父親並不總能做到，故
而覺得父親言行不一，容易導致反彈和逆反心
理。孟子解釋易子而教的原因，還是有合理的地
方的。易子而教，是因為對自己的小孩要求高，
不容易寬容，對別人的小孩會比較寬容。這大概
適合正規的道德倫理教育，至於一般的認字、科
學常識教育，只要父母不像學校裏那樣測試打
分，對孩子不形成太大精神壓力，還是應該鼓勵
的。

　　父子相處，父親感情也不能太壓抑，以為自
己真的是人生楷模，一舉手一投足都要為兒子

Mencius said, "Because it will not work. When one teaches, one will certainly resort to correction. If the correction does not have any effect, one will lose one's temper. If one loses one's temper, it will spoil the relationship. The son might think, 'You wanted to correct me, yet you are not correct yourself.' This is how both father and son end up hurting each other. It is bad for a father and his son to hurt each other. In the past, people taught one another's sons, and fathers and sons never rebuked each other; for rebuke causes estrangement, and estrangement is the worst misfortune for a family." (Chapter 7.18)

Contemporary interpretation:

In the West, the term "preacher's kid" refers to the child of a clergyman who becomes fed up with being indoctrinated on how to behave, but at the same time witnesses the discrepancy between what his father preaches and what he does, and thus becomes rebellious. So, there may be good reason for Mencius to call for teaching one another's children instead of one's own. For very often we are particularly demanding of our own children, while we are tolerant to other kids. Such a principle may be properly applied to moral education, while parents may still be encouraged to teach their kids language and other subjects, provided they don't pressure them with tests and grades as the school usually does.

「立範」，放下架子，與兒子打成一片才好，如
作家汪曾祺所說，「父子多年成兄弟」。做父親
的有情緒時自己要疏通一下，兒子做錯了事就適
當地批判教育一下，這樣父親才能成為一個真實
的人，而不是甚麼完美的聖人。父親要走下神壇，
兒子早早認清這一點，可能有助於其自立。

十一

逢蒙學射於羿，盡羿之道，思天
下惟羿為愈己，於是殺羿。孟子曰：
「是亦羿有罪焉。」公明儀曰：「宜
若無罪焉？」曰：「薄乎雲爾，惡得
無罪？鄭人使子濯孺子侵衛，衛使庾
公之斯追之。子濯孺子曰：『今日我
疾作，不可以執弓，吾死矣夫！』問
其僕曰：『追我者誰也？』其僕曰：
『庾公之斯也。』曰：『吾生矣。』
其僕曰：『庾公之斯，衛之善射者也，
夫子曰吾生，何謂也？』曰：『庾公
之斯學射於尹公之他，尹公之他學射
於我。夫尹公之他，端人也，其取友
必端矣。』庾公之斯至，曰：『夫子
何為不執弓？』曰：『今日我疾作，

Actually, when it comes to the father and son relationship, even though the father may want to establish a lofty role model for the son to follow, he should not sacrifice parental intimacy for the sake of modeling. As writer Wang Zengqi said, "After years of living together, a father and his son will become friends." Disciplining is necessary for wrongdoings; yet we must also acknowledge that none of us are saints, and we ourselves might do wrong, too. Fathers therefore should be tolerant to sons' misdeeds and be sensitive to their emotional needs. If a son knows at an early stage that his father is not perfect, it may help him to become independent.

Eleven

Translation:

Peng Meng learned archery from Yi. Having learned everything he could from Yi, he thought that Yi was the only one in the world who surpassed him in archery, so he killed him. Mencius said, "Yi was also to blame."

Gong Ming Yi said, "Wouldn't he be blameless?"

Mencius said, "His blame was sky-high, how could one say he was blameless? The people of Zheng sent Zi Zhuo Ru Zi to

不可以執弓。』曰：『小人學射於尹
公之他，尹公之他學射於夫子。我不
忍以夫子之道反害夫子。雖然，今日
之事，君事也，我不敢廢。』抽矢叩
輪，去其金、發乘矢而後反。」（卷
八 離婁章句下・二十四）

【今譯】

逢蒙跟羿學射箭，把羿的本事全學到了手，
他想到普天下只有羿比自己強，就把羿殺害了。
孟子說：「在這件事上，羿自己也是有罪的。」
公明儀說：「羿應該沒有甚麼罪吧。」孟子說：
「他的罪高到天上去了，怎能說沒有罪？鄭國曾
經派子濯孺子侵犯衛國，衛國就派庾公之斯追擊
他。子濯孺子說：『今天我的病犯了，不可以拿
弓，我要完蛋了！』然後問他的僕人說：『追我
的那個人是誰？』僕人說：『是庾公之斯。』子
濯孺子說：『我有救了。』僕人問：『庾公之斯，
是衛國善於射箭的人，先生您說「我有救了」，
是甚麼意思？』子濯孺子說：『庾公之斯曾跟尹
公之他學射，尹公之他曾跟我學射。尹公之他這
個人，是一個品行端正的人，他交的朋友一定也
是品行端正的。』庾公之斯追到了，問：『先生
您怎麼不拿弓？』子濯孺子說：『今天我犯病了，

attack Wei, and Wei sent Yu Gong Zhi Si to chase after him. Zi Zhuo Ru Zi said, 'I'm ill today and cannot hold my bow; I am going to die!' He asked his servant, 'Who is chasing after me?' His servant replied, 'It's Yu Gong Zhi Si.' He said, 'Then I will not die.' His servant said, 'Yu Gong Zhi Si is one of the best archers in Wei, sir; why did you say you would not die?' He said, 'Yu Gong Zhi Si learned archery from Yin Gong Zhi Ta, and Yin Gong Zhi Ta learned it from me. Yin Gong Zhi Ta is an upright man, the one he befriends must be an upright man, too.' Then Yu Gong Zhi Si came and asked, 'Sir, why aren't you holding your bow?' Zi Zhou Ru Zi replied, 'I'm ill today and cannot hold my bow.' Yu Gong Zhi Si said, 'I learned archery from Yin Gong Zhi Ta and Yin Gong Zhi Ta learned it from you. I can't bear to hurt you with your own art. Nevertheless, today I am under my ruler's command and I dare not ignore it.' He drew out his arrows and knocked off the metal tips against the chariot wheels, shot four times and went back." (Chapter 8.24)

Contemporary interpretation:

To teach students successfully, one has to select those of good character, or one has to nurture good character in the students. This is of particular importance nowadays as we live

不可以拿弓。』庾公之斯說：『我跟尹公之他學
射，尹公之他跟先生學射。我不忍心用先生您的
射箭之術反過來害先生。雖然如此，今天的事卻
是君主委派的國事，我不敢不執行。』他抽出箭
來，在車輪上敲了幾下，把箭頭敲掉，射了四箭，
然後就回去了。」

【時析】

　　教學生，要選人品好的學生教，或者要把學
生品德教好，這在今天尤其重要。現今的高科技
越來越厲害，掌握了高科技的人如果品德差，越
是本事大，越可能造成巨大的損害，比如霸菱銀
行事件（1995 年 2 月 26 日，該銀行倒閉，原
因是一名其新加坡分行任職的交易員在衍生性金
融商品進行超額交易投機失敗）、常見的電腦系
統駭客事件。對將來可能掌握政治權力的學生的
培養，更要注重品德。如果品行不端，將來他們
掌握巨大的權力之後，難免不貪污腐化，利用公
權力牟取私利，危害公眾、國家安全。讓學生德
才兼備，一直是教育的理想。孟子責備羿，認為
羿選人不善，自取其禍。子濯孺子擇徒重品，故
能揀回一條命。中國傳統一直重視品德教育，這
是正確的。如果學生品德差，你還將知識技能教

in an ever-advancing technological world. If an evil-minded person were to master any kind of advanced technology, he could bring huge damage to society. Examples are the collapse of Barings Bank (caused by fraudulent trading by one of its employees in Singapore resulting in a massive trading loss), as well as the frequently seen network hacking attacks.

Character education is especially important for students who may become our future political leaders. If they lack integrity, they may use the vast political power they acquire for personal gain, putting the public and state interests in jeopardy. It has always been an ideal to educate students to attain both uprightness and talent.

Mencius blamed Yi for recruiting people of doubtful character to be his students, and in doing so he paid the price with his life. Zi Zhuo Ru Zi recruited students only if they were virtuous, and thus saved his life. The Chinese tradition rightly places importance on character education. If we teach a student to become knowledgeable while ignoring his bad character traits, we then increase his ability to harm society. To select students of good character and to nurture students' good character and moral values is the foremost task for teachers and schools alike.

給他，不過是培養了一個更有能力危害社會的人。所以選擇人品好的學生或者培養學生品德，使他們建立正確的價值觀，是學校和老師應有的責任。

十二

孟子曰：「人之患，在好為人師。」（卷七 離婁章句上・二十三）

【今譯】

孟子說：「人的毛病，在於總喜歡當別人的導師。」

【時析】

這裏說的「好」，不是說好得夠資格當老師，而只是說，某些人喜歡說教，常常根據自己一隅之見，覺得自己識見高人一籌，其他人都無知無識，所以要去「教導」一下，滿足自己的虛榮快感。這種毛病的人，在各個階層、各個行業都有。今日很多人誤讀孟子這句話，將當老師說成是「人之患」，讓大家誤以為孟子對教師反感，反對人們當老師，其實這並不是孟子的原意。

Twelve

Translation:

Mencius said, "The trouble with people is that they are too keen on taking up the role of the teacher." (Chapter 7.23)

Contemporary interpretation:

The word "keen" in this passage does not imply that one is qualified to be a teacher. Instead, it refers to a person who regards himself as more knowledgeable than others, and so would take any chance to indoctrinate others with his narrow views just for the sake of gratifying his own vanity. People with this kind of problem exist in every social class or trade.

Nowadays, many people misread this passage and interpret it as meaning that teachers are "the trouble of people." This has led people to think that Mencius was against people becoming teachers, which absolutely was not his intended message!

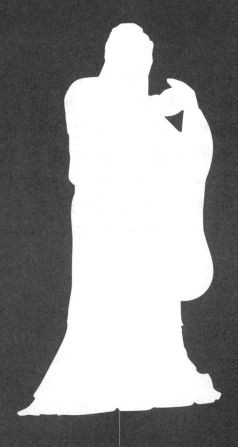

聖人 *The Sage*

一

孟子曰：「聖人，百世之師也，伯夷、柳下惠是也。故聞伯夷之風者，頑夫廉，懦夫有立志。聞柳下惠之風者，薄夫敦，鄙夫寬。奮乎百世之上，百世之下聞者莫不興起也。非聖人而能若是乎？而況於親炙之者乎？」（卷十四　盡心章句下・十五）

【今譯】

孟子說：「聖人，是一百代人的導師，伯夷、柳下惠就是這樣的人。所以聽到伯夷的風範的，貪婪的人也會變得廉潔，懦弱的人也會立志幹一番大事。聽到柳下惠的風範的，刻薄的人也會變得厚道，心胸狹窄的人也會變得寬容。聖人在百代以前奮發有為，百代之後聽到的人也無不倍受鼓舞，奮起效仿。不是聖人怎能在一百代之後還產生這樣的影響呢？（一百代尚且如此，）何況那些親自接受過聖人薰陶的人呢？」

【時析】

聖人為後世起到一個榜樣的作用，通過語言、教育、形象在後世流傳，在某種程度上塑造了那時的文化和風俗傳統。比如孔子對於山東的

One

Translation:

Mencius said, "A sage is teacher to a hundred generations; Bo Yi and Hui of Liu Xia were truly such sages. Upon hearing of Bo Yi's demeanor, a covetous man will become incorruptible, a weak-willed man will aspire to become great. Upon hearing of Hui of Liu Xia's demeanor, a harsh man will become kind-hearted and a small-minded man will become generous. The sages who roused themselves to accomplish a hundred generations ago will for sure arouse those a hundred generations later. Could anyone but a sage possibly have such influence after a hundred generations? And how much more rousing could it have been for those who were taught by the sages personally [compared with those who come a hundred generations after]?" (Chapter 14.15)

Contemporary interpretation:

A sage offers a role model for future generations through his words, teachings and image. As a result, he may help shape the ethos and customs of a local culture and offer guidance for generations to come. For example, Confucius most probably had a subtle influence on the folk culture of Shandong. But this influence should not be overstated. As seen from history, many sages have come and gone leaving no traces, and thus

民風，可能確實是有一種潛移默化的影響。但是，有時聖人的影響也不應誇大。歷史上許多聖人在後世被湮滅，變得默默無聞，這種情況也是有的。跟「封神榜」一樣，聖人也有地方級的、短時期級的，有全國級的、長時段級的。如孔子就是全國級的，千年級的。

孟子的時代接近孔子，工作和居住地也靠近魯國，他跟孔子的再傳弟子學習過，所以，他可以說離聖人很近，能夠學到一些鮮活的東西。對於他來說，孔子還是一個活生生的榜樣，激勵他希聖希賢，自己也做出一番偉業。

人們容易受身邊人的影響。比如，一個學校裏有一個同學畫畫得獎，就會激勵周圍的一些同學也去學畫畫，學的人多了，獲獎的多了，就會漸漸形成一種風氣，乃至漸漸變成學校的一個傳統，時間久了，就會湧現出高端的人才。如果這個學校能存在一百年、兩百年，將這個傳統傳承下去，可能就會幅射到整個城市和地區，學校出現了大畫家可能就對當地藝術界產生長遠的影響，改變當地乃至外地的藝術觀念和市場，後來學畫畫的人在接受其影響的同時也想着超越他，結果這裏就形成一個人才輩出，畫風熾盛的傳

were unable to make any lasting impact. As with the gods in the mythical Chinese novel *Feng Shen Bang* (Investiture of the Gods), hierarchy does exist among the sages; while some are more locally active and have a rather short-term influence, others are more widely known and have had a long-term impact. Confucius is an example of the latter. Although Mencius was born a couple of centuries after Confucius, he lived close to the state of Lu, and had studied under a second-generation disciple of Confucius. We may even say that he was so close to Confucius that he should have been able to learn from the sage in a lively way. Confucius, in fact, was still such a vivid a role model that he was able to inspire Mencius to become as virtuous, as wise and as great.

We are prone to be influenced by people around us. For example, if a student has won a painting award, his efforts may stimulate other students to start to learn to paint; as more students become interested and gain achievements in painting, an artistic ethos will gradually form in the school, and after a while it will become a tradition of the school where more and more outstanding artists are inspired and nurtured. If this school keeps such a tradition alive for a hundred or even two hundred years, the influence may spill out into the city and even the nearby region. In this way, the great painters

統。孔孟之鄉的儒學傳統，也可以這樣來理解。

二

孟子曰：「富歲，子弟多賴；兇歲，子弟多暴。非天之降才爾殊也，其所以陷溺其心者然也。今夫麰麥，播種而耰之，其地同，樹之時又同，浡然而生，至於日至之時，皆熟矣。雖有不同，則地有肥磽，雨露之養、人事之不齊也。故凡同類者，舉相似也，何獨至於人而疑之？聖人與我同類者。故龍子曰：『不知足而為屨，我知其不為蕢也。』屨之相似，天下之足同也。口之於味，有同嗜也。易牙先得我口之所嗜者也。如使口之於味也，其性與人殊，若犬馬之與我不同類也，則天下何嗜皆從易牙之於味也？至於味，天下期於易牙，是天下之口相似也。惟耳亦然，至於聲，天下期於師曠，是天下之耳相似也。惟目亦然，至於子都，天下莫不知其姣者。不知子都之姣者，無目者也。故

nurtured by the school will have a long-term impact on the local arts culture, thus reshaping local as well as foreign aesthetic ideas and market trends. Subsequent painters who are inspired by the great painters will at the same time try their best to surpass them. In consequence, many talented painters will be nurtured, and a vibrant artistic tradition will flourish. This example is useful for us to understand how the Confucian culture which germinated in the homelands of Confucius and Mencius has developed into the current Confucian tradition.

Two

Translation:

Mencius said, "In good years, the children are mostly lazy; in bad years, the children are mostly violent. This is not due to their endowed differences, rather it is the environmental influence that has ensnared their hearts. Let's take barley as an example. If we sow the seeds and weed them in the same soil, and at the same time, then all the barley will thrive and be ripe when summer comes. Even if some of the barley turns out to be different, the cause will lie in the difference in soil fertility, rainfall and human effort. Therefore, for all things that are the same in kind, they resemble each other. Why then does it sound doubtful only when we talk about human beings? The

曰：口之於味也，有同嗜焉；耳之於聲也，有同聽焉；目之於色也，有同美焉。至於心，獨無所同然乎？心之所同然者，何也？謂理也，義也。聖人先得我心之所同然耳。故理義之悅我心，猶芻豢之悅我口。」（卷十一 告子章句上・七）

【今譯】

　　孟子說：「豐收之年，少年子弟懶惰的多；欠收之年，少年子弟兇暴的多。並不是天降的才這樣不同，而是由於環境把人心變壞了。好比那大麥，播了種，耘了地，如果地質一樣，栽種的時間一樣，那就會蓬勃生長，到夏至時就都成熟了。即使有長得不一樣的，那也是因為地有肥瘠的不同，和雨露多少、人工勤惰的不同。所以一切同類的事物，都是相似的，為甚麼一談到人類就懷疑這一點呢？聖人是跟我同一類的。所以龍子說：『即使你不知道腳的大小就去編鞋，我也知道你不會編出一個筐子來。』鞋是相似的，因為天下人的腳是相似的。人的嘴巴對於味道，是有同樣的嗜好的，易牙是搶先一步懂得人們的嗜好的人。假如嘴巴對於味道，性質因人而易，就像狗、馬和人不同類那樣，那麼天下人怎麼都會

sage and I are the same in kind. As Lung Zi said, 'When you make a sandal, even if you do not know the foot size, you will not end up making a basket.' Sandals all resemble one another because our feet are the same in kind. Similarly, we all savor food with our mouths, and thus we all have similar palates. Yi Ya is simply the first man to have captured what is most pleasing to our palates. Were it the case that our mouths all experienced different tastes, just as humans are different in kind from dogs and horses, how would it be possible for the whole world to admire Yi Ya's taste for food? The fact that the world follows Yi Ya's taste shows that our mouths are all alike. The same applies to our ears. When we talk about good sound, the whole world looks to Shi Kuang for good music; this shows that we as humans all resemble one another in our hearing. The same also applies to our eyes. The whole world knows that Zi Du is a true beauty; anyone who doesn't is blind. Hence, I say, with our mouths we savor and thus can have shared standards of taste; with our ears we listen and thus can have shared standards of melody; and with our eyes we see and thus can have shared standards of beauty. So, would it only be the case for hearts not to have anything in common? If they do, what would they share? I would say, our hearts all share reason and righteousness in common. The sage is just the one who was first to grasp what is shared among our

跟隨易牙的口味呢？一說到味道，天下人都期望
達到易牙的水準，這就說明天下人的味覺是相似
的。耳朵也是一個道理。一說到聲音，天下人都
期望達到師曠的水準，可見天下人的耳朵是相似
的。眼睛也是一個道理。一說到子都，天下人沒
有不知道他的俊美的。不知道子都的俊美的，是
沒有眼睛的人。所以說：嘴巴對於味道，有相同
的嗜好。耳朵對於聲音，有相同的聽覺。眼睛對
於形色，有相同的美感。至於人心，難道就偏偏
沒有相同之處嗎？人心共有的東西，是甚麼呢？
可以說是理，是義。聖人先我一步知道了人心共
同的東西。所以，理義之令我心愉悅，正如肉類
令我口感良好一樣。」

【時析】

　　孟子前面說到性善，這裏要解釋為甚麼現實
生活中有的人性善有的人不善，有的善多有的善
少。他認為，雖然天賜予每個人的才（材質，指
四端）是一樣的，只是由於環境的不同呈現出差
異。但就根本而言，在性善上，普通人跟聖人是
一樣的，差異只不過在於聖人充分實現了自己的
「才」，擴充了善性，先我一步覺悟，成了楷模；
而普通人不加保養維護，加上有時外部環境欠
佳，差距才越來越大。

hearts. Thus, reason and righteousness please my heart, just as good meat pleases my mouth." (Chapter 11.7)

Contemporary interpretation:

In previous chapters, Mencius talked about the intrinsic goodness of human beings. This passage serves to explain why in reality good people as well as bad people exist, and some have more goodness while others have less. According to Mencius, even though we as humans are born with similar capability ("capability" refers to the four budding senses), we are exposed to different environmental influences that have shaped us into people with vastly individual differences. Nevertheless, the average person is essentially no different from a sage regarding the goodness of his heart. Instead, the difference lies in the sage's ability to fully actualize his capability — his advancement of goodness and early enlightenment made him the role model for all. The average man is simply mindless about his capability to do good and is more affected by a detrimental environmental influence, and gradually forsakes his own goodness. The last sentence, "reason and righteousness please my heart, just as good meat pleases my mouth" echoed well with the moral joy shared by Confucius and his beloved student Yan Hui. Mencius's view is contrary to Kant's dispassionate deontology (the study of

最後一句「理義之悅我心猶芻豢之悅我口」，與孔顏樂處可承接。此與康德義務論不動情恰恰相反，這位德國哲學家提出義務倫理學，認為一個行為是否道德，僅出於責任，而非感情或結果。

三

曹交問曰：「人皆可以為堯舜，有諸？」孟子曰：「然。」「交聞文王十尺，湯九尺；今交九尺四寸以長。食粟而已，如何則可？」曰：「奚有於是？亦為之而已矣。有人於此，力不能勝一匹雛，則為無力人矣。今日舉百鈞，則為有力人矣。然則舉烏獲之任，是亦為烏獲而已矣。夫人豈以不勝為患哉？弗為耳。徐行後長者，謂之弟；疾行先長者，謂之不弟。夫徐行者，豈人所不能哉？所不為也。堯舜之道，孝弟而已矣。子服堯之服、誦堯之言、行堯之行，是堯而已矣。子服桀之服、誦桀之言、行桀之行，是桀而已矣。」曰：「交得見於鄒君，可以假館，願留而受業於門。」曰：「夫道若大路然，豈難知

the nature of duty). The German philosopher advocated a deontological style of ethics that defines moral agency with deontic reasoning, rather than emotion or consequence.

Three

Translation:

Cao Jiao asked, "Is it true that every man is capable of becoming a Yao or a Shun?"

Mencius replied, "Yes."

Cao Jiao went on, "I heard that King Wen of Zhou was ten _chi_ tall, King Tang of Shang was nine _chi_ tall. Now I am a little more than nine _chi_, four _cun_ tall, yet I know nothing other than eating my meal. What should I do?"

Mencius replied, "Why does your height matter? Just try to live up to them. Here is a man who cannot lift even a chick, he is, indeed, weak in strength. If it turns out that he can lift 3,000 catties, then he is full of strength. Likewise, if he can lift a weight as heavy as that which the strong man Wu Huo lifted, then we say he is just another Wu Huo. Why should people worry about not being capable of it? It is only that they have

哉？人病不求耳。子歸而求之，有餘
師。」（卷十二　告子章句下‧二）

【今譯】

　　曹交問：「人都可以成為堯舜，有這樣的話
嗎？」孟子說：「有的。」曹交說：「我聽說周
文王有十尺高，商湯有九尺高；如今我有九尺四
寸多高，卻只會吃飯罷了，要怎麼做才行呢？」
孟子說：「這有甚麼關係呢？去做就行了。這裏
有個人，力氣連個小雞都提不起來，那他就是一
個毫無力氣的人。如果說能舉起三千斤，那他就
是個有力氣的人。同樣的道理，如果他舉得起大
力士烏獲所舉的重量，那他也就成為烏獲了。人
哪裏會以勝不過為憂呢？只是不去做罷了。走慢
點，跟在長者後面，叫做悌；走快點，搶在長者
前面，叫做不悌。走慢一點，豈是人做不到的嗎？
只是不那樣做罷了。堯舜之道，也不過就是孝悌
罷了。你穿堯的衣服，唸誦堯的話，做堯做的事，
便就是堯。你穿桀的衣服，唸誦桀的話，做桀做
的事，便就是桀。」曹交說：「我能謁見鄒君，
可以向他借到住處，我願意留下來當您的弟子。」
孟子說：「道就跟大路一樣，難道不容易瞭解嗎？
人的毛病在於不去尋求它。你還是回去尋找吧，
老師多得很。」

not tried? When one walks with an elder and can slow one's pace to follow behind, one is considered a well-mannered younger brother; while if one walks hastily past the elder, one is considered an ill-mannered younger brother. Is it too hard for someone to slow his pace? One simply chooses not to do it. The way that Yao and Shun show us is simply that of a good son and a good younger brother. If you dress like Yao, speak in the tone of Yao and act in the way of Yao, then you become a Yao. If you dress like Jie, speak in the tone of Jie and act in the way of Jie, then you become a Jie." Cao Jiao said, "If I can meet with the ruler of Zou and am offered a place to lodge, I wish to stay and study under you." Mencius said, "The Way is like a wide road, is it so hard to find? One fails only when he does not look for it. You may go home and continue your pursuit; there should be many teachers around." (Chapter 12.2)

Contemporary interpretation:

Often people tend to idolize the sage and think that their standards are so high that a common person simply cannot attain them. In other passages, Mencius talks about the sublimity of the sages, like the perfection of their character and their extraordinary ability to do good. Nevertheless, based upon his doctrine on human goodness, every human possesses the four budding senses for becoming good; once we actualize

【時析】

人們有時會把聖人神化，認為聖人高不可攀，你我凡人做不到那個高度。孟子在別的地方也會說聖人的神聖、人格的完善、能力的超凡等，但基於他的性善論，人人都有為善的四端，只要擴而充之，任何人跟聖人並沒有本質上的差異。因此，只要能學習聖人的言行，有樣學樣，把聖人當作日常生活的榜樣，就算未能立刻成為聖人，也能一步一步接近達到聖人的水準。

在別的宗教和傳統中，也有類似的做法。比如基督教有本名著叫《效法基督》，就是鼓勵信徒向基督這個榜樣學習，學他的話，學他的行為。中國大陸也樹立了一些榜樣人物，如雷鋒等。孟子在這裏是向普通人指出一條簡易的學習捷徑，例如穿堯的服裝，從外面學習久了，浸泡在那種氛圍裏就會受到薰陶，形成社會風俗後，也許就真會有效果。為甚麼要穿堯舜的服裝，也許是用這個行為向別人表示，我在向聖人學習，你們監督我吧。因此，服裝不僅僅是一個外在的行為，而且是一種內心想要轉變更新的象徵，服裝會對行為起到規範的作用。這跟學生穿校服有一定的相似：穿上校服表明你的身份，你的言行就跟學校傳統聯繫起來，因此要注意，不要有違反紀律

them to the fullest extent, we are essentially no different from the sages. Therefore, we can follow the examples of the sages — to learn the words and deeds of the sages and to put them into practice in everyday life — then even though we may not become a sage straight away, we can gradually become closer to the standards of the sage.

There are similar teachings in other religions or cultural traditions. For example, *The Imitation of Christ*, a Christian classic, encourages Christians to look upon Christ as the good example to follow — to learn his words and to imitate his deeds. In modern China, some role models have been promoted, such as Lei Feng. Mencius's point is to offer an easy way for everyone to learn. This involves dressing like Yao and nurturing oneself in a cultural outlook that may in the end reshape the ethos of the community. Why dress like Yao? This may be a way to tell people that one is a dedicated student of the sage, thus welcoming any advice from people around. Indeed, how we dress is not only a matter of appearance, it is also a symbol for our dedication to self-betterment, and our choice of outfit very often obliges us to behave. This may also make a point for the wearing of school uniforms: putting on the school uniform identifies us as members of the school, and any of our words and deeds would present ourselves as

的行為，要符合學校內部和社會上對你的期待。

四

孟子曰：「舜生於諸馮，遷於負夏，卒於鳴條，東夷之人也。文王生於岐周，卒於畢郢，西夷之人也。地之相去也，千有餘里；世之相後也，千有餘歲。得志行乎中國，若合符節。先聖後聖，其揆一也。」（卷八離婁章句下・一）

【今譯】

孟子說：「舜出生在諸馮，搬遷到負夏，死於鳴條，他是東夷人。周文王出生在歧周，死在畢郢，他是西夷人。這兩個人，居住的地方相差一千多里，生活的年代相差一千多年，但他們在中原地區推行的仁政，簡直像符節的兩半一樣絲毫不差。儘管他們一個是前代的聖人，一個是後代的聖人，他們的治國原則卻是一樣的。」

【時析】

原文中「東夷」、「西夷」中的夷，是跟華相對的。夷是野蠻人的意思。孟子在批判許行的

part of our school tradition. In order to live up to reasonable expectations from the school as well as from the society, we should act with prudence and compliance.

Four

Translation:

Mencius said, "Shun was born in Zhu Feng, then moved to Fu Xia and died in Ming Tiao; he is from Eastern Yi. King Wen of Zhou was born in Qi Zhou and died in Bi Yin; he is from Western Yi. The places where they lived are more than one thousand miles apart; their lives span more than one thousand years. Yet both of them ruled the central regions with benevolent policies that were so matched with one another as if they were the two halves of a tally. Even though they were sages across so many generations, the principle they shared in governance is the same." (Chapter 8.1)

Contemporary interpretation:

The "Yi" in "Eastern Yi" and "Western Yi" were used in contrast to "Hua" in the original text. "Yi" means barbarians. When Mencius criticized the doctrine of Xu Xing, he made a sharp distinction between "Hua" and "Yi," in which "Hua" should be understood as Confucian doctrine: "Hua" implies

學說時有較強的「華夷之辨」，但我們可以理解為他把孔子的學說當作「華」，是「文化中國」，而不是種族或民族中國。在這裏，根據孟子一貫的仁義思想，他應當是說，雖然舜與文王原先都是夷，但由於他們有仁義思想，因此就取得了華的中心地位。可見孟子只以思想理念來判斷一個人，而不是根據地域和種族出身來判斷一個人。

這種以理想為中心的華夷之辨，為後來佛教、基督教順利傳入中國準備了思想上的條件。比如，當天主教傳教士來華時，他們強調「東海西海，心同理同」——雖然我們是西方人，來自遙遠的西方，但在倫理道德上，在仁愛精神上，跟儒家是一致的。徐光啟等中國儒士很快就接受了利瑪竇等人，也跟這種重視文明而不看重種族的「從道不從種」傳統有關。耶穌會傳教士艾儒略長期在福建活動，他甚至被當地儒士稱為「西來孔子」。

孔孟注重從文明程度上來劃分華夷之辨，應該說是一種開放的心態。近代的問題是傳統儒家治理理念遇到了西方治理理念，儒教禮制遇到了西方制度，從而在文明上出現了比較危機。即使在這種情況下，如果把孟子所重視的「其揆一

a "cultural China" but not an "ethnic China." If we can read according to Mencius's ethical doctrine on benevolence and righteousness, this passage should be given the following interpretation: despite the fact that Shun and King Wen were barbarians by birth, they became rulers of central China because they adopted a benevolent doctrine as the foundation of their governance. It is thus clear that Mencius does not judge a person by his birthplace or ethnicity; instead, he judges a person according to his thoughts and ideas.

Later, when Buddhism and Christianity were introduced to China, this "Hua/Yi distinction" based upon the benevolent ideal enabled an easy acceptance of these foreign doctrines. For example, when Catholic missionaries came to China, their message was, "Whether in coming from the Eastern or Western sea, the heart and the reason are the same." In other words, "Even though we are Westerners coming from a faraway land, our ethical ideals and spirit of benevolence are congruous with Confucianism." The Confucian tradition of "serving the Tao, not the race" (with emphasis on cultural rather than ethnic unity) to a certain extent prompted Confucian scholars like Xu Guang Qi to acknowledge missionaries like Matteo Ricci. The long-time Jesuit missionary Giulio Aleni, who was active in Fujian province, was even called "Confucius from the

也」理解為人道主義、仁政、民生主義，未嘗不可以將它當作普世價值。甚至孟子的「義戰」（救民於水火）的觀念，都跟今天的人道主義干涉（人權高於主權）或人道主義救援相似，有可取之處。

五

孟子曰：「霸者之民，驩虞如也；王者之民，皞皞如也。殺之而不怨，利之而不庸，民日遷善而不知為之者。夫君子所過者化，所存者神，上下與天地同流，豈曰小補之哉！」
（卷十三 盡心章句上・十三）

【今譯】

孟子說：「霸主治下的百姓過得歡喜快樂，聖王治下的百姓過得自由自在。百姓被殺了也不怨恨，得到好處也不感恩戴德，只是一天天地變得善好，而不知是誰使他變得善好。君子經過哪裏，哪裏的風氣就好轉。君子停在哪裏，哪裏的境界就高妙。上上下下的人，行為都合乎天地的運行，君子對社會的影響，怎麼能說補益不大呢？」

West" by local Confucian scholars. The Confucian emphasis on cultural enlightenment as the sole criterion of "Hua/Yi distinction" in fact represents a liberal attitude towards foreign culture. One of the modern challenges we face is caused by the tensions between Chinese and Western cultures, including the tensions between traditional Confucian ideas of governance and Western ideas of governance, and tensions between the Confucian social system of rites and the Western social system. In the face of such a situation, Mencius's point in "the principle they share in governance is the same" may indicate a solution, since it endorses a form of governance that upholds humanitarianism, benevolence and righteousness, and the livelihood of people. It can be considered as a universal value. Even Mencius's idea about "just wars" (to save the people from hardship), which is similar to the humanistic intervention and rescues of today (placing human rights above sovereignty), has some worth.

Five

Translation:

Mencius said, "Under the rule of a hegemon, people's lives are happy; under the rule of a sage king, people's lives are carefree. When they are put to death, they bear no grudge;

【時析】

孟子這段話，如果掩去作者的名字，也許會讓大家以為是老莊寫的呢！看來，正如孔子所嚮往的人生境界，是其弟子曾點所說的逍遙春遊，跟老莊的適性自在類似，在對於教化的最高境界上，孟子也跟老、莊不謀而合。

這裏所說的君子化人的功夫，跟老莊所說的真人至人神人是不是沒有多大差別呢！聖王所化之民，正如老莊上古沌混世界之民，聖王之化民，正如老莊筆下的真人至人神人。

說到底，能化，是因為有軟實力，有超凡魅力，讓人情不自禁就信了你的話，跟着你跑。現在美國出現了很多問題，不過美國的吸引力還是有的，例如其一流的高等教育與科技創新環境，不然，怎麼會有那麼多國家的官員和百姓，都爭着把孩子送到美國去留學呢？可見美國是有讓人信服的地方。

六

孟子曰：「伯夷目不視惡色，

when they receive benefit, they give no thanks. Day by day, they move towards goodness, yet they do not know who guides them there. Indeed, wherever the gentleman passes by, the ethos becomes transformed; wherever his mind resides, things turn sublime. Those at the top and those at the bottom are in harmony with the sky and the earth; how could one say his contribution is small!" (Chapter 13.13)

Contemporary interpretation:

If the author of this passage was unknown to us, we might have guessed it was written by Laozi or Zhuangzi! As pointed out by Zeng Dian in the *Analects*, the life that Confucius longed for was a spring outing with joyful company. Indeed Confucius's outlook on life was comparable to that of Laozi and Zhuangzi's pursuit of an authentic and carefree life. In a similar way, on the ultimate goal of nurturing, Mencius's view echoes with that of Laozi and Zhuangzi. In this passage, Mencius talks about the subtle transformation that the gentleman brings to people. Doesn't it fit well with Laozi and Zhuangzi's understanding of the "pure man/perfect man/godly man"? The people whom the sage king transforms are the same people in the benighted world of Laozi and Zhuangzi; the sage king who transforms everyone mirrors the "pure man/perfect man/godly man" depicted by Laozi and Zhuangzi.

耳不聽惡聲。非其君不事，非其民不
使。治則進，亂則退。橫政之所出，
橫民之所止，不忍居也。思與鄉人
處，如以朝衣朝冠坐於塗炭也。當
紂之時，居北海之濱，以待天下之清
也。故聞伯夷之風者，頑夫廉，懦夫
有立志。

「伊尹曰：『何事非君？何使非
民？』治亦進，亂亦進。曰：『天之
生斯民也，使先知覺後知，使先覺覺
後覺。予，天民之先覺者也；予將以
此道覺此民也。』思天下之民匹夫匹
婦有不與被堯舜之澤者，若己推而內
之溝中。其自任以天下之重也。

「柳下惠不羞污君，不辭小官。
進不隱賢，必以其道。遺佚而不怨，
厄窮而不憫。與鄉人處，由由然不忍
去也。『爾為爾，我為我，雖袒裼裸
裎於我側，爾焉能浼我哉？』故聞柳
下惠之風者，鄙夫寬，薄夫敦。孔子
之去齊，接淅而行。去魯，曰：『遲
遲吾行也。』去父母國之道也。可以

After all, the power of transformation rests in one's "soft power" — the extraordinary charisma that draws people's admiration and compliance. Even now that America is being troubled by several issues, the nation is still attractive to many, such as by its environment that contributes to the country's excellent higher education and technological creativity. Why otherwise would officials and people of influence from so many countries keep sending their children to study there even when they play an anti-American role in their professional lives?

Clearly America retains its persuasive global influence.

Six

Translation:

Mencius said, "Bo Yi would not set his eyes on improper sights, nor allow his ears to listen to improper sounds. He would not serve a ruler whom he did not honor; he would not use people who were not upright. He served in the government when there was good governance; he retired during chaotic times. He could not bear to live under a tyrant's rule or among unruly people. He considered being with a vulgar person like sitting on dirt in his court robes. When Zhou came into power

速而速，可以久而久，可以處而處，
可以仕而仕，孔子也。」

孟子曰：「伯夷，聖之清者也；
伊尹，聖之任者也；柳下惠，聖之和
者也；孔子，聖之時者也。孔子之謂
集大成。集大成也者，金聲而玉振之
也。金聲也者，始條理也；玉振之也
者，終條理也。始條理者，智之事也；
終條理者，聖之事也。智，譬則巧也；
聖，譬則力也。由射於百步之外也，
其至，爾力也；其中，非爾力也。」
（卷十 萬章章句下・一）

【今譯】

　　孟子說：「伯夷，眼睛不看不好的顏色，耳
朵不聽不好的聲音。不是好的君主，他不事奉，
不是好的百姓，他不使喚。天下太平，就出來做
事；天下動亂，就退隱獨處。實行暴政的國家，
住有暴民的地方，他都不願意住。他認為和低俗
的人在一起，就跟穿着上朝廷的衣冠坐在泥炭上
一樣。商紂在位的時候，他住到北海之濱，等待
天下變得清平。所以，聽到伯夷風範的人，貪婪
的也變得廉潔，懦弱的也樹立志向。

as the King of Shang, he lived far away in the Northern shore, and waited for the state to be restored. So, when a man hears about Bo Yi's good example, the covetous man will become incorruptible, the weak-willed will cherish aspiration.

"Yi Yun said, 'Whom may I not serve? Whom may I not use?' He [Yi Yun] offered his service, no matter whether the country was at peace or in chaos. He said, 'Heaven has my people born in such a way that those who attain understanding first are obliged to enlighten those who are slow to learn, and those who have mastered the Way can show it to those who have not. I am among those who have already mastered the Way and I am ready to show my people how they can, too.' Yi took it to be his foremost obligation to have everyone — man or woman — to be nurtured by the good examples shown by Yao and Shun. For if he failed to do so, he would feel like pushing them into a ditch to drown.

"Hui of Liu Xia was not ashamed to serve tyrants, nor would he decline a minor post. When he worked, he did not hide his talents, yet he served always with a righteous mind. When he was dismissed, he did not grudge it; when he was penniless, he did not worry. When he met a vulgar person, he was delighted to be in his company. He once said, 'You are you

「伊尹說：『哪種事奉不是事奉君主？哪種使喚不是使喚百姓？』天下太平，他出來做事，天下動亂，他也出來做事。他說：『上天生育這些百姓，就是要讓先知喚醒後知，讓先覺喚醒後覺。我，是天的子民中的先覺者。我要用這大道喚醒這些百姓。』他認為，天下百姓只要有一個男子或一個女子還沒有享受到堯舜的恩澤，那就好像是他把他們推到了溝裏似的——他一個人扛起了拯救天下的重擔。

「柳下惠不以事奉壞君為羞恥，不因官小而辭去。當官時不隱藏自己的賢能，但一定要按他的原則行事。被撤職也不埋怨，處在窮困之中也不發愁，跟低俗的人在一起，高高興興地不忍離開。『你是你，我是我，即使你在我身邊赤身露體，你哪能髒了我呢？』所以，聽到柳下惠風範的，小氣鬼也胸襟寬大起來，刻薄鬼也厚道起來。

「孔子離開齊國的時候，米還沒淘完濾乾就走了。離開魯國的時候，卻說：『我們慢慢走吧。』這是離開父母之國的態度。應該馬上走就馬上走，應該繼續幹就繼續幹，可以不做官就不做官，可以做官就做官，這便是孔子。」

and I am me, even if you stand naked next to me, how can your nudity defile me?' So, when a man has heard about Hui's good example, even the small-minded will become generous, the harsh ones will become kind-hearted.

"When Confucius left Qi, he had not even finished rinsing the soaked rice. Yet when he was leaving Lu, he said 'Let us take our time.' This is indeed the proper way for one to leave his homeland. Confucius is such a person that when it is proper for him to go at once, he goes at once; when it is proper for him to stay long, he stays long; when it is proper for him to retire, he retires; and when it is proper for him to take office, he takes office."

Mencius then went on to say, "Among the sages, Bo Yi is the unsullied one, Yi Yun is the dutiful one, Hui of Liu Xia is the gracious one, Confucius is the timely one. Among them, Confucius was the one who harmonized all that was good. He acted like playing a tune that starts with bronze bells and closes with jade chimes: the sound of the bells suits well as the overture and the chimes suit well as the finale. To start properly is a wise deed; to close properly is a sublime deed. Wisdom resembles skillfulness as sagacity resembles strength. It is like shooting an arrow beyond a hundred paces: for the

孟子說：「伯夷，是聖人中清高的人；伊尹，是聖人中負責任的人；柳下惠，是聖人中隨和的人；孔子，是聖人中識時務的人。孔子可以稱為集大成者。『集大成』的意思，就像演奏音樂時，以敲銅鐘開始，以擊玉磬結束。先敲銅鐘，是奏響音樂節奏。最後擊玉磬，是結束音樂節奏。奏響音樂節奏，是智慧的事。結束音樂節奏，是聖明的事。智慧好比技巧，聖明好比力氣。這就像朝百步外的目標射箭，能射到那麼遠的地方，靠的是你的力氣；但能否射中，卻不是由於你的力氣，（而是由於你的技巧）。」

【時析】

如果看世界上的宗教，各宗教都有自己的聖人、聖徒、先知系統。這些聖人、聖徒、先知都體現了一致的價值觀，但又各具性格特色，是一元與多元的統一。比如佛教的諸佛、五百羅漢、諸菩薩，猶太教、基督教、伊斯蘭教的眾多先知和聖徒。各個宗教都有自己的「集大成者」，比如，佛教的釋迦牟尼，猶太教的摩西，基督教的耶穌，伊斯蘭教的穆罕默德。孟子在這裏也為儒家的聖人傳統列出了一個譜系，伯夷、伊尹、柳下惠、孔子各具特色，都體現了「聖」的道德和操守，同時，相對而言，孔子是聖人中的「集大

arrow to reach the target depends on the archer's strength, whereas for it to hit the mark does not. [It depends on his skillfulness as well.]" (Chapter 10.1)

Contemporary interpretation:

If we look at the different religions of the world, each religion has its own sages, saints and prophets. Even though these sages, saints and prophets may be unique in their characters, they all seem to share a compatible set of values. We can say this is a unity of monism and pluralism: a panoply of Buddhas, the five hundred arhats, the various bodhisattvas in Buddhism, and many prophets and saints in Judaism, Christianity as well as Islam. Besides, in each of the religions, we can identify "the harmonizing sage": Buddha in Buddhism, Moses in Judaism, Jesus in Christianity and Muhammad in Islam. In this passage, Mencius produced a genealogy of Confucian sages, including Bo Yi, Yi Yun, Hui of Liu Xia and Confucius; these sages are unique in their own ways, yet they all exemplify the moral character of a sage in the Confucian tradition, among whom Confucius is the harmonizing sage.

What all sages share in common is the embodiment of the human ideal of a "perfect man": their lives are more honorable and consummate when compared with the common people.

成者」，是一個總結。

　　聖人體現「完人」的理想，他們的道德比一般人要高尚、完善，在跟普通人、社會、國家的關係上，他們也各自有不同的應對模式，有的更加出世一些，有的更加入世一些，有的不妥協，有的會妥協一些，但無論哪種情況，他們都代表了一種理想，可以作為世人的楷模。比如，基督教有隱修主義，修士們跑到世俗社會之外，建立一種理想的新的小社會、一種新社會模型。再比如，在元朝和清朝初期，面對異族入主中原，漢族儒家知識份子是否要跟異族統治者合作，也出現了不同的反應模式。有的主張反抗或回避，不入仕，相當於伯夷。有的仍然認為可以入仕，為天下百姓辦事，相當於伊尹和柳下惠。就宗教總體而言，佛教更加強調與所在社會的適應，基督教更加強調對所在社會的改造。不過，即使如此，在每一宗教的內部，面對同一個社會，同一個問題，總是會有不同的反應的，每種反應都有代表人物。反映在聖人上，就是聖人具有多元性、多樣性。

　　可以看到，孟子的「聖」觀念跟孔子的已有所不同。孔子在《論語》中以堯舜禹周這樣的「聖

The sages are unique in their relationships to other people, to society, as well as to the country: some are inclined to stand aloof from worldly affairs, while others are inclined to become involved with worldly matters some are uncompromising, while others are more accommodating. Every one of them represents a human ideal that deserves to be a role model for all of us to follow. For example, monasticism in Christianity seeks to establish an ideal, alternative, small community beyond the secular society.

Another example can be taken from Confucian scholars of Han nationality during the early Yuan and Qing dynasties: in the face of the invasion by another nationality, they opted for different ways of dealing with the governing power. Some, like Bo Yi, chose to resist or stay away from official public roles. Others, like Yi Yun and Hui of Liu Xia, chose to work for the government as a better way to serve their own people.

Generally speaking, Buddhism puts more emphasis on accommodating to society while Christianity stresses reforming society. Nevertheless, even when rooted in the same religion, there is always more than one way to respond to the same social challenges, and this is represented by a variety of sages.

王」的事功來談「聖」,從而認為自己並不是「聖
人」。孟子則將孔子與伊尹這樣有大功的臣子相
提並論,並且認為孔子已經超出伊尹,是「集大
成者」,可見,在孟子的時候,「聖」的標準已
有所改變,逐漸側重道德文章,跟孔子時代側重
於事功不同了。

孟子說孔子是「聖之時者」,這個「時」如
何解?適時?順應時勢?從文中來看,孟子可能
是指,孔子根據不同情況而行事,如離齊離魯,
時機不同,環境不同,態度也不同。同時,孔子
不像伯夷等聖人,他不固執一偏,而是兼具各種
美德,原則與權變都有,正如奏樂,有始有終,
旋律隨樂曲進行而隨時變化,沒有機械之感。再
如射箭,是巧智與力量的結合,才能達到目標。

In addition, it can be seen from the passage that Mencius held a different idea of "sagacity" from Confucius. When Confucius talked about the achievement of "sage kings" like Shun and Yao in the *Analects*, he considered himself as excluded from sagacity. Mencius, however, mentioned Confucius alongside officials like Yi Yun who rendered outstanding service, and thought that Confucius surpassed Yi Yun to become the harmonizing sage. It is clear that in Mencius's time, the criterion of sagacity shifted from one's social contribution to one's cultural influence by way of moralizing texts.

Mencius said that Confucius was "the timely one." How should we understand this? What does "timely" mean? Does it mean Confucius did things at the right time and conformed to circumstances? Reading from the passage, "timely" may refer to Confucius's ability to act according to circumstance, like leaving Qi and Lu, acting in different ways to suit the existing situation. Unlike Bo Yi and the other sages, Confucius did not stick to a certain way of doing things; instead, he mastered all the virtues and adopted principles with flexibility, thus making him the harmonizing sage. After all, like playing music, the tune changes according to the rhythm, displaying no rigidity; or like archery, it is combination of skillfulness and strength that helps hit the target.

孟子其人 *About Mencius*

一

公孫丑問曰：「夫子加齊之卿相，得行道焉，雖由此霸王不異矣。如此則動心否乎？」

孟子曰：「否，我四十不動心。」

曰：「若是，則夫子過孟賁遠矣。」

曰：「是不難。告子先我不動心。」

曰：「不動心有道乎？」

曰：「有。北宮黝之養勇也，不膚撓，不目逃。思以一豪挫於人，若撻之於市朝。不受於褐寬博，亦不受於萬乘之君。視刺萬乘之君若刺褐夫。無嚴諸侯。惡聲至，必反之。孟施舍之所養勇也，曰：『視不勝猶勝也。量敵而後進，慮勝而後會，是畏三軍者也。舍豈能為必勝哉？能無懼而已矣。』孟施舍似曾子，北宮黝似

One

Translation:

Gongsun Chou asked, "Sir, if you were appointed as a top official of Qi and were able to put the proper way into practice, your achievement would definitely be comparable to that of a king or hegemon. If this happened, would you be anxious?"

Mencius said, "No. Since the age of forty, my heart has been free from any anxieties."

Gongsun Chou said, "In that case you have surpassed Meng Ben by far!"

Mencius said, "That is not hard. Gao Zi had attained an undisturbed heart sooner than I did."

Gongsun Chou said, "Are there any ways to attain an undisturbed heart?"

Mencius said, "Yes, there are. Bei Gong You nurtured his courage by trying not to flinch when pricked nor to blink when poked. He considered the slightest insulting remark as humiliating as being whipped before the public. He accepted no humiliations from anyone, whether from common folk

子夏。夫二子之勇，未知其孰賢，
然而孟施舍守約也。昔者曾子謂子襄
曰：『子好勇乎？吾嘗聞大勇於夫子
矣：自反而不縮，雖褐寬博，吾不惴
焉；自反而縮，雖千萬人吾往矣。』
孟施舍之守氣，又不如曾子之守約
也。」

日：「敢問夫子之不動心與告子
之不動心，可得聞與？」

「告子曰：『不得於言，勿求於
心；不得於心，勿求於氣。』不得於
心，勿求於氣，可；不得於言，勿求
於心，不可。夫志，氣之帥也；氣，
體之充也。夫志至焉，氣次焉。故曰：
『持其志，無暴其氣。』」

「既曰『志至焉，氣次焉』，又
曰『持其志，無暴其氣』者，何也？」

日：「志壹則動氣；氣壹則動志
也。今夫蹶者趨者是氣也，而反動其
心。」

or the ruler of a major state. He considered assassinating the ruler of a major state as no different from stabbing a common person. He had no fear of any of the vassal state rulers. If anyone insulted him, he would always strike back.

"Meng Shi She described how he nurtured his courage in this way: '[I] treat defeat as victory. If a man makes an attack only after sizing up the enemy or strikes only after weighing up the chance for victory, he is actually fearful of the enemy. How can I be sure of winning? All I need do is to be fearless.'

"Meng Shi She resembled Zengzi, while Bo Gong You resembled Zi Xia. I do not know which of these two men's courage is finer, all I know is that Meng Shi She was a man who had a firm grasp of the spirit.

"Zengzi once said to Zi Xiang, 'Do you desire courage? I once heard the Master talk about great courage:

>If, upon reflection, I find myself to be wrong, I shall feel awful even though it is just a common person whom I hurt. If, upon reflection, I find myself to be right, I shall press on even though I am against men in the thousands.

The way in which Meng Shi She nourished his vital energy (qi) was not as fine as the way Zengzi grasped the essentials."

「敢問夫子惡乎長？」

曰：「我知言，我善養吾浩然之氣。」

「敢問何謂浩然之氣？」

曰：「難言也。其為氣也，至大至剛，以直養而無害，則塞於天地之間。其為氣也，配義與道，無是餒也。是集義所生者，非義襲而取之也。行有不慊於心則餒矣。我故曰：告子未嘗知義。以其外之也。必有事焉，而勿正，心勿忘，勿助長也。無若宋人然。宋人有閔其苗之不長而揠之者，芒芒然歸，謂其人曰：『今日病矣，予助苗長矣。』其子趨而往視之，苗則槁矣。天下之不助苗長者寡矣。以為無益而舍之者，不耘苗者也。助之長者，揠苗者也，非徒無益，而又害之。」

「何謂知言？」

Gongsun Chou said, "May I ask about the undisturbed heart as in your case and in Gaozi's? Can I hear about it?"

Mencius said, "According to Gaozi, 'Anything you cannot explain well in words, you should not try to seek in your heart. Anything you cannot appreciate with your heart, you should not not try to seek in your vital energy.' It is fine for one not to seek in his vital energy anything he cannot appreciate with his heart. It is, however, not acceptable for one not to seek in his heart whatever he cannot explain well in words. The will is the commander of vital energy, and vital energy vitalizes the body. Wherever the will leads, vital energy follows. Hence, it is said, 'Take hold of your will and do not scatter your vital energy.'"

Gongsun Chou said, "On the one hand you have said, 'Wherever the will leads, vital energy follows.' But then you have also said, 'Take hold of your will and do not scatter your vital energy.' What do you mean?"

Mencius said, "When the will is focused, it moves vital energy. When vital energy is focused, it moves the will. For example, when you see a man stumble or rush, it is vital energy that energizes his body into action, and thereby arousing his heart."

曰：「詖辭知其所蔽，淫辭知其所陷，邪辭知其所離，遁辭知其所窮。生於其心，害於其政；發於其政，害於其事。聖人復起，必從吾言矣。」

「宰我、子貢善為說辭，冉牛、閔子、顏淵善言德行；孔子兼之，曰：『我於辭命，則不能也。』然則夫子既聖矣乎？」

曰：「惡！是何言也！昔者子貢問於孔子曰：『夫子聖矣乎？』孔子曰：『聖則吾不能，我學不厭而教不倦也。』子貢曰：『學不厭，智也；教不倦，仁也。仁且智，夫子既聖矣。』夫聖，孔子不居，是何言也！」

「昔者竊聞之：子夏、子游、子張皆有聖人之一體，冉牛、閔子、顏淵則具體而微，敢問所安。」
曰：「姑舍是。」

曰：「伯夷、伊尹何如？」

Gongsun Chou said, "May I ask, sir, what your strengths are?" Mencius said, "I understand the language, and I nurture well my boundless vital energy."

Gongsun Chou said, "What do you mean by 'boundless vital energy'?'" Mencius said, "It is hard to explain. This is an energy that is as great and as unyielding as can be. If one nurtures it with integrity and never impairs it, it will infuse the space between the sky and the earth. Vital energy must go hand in hand with righteousness and the Way, otherwise it will wane. It gradually grows out of one's persistent effort in righteous acts and cannot be attained by just an occasional display of righteousness.

"Whenever one acts with a guilty conscience, vital energy weakens. This is why I consider that Gaozi never really understood righteousness because he takes righteousness as external to one's heart. We must keep on nurturing righteousness within our heart, be mindful of it, yet at the same time try not to force it to grow too fast. Don't act like the man from the state of Song.

"There was a man from Song who was anxious about his seedlings not growing well, so he tried to give them a pull.

曰：「不同道。非其君不事，非其民不使，治則進，亂則退，伯夷也。何事非君？何使非民？治亦進，亂亦進，伊尹也。可以仕則仕，可以止則止，可以久則久，可以速則速，孔子也。皆古聖人也。吾未能有行焉，乃所願，則學孔子也。」

「伯夷、伊尹於孔子，若是班乎？」

曰：「否，自有生民以來，未有孔子也。」

「然則有同與？」

曰：「有，得百里之地而君之，皆能以朝諸侯有天下；行一不義、殺一不辜而得天下，皆不為也。是則同。」

曰：「敢問其所以異。」

曰：「宰我、子貢、有若，智

Then he went home without realizing what he had done and told his family, 'I'm exhausted today! I've been out helping the seedlings to grow.' His son rushed out to take a look and found the seedlings all withered. Indeed, there are few in the world who can resist pulling the seedlings to speed up their growth. Those who think nurturing vital energy is of no benefit and choose to give up are like those not weeding the fields. Those who try to speed up the growth of vital energy are like those who try to speed up the growth of seedlings by giving them a pull. By doing so, not only have they failed in nurturing vital energy but also in causing damage to it."

Gongsun Chou said, "Would you tell me more about your being able to understand the language?"

Mencius said, "For this I mean: I can tell from a biased speech what has been obscured; I can tell from an exaggerated speech what has been misled; I can tell from a heretical speech what has been erred; and I can tell from an evasive speech what has been ill-founded. When such crooked thoughts arise in one's mind, they bring harm to one's conduct of politics. When they are manifested in politics, they bring harm to governance. If a sage were to arise again, he would surely agree with what I have said."

足以知聖人，污不至阿其所好。宰
我曰：『以予觀於夫子，賢於堯舜遠
矣。』子貢曰：『見其禮而知其政，
聞其樂而知其德。由百世之後，等百
世之王，莫之能違也。自生民以來，
未有夫子也。』有若曰：『豈惟民哉！
麒麟之於走獸，鳳凰之於飛鳥，泰山
之於丘垤，河海之於行潦，類也。聖
人之於民，亦類也。出於其類，拔乎
其萃。自生民以來，未有盛於孔子
也。』」（卷三　公孫丑章句上・二）

【今譯】

　　公孫丑問道：「先生假如做了齊國的卿相，
能夠實現自己的主張，由此小則可以成就如霸
業，大則可以成就如王業。如果遇到這種情況，
您會不會因有壓力而心裏忐忑不安、動個不停
呢？」

　　孟子說：「不會的，我四十歲的時候就不動
心了。」

　　公孫丑說：「如果這樣，那先生比孟賁厲害
多了。」

Gongsun Chou said, "Zai Wo and Zi Gong excelled in rhetoric while Ran Niu, Minzi and Yan Yuan excelled in spelling out the virtues. Confucius excelled in both, yet he said, 'I am not good at rhetoric.' In that case, sir, you must already be a sage."

Mencius said, "What did you just say of me! Zi Gong once asked Confucius, 'Sir, aren't you a sage?' and Confucius replied, 'Sage? I am still very far from being a sage. I am just a person who has never been bored by learning and never tired of teaching.' Zi Gong said, 'To have never been bored by learning is wisdom; to have never been tired of teaching is benevolence. Being both wise and benevolent, sir, you are indeed a sage.' You see, even Confucius did not consider himself a sage. What did you just say of me!"

Gongsun Chou said, "I once heard that Zi Xia, Zi You and Zi Zhang each acquired one aspect of the sage, whereas Ran Niu, Minzi and Yan Yuan acquired every aspect of the sage, but in a lesser degree. Which would you rather be?"

Mencius said, "Let us put that question aside for now."

Gongsun Chou said, "What would you say then of Bo Yi and Yi Yin?"

孟子說：「做到這點並不難。告子不動心比我還早。」

公孫丑問：「做到不動心，有甚麼辦法嗎？」

孟子說：「有的。北宮黝培養勇氣，皮膚被刺了也一動不動，眼睛被戳了也一眨不眨。他覺得，被別人拔了一根毫毛，就相當於在廣場上被人用鞭子打了一頓，引為奇恥大辱。他既不能忍受來自卑賤者的羞辱，也不能忍受來自大國君主的侮辱。他把刺殺大國君主，看得跟刺殺卑賤者一樣。他一點也不怕諸侯，誰要罵他，他一定還擊。有關孟施舍培養勇氣的法子，他自己說：『把打不過看得跟打得過一樣。估量敵人的力量後才前進，考慮勝敗後才交手，這是怕敵人人多勢眾。我哪能次次都打勝仗呢？我不過是無所畏懼罷了。』孟施舍像曾子，北宮黝像子夏。這兩個人的勇敢，不知道哪個更勝一籌，然而孟施舍保持的是一種氣概。從前曾子對子襄說：『你喜歡勇敢嗎？我曾聽孔夫子談到最大的勇敢：如果自我反省，發現是自己不對，即使面對一個最卑賤的人，我也會害怕，如果自我反省，發現自己是對的，即使面對成千上萬的敵人，我也會勇往直前。』這樣看來，孟施舍的保持氣概，還是不如

Mencius said, "Their ways were different from mine. For Bo Yi, he served only a ruler he admired, and chose to use only people whom he acknowledged. He took office when the world was orderly, he quit whenever chaos set in. For Yi Yin, he would serve any ruler or any people. He took office no matter whether the world was in good order or in chaos. For Confucius, he would serve when it was proper to serve, quit when it was proper to quit, stay long when it was proper to stay long and leave quickly when it was proper to leave quickly. These were all sages of the past. I am not yet able to achieve what they did; but it is my wish to follow the example of Confucius."

Gongsun Chou said, "Were Bo Yi and Yi Yin the equals of Confucius?"

Mencius said, "No. Since the birth of mankind, there has never been another like Confucius."

Gongsun Chou said, "But did they share anything in common?"

Mencius said, "Yes. Had they ruled over a land of a hundred Chinese miles, they would receive tribute by all the vassal

曾子的堅持原則。」

公孫丑問：「我大膽地問一下，先生的不動心和告子的不動心，到底是甚麼情況呢？」

孟子說：「告子說：『你搞不清所說的意思，就不要在心裏去尋求；你自己心裏還沒有弄明白，就不要往氣處找。』你自己心裏還沒有弄明白，就不要往氣處找，是可以的；你搞不清所說的意思，就不要在心裏去尋求，卻不可以。志向，是氣的統帥；氣，是體力的充實。志向到哪裏，氣才會跟到哪裏。所以說：堅定志向，別濫用氣。」

公孫丑問：「您既說『志向到哪裏，氣才會跟到哪裏』，又說『堅定志向，別濫用氣』，為甚麼呢？」

孟子說：「志向專一，就會影響氣；氣專一，也會影響志向。比如跌倒的人和正在快步走的人，他們的氣都會反過來讓他們心動。」

公孫丑說：「請問，先生擅長哪方面呢？」

孟子說：「我擅長分析別人的話，我善於培

state rulers and have the world united. Had it been necessary for them to do wrong for just once or to kill just one innocent man in order to rule the world, none of them would do it. This is how they were alike."

Gongsun Chou said, "May I ask in what way they were different?"

Mencius said, "Zai Wo, Zi Gong and You Ruo were all intelligent enough to appreciate the sage, and none would have been so base as to show bias in favor of the man they admired. Zai Wo said, 'In my view, the Master has greatly surpassed Yao and Shun.' Zi Gong said, 'Observing the rites of a state, the Master knows how it is governed; listening to the music of a state, he knows the conduct of the ruler. Looking back over a hundred generations, he gives fair appraisals of all the kings that no one can reasonably object to. Since the birth of mankind, there has never been another like the Master.'

"You Ruo said, 'It is the case not only of men. As the unicorn is to animals, the phoenix is to birds, Mount Tai is to mounds, the Yellow River and the Yellow Sea are to pools of water — they are all of the same kinds. The sage is also one of mankind. Yet all of them stand out from their kind, far above the crowd.

養自己的浩然之氣。」

公孫丑問：「請問甚麼是浩然之氣？」

孟子說：「不容易說清楚。這個浩然之氣，作為氣可是最偉大、最剛強的，如果用正直去培養它，一點都不傷害它，它就會彌漫於天地之間。它作為一種氣概，必須和正義、正道配合，如果沒有這兩者，就會虛浮無力。它是正義經常積累產生出來的，不是偶然做幾件正義的行為就能具備的。只要做了一件於心有愧的事，這氣就變虛變軟。所以我要說：告子不知道正義是怎麼回事，因為他把正義看作外在的東西。一定要培養正義，不要停止，心裏時時刻刻不能忘記它，但也不要揠苗助長，像那個宋國人那樣。那個宋國人嫌禾苗長得不快而將它們拔高，他十分疲憊地回家，對家人說：『今天累死了，我幫禾苗長高了！』他的兒子跑到田裏一看，禾苗都枯死了。天下不揠苗助長的人很少。以為養氣沒有好處而放棄的人，相當於種地卻不除草。不顧實際地幫助氣生長的人，相當於揠苗助長，不但沒有好處，還帶來損害。」

公孫丑問：「怎麼才算得上擅長分析別人的話？」

Since the birth of mankind, there has been no one greater than Confucius.'" (Chapter 3.2)

Contemporary interpretation:

This passage can be divided into two parts. The first part discusses the cultivation of courage, the boundless vital energy and understanding the language. The second part offers an appraisal of Confucius and the other sages.

In the first part, Mencius mentions that his heart has been free from any anxiety since the age of forty; thus he would not be disturbed by fortune or misfortune, or favors or humiliation from others. He then points out the significance of courage in the cultivation of such an undisturbed heart and explains how courage could be nurtured through the various practices of Bei Gong You, Meng Shi She and Zengzi. While Bei Gong You and Meng Shi She stressed nurturing physical courage, Zengzi emphasized nurturing moral courage.

Zengzi's way was considered by Mencius as superior to that of the others. Though Gaozi attained an undisturbed heart sooner than himself, Mencius considered Gaozi's version of the undisturbed heart as mistaken (in the same way as Yang Zhu and Mozi were) because he contended that in reality one

　　孟子說：「偏頗的話能看出它所掩蓋的事實，過頭的話能看出它所要陷害的目標，歪理邪說能看出它與正道的偏離之處，躲躲閃閃的話能看出它理屈之處。這些言詞，在心裏產生，在政治上產生惡果；如果在政治上體現出來，就會損害政事。聖人如果復活，也一定會同意我的話。」

　　公孫丑說：「宰我、子貢擅長組織辭令，冉牛、閔子、顏淵擅長講述德行；孔子兼具這些長處，但還是說：『我在辭令方面還是不行的。』這樣看來，先生是聖人了吧？」

　　孟子說：「哎！你這是甚麼話！從前子貢問孔子說：『老師是聖人了嗎？』孔子說：『聖人我做不到，我不過學而不厭，教而不倦罷了。』子貢說：『學而不厭，是智；教而不倦，是仁。有仁又有智，老師已經是聖人了。』聖人，連孔子都不敢自居，你這是甚麼話！」

　　公孫丑說：「我以前聽說過，子夏、子游、子張都具備了聖人的一個方面，冉牛、閔子、顏淵則具備了所有方面，只不過微小一些罷了。請問老師，您自居哪一種人？」

should pursue in his heart whatever he could explain well in words. According to Mencius, such a claim undermines the heart's commanding role in moral discernment and is thus unacceptable.

Mencius then turns to explain the relationship between the will and vital energy. He took vital energy as the basis of life, while the will, as the reasoning power, is the controller of vital energy. He also talks about how he nurtured his famous "boundless vital energy" through persistent moral practice, and that it was associated with benevolence and righteousness (similar in meaning to the proverb "with justice on one's side, one is bold and assured"). He says that while one should not ignore the way to nurture boundless vital energy, one should also not hasten its nurturing in the same way as one might in speeding up the growth of seedlings by giving them an unnecessary pull.

As for understanding the language, Mencius points to the importance of a skeptical mindset towards any kind of speech (such as the schools of Yang and Mo in Mencius's time). He reckons that one should thoroughly scrutinize the intentions and dangers as well as the limits of any claims before coming to a conclusion.

孟子說：「這個話題還是不談了吧！」

公孫丑說：「伯夷、伊尹怎麼樣？」

孟子說：「也不相同。不是他的君主，他不服事；不是他的百姓，他不役使，天下太平就出來做官，天下動亂就退而隱居，這是伯夷的做法。哪件事不是服事君主呢？哪件事不役使百姓呢？天下太平時做官，天下動亂時也做官，這是伊尹的做法。可以做官就做官，應該辭職就辭職，可以幹得久一點就幹久一點，應該馬上走就馬上走，這是孔子的做法。他們都是古代的聖人。可惜我都沒有做到，至於我的願望，則是向孔子學習。」

公孫丑說：「伯夷、伊尹跟孔子相比，是一樣的嗎？」

孟子說：「不一樣。自從有人類以來，還沒有比孔子更偉大的人。」

公孫丑說：「那麼，這三個聖人有相同之處嗎？」

孟子說：「有的。如果他們都能得到方圓

In the second part of the passage, Mencius highly commends Confucius and considers him to be the greatest sage that ever lived. In fact, during Mencius's time, Confucius was yet to acquire the status of sage as Yao and Shun had. Based upon the principle of benevolence, Mencius claimed that Confucius successfully embodied the principle of benevolence through his timely moral decisions and actions. In reaffirming Confucius's moral greatness, Mencius made a significant contribution to promoting Confucius's moral status to that of a sage.

Mencius's conception of "the boundless vital energy" has become a motivational motto for generations of people endeavoring to fight against injustice even at the cost of their own lives. One example is the loyal Song dynasty official Wen Tianxiang, who chose to give up his life rather than surrender to a foreign enemy. His famous poem, "Song of Vital Energy," shows inspirations from Mencius: "Infusing the universe is a vital energy that transforms into a variety of forms: when it goes down, it becomes the rivers and mountains; when it goes up, it becomes the sun and the stars. In man it is called the boundless vitality..."

As for the pursuit of "understanding the language," Mencius was certainly right in emphasizing the importance of critical

一百里的地方做君主，那他們都能使諸侯朝覲，
一統天下。讓他們做一件不義的事，殺一個無辜
的人以得到天下，他們都不會做。這是他們相同
的地方。」

公孫丑說：「那他們的差別何在？」

孟子說：「宰我、子貢、有若，以他們的聰
明才智都足以瞭解聖人，他們的品格往低裏說，
也不會無原則地吹捧所喜歡的人。宰我說：『以
我來看老師，要比堯舜賢明多了。』子貢說：『見
到一國的禮制就知道它的政治如何，聽到一國的
音樂就知道它的品格如何。從一百代以後，來評
價一百代君主的高下，還沒有一個君主能違背孔
子的評價的。自從有人類以來，還沒有老師這樣
的偉人。』有若說：『豈只人類才有高下之分？
麒麟對於走獸，鳳凰對於飛鳥，泰山對於土堆，
河海對於小溪，都是同一類。聖人對於人類，也
是同一類。從自己的同類中突顯出來，從自己的
群體中挺拔而出，自從有人類以來，還沒有比孔
子更偉大的。」

【時析】
　　這段長文內容豐富，涉及諸多主題，大致可

thinking, yet at the same time he might have put people off because he gave no intimation as to how to go about it. Perhaps Mencius was an advocate of the intrinsic goodness of human nature and he felt that there was no need for man to learn it in a hard way. That might be the case for talented people, but for ordinary people, guidance and instructions are necessary for "understanding the language."

Two

Translation:
When Mencius left Qi, Chong Yu asked him on the way, "Sir, you look rather unhappy. The other day I heard you say, 'The gentleman does not bear grudges against heaven, neither does he bear grudges against men.'"

Mencius said, "That was one time, this is another. Every five hundred years a king should arise, and in between reputable people should appear. It has been seven hundred years since the Zhou dynasty. If we count the years, it is overdue; if we observe what is happening, the time is right. It must be that heaven does not yet wish to bring peace to the world. If it did, in the present world, who else other than myself would do it? Why should I be unhappy?" (Chapter 4.13)

以分為兩部份。第一部份由養勇講到培養浩然之氣，再到知言。第二部份是對孔子等人的評價。

第一部份，孟子說自己四十歲做到了「不動心」，不為窮達禍福所擾，寵辱不驚，跟孔子「四十不惑」類似。然後講到，不動心跟「勇」相關，只有做到「勇」，才能不動心，而勇是可以培養的。北宮黝、孟施舍培養的是血氣之勇，曾子培養的是道義之勇，孟子認同曾子的方法。雖然告子早於孟子做到「不動心」，但在孟子看來，告子的「不動心」（不得於言，勿求之於心，實即「得於言，求於心」）是不正確的，是把心的作用置於外在之言（楊墨那樣的學說）的控制下，沒有顯出心的主導作用。然後轉入「志」與「氣」的關係。志（理性能力）是氣的統帥，氣是生命的基礎。孟子談到自己時，指出著名的「浩然之氣」是由長期的道德修養培養出來的一種氣，跟仁義等相關。（成語「理直氣壯」與此類似。）他說，培養浩然之氣的辦法，既不能忽略，也不能揠苗助長。至於知言，孟子談到對各類言辭（如楊墨之言）要持深入分析的態度，看出其動機、危害、弊端，要有懷疑批判精神，不能輕信盲從。

Contemporary interpretation:

Mencius had traveled around the vassal states trying to persuade the rulers to adopt benevolent governance, yet none of them had accepted his governance measures.

This dialogue took place at a time when Mencius decided to retire from politics.

According to Mencius, if a ruler has the ambition to rule the world, it is essential for him to adopt the kingly way, which is based on the interests of the people. Mencius considered that this was the only way that was shown to have worked in history. However, no matter how hard he tried, none of the rulers was willing to listen to him. So reluctantly he reckoned that the conditions were not yet ripe for benevolent governance to be put into practice. In the historical estimations that he made, for every five hundred years, a sage king would arise and lead the people out of the chaotic situation.

Yet seven hundred years had already passed since the rise of King Wen of Zhou, and still there was no sign of the next sage king appearing. Mencius could only speculate that the time, as mandated by heaven, had not yet come for the world to regain the peace for which he longed.

第二部份讚美孔子。孔子在當時「至聖」地位尚未確立，當時的人並不把他跟堯舜禹等聖王相提並論。但是孟子從仁道出發，認為孔子完美地體現了仁道思想，實踐上也做得恰到好處。孟子在提高孔子的地位上，起到很大的作用。孟子在這裏提出的「浩然之氣」，在後世鼓勵很多人勇往直前為仁義、為真理而奮鬥，不苟且偷生，不惜殺身成仁。文天祥殺身成仁，其在《正氣歌》中寫道：「天地有正氣，雜然賦流形。下則為河嶽，上則為日星。在人曰浩然……」顯然是受孟子浩然之氣的影響。至於「知言」，孟子的批判分析是正確的，可惜孟子沒有給出他能夠做到知言的方法，別人無法從他那裏學到方法。也許因為孟子是性善論者，因此人有良知良能，不必辛苦地在後天去學習。這對於才高者適用，但對於普通人來說，卻不得其門而入。

二

孟子去齊，充虞路問曰：「夫子若有不豫色然。前日虞聞諸夫子曰：『君子不怨天，不尤人。』」曰：「彼一時，此一時也。五百年必有王

Mencius was very concerned about the situation because he had deep faith in the political doctrine grounded in Confucianism, and he was confident that he had the virtue and the talent to implement the policies in order for peace and order to be restored. What he lacked, in fact, was the necessary legitimate political power — he was neither a vassal ruler nor a prince — for the execution of his political measures.

Mencius deeply felt the calling by heaven to realize the Way of the sage kings. Confucius emphasized self-edification in virtues and was considered a sage. Mencius tried to apply the moral principles of Confucianism to governance, claiming himself to be a dedicated follower of the sage kings of the past. Failing to convince the vassal rulers to accept his governance measures, he found himself in the same situation as Confucius: he was in no position to carry out benevolent policies to save the world from chaos. So he chose to emulate Confucius in preserving "the moral culture entrusted by heaven" and dedicated himself to safeguarding the Way of the sage kings from being lost. The idea underlying the belief in "the rise of a sage king for every five hundred years" was not exclusive to Chinese culture, as Muslims also believe in "the rise of a sage in every one hundred years" to restore peace and order in society.

者興，其間必有名世者。由周而來，七百有餘歲矣；以其數則過矣，以其時考之則可矣。夫天，未欲平治天下也，如欲平治天下，當今之世，舍我其誰也？吾何為不豫哉？」（卷四　公孫丑章句下‧十三）

【今譯】

孟子離開齊國，充虞路問他說：「先生好像有不高興的樣子。可是，以前我聽先生講過：『君子不怨天，不尤人。』」孟子說：「那是一個時候，現在又是一個時候。每過五百年一定會有聖王興起，其間一定會出顯赫於世的人物。從周代以來已有七百多年，論年數，已經超過五百，從時勢來看，現在正是時候。也許是老天還不想治理好天下吧！如果老天想治理好天下，當今之世，除了我，還能有誰呢？我怎麼會不高興呢！」

【時析】

這段對話發生在孟子告別政治舞台的時候。孟子周遊列王，游說諸侯，勸以王道，但無人接受。孟子認為，統一天下，一定要實行王道，因為王道以民為本，得民心者得天下，這是歷史的必然趨勢。但是，在戰國這段時間，實行王道的

Since ancient times, philosophers have been seen engaging themselves in politics in the hope of creating the ideal state they dreamed of. Examples include Plato's plan to influence the rule of Syracuse, Heidegger's involvement with Nazism, as well as Chinese scholars' aspirations to become "advisors to the state" in modern China. Regrettably, rarely has success been seen. Very often, utopias based on political ideals turned out to be the worst political experiments. In reality, human nature is complicated, and a country is multifaceted. Ruling a country with morality is bound to produce its own problems. If Mencius had become a sage king and unified the world, would he have created "a Confucian utopia" in which the people were obliged to carry out unattainable things?

Three

Translation:

Gong Du Zi said, "Sir, outsiders always say you are fond of argument. May I ask why?"

Mencius said, "How could it be that I am fond of argument? I simply have no choice. The world has existed for a long time, now in order, now in chaos. In the time of Yao, the water reversed its course and flooded the Central Plain region;

機會和條件還不具備，因此他也無能為力。他的
主張無人聽取，看來這是天命了，只能說老天還
不想天下現在就得到平治。根據孟子的計算，
五百年就會出一個收拾天下亂局的聖王，現在從
周文王開始，已有七百年，超過五百年已有兩百
年，但還是亂糟糟的樣子，只能說老天還沒有想
平治天下。假如老天想平治天下，那只有孟子這
樣的人和主張才能實現，因為孟子的仁政主張，
繼承的正是前代聖王，孟子也有道德和才能去實
現——但是實際上，孟子沒有「位」（非諸侯，
非「王二代」），亂世之中也無人聽取他的主張，
因此，只能說時機未到。

孟子是有「天命感」的人，他認為自己繼承
了聖王（「王者」）的治國理念。聖王跟聖人有
差別，孔子是聖人，但不是聖王，因為孔子未曾
為王。聖人是道德教化的化身，而王跟掌權治理
百姓有關，聖王則是既有道德又有政權的人。跟
孔子一樣，孟子無「位」，便沒有機會自己平濟
天下。正如孔子自視為天之木鐸，使「天不喪斯
文」一樣，孟子也認為自己保存了王道，使不中
絕。在別的文化中，也有類似於「五百年必有王
者興」的思想，比如伊斯蘭教，就認為百年必有
聖人出，重振社會風氣，收拾亂局。思想家想搞

reptiles made their homes there and people had no safe place to live. In the lowlands, people lived in nests; in the highlands, people lived in caves. The *Book of Documents* says: 'The deluge was a warning for us.'

"'The deluge' referred to this flood. Yu was sent to control the floods. He cut channels through the land to guide the water to the sea and drove the reptiles away into the marshlands. The water that flowed through the channels formed the Yangzi, Huai, Yellow River and Han. As people were free from danger and the threat of the beasts, they at last were able to level the ground and build their homes.

"But after the death of Yao and Shun the Way of the sages declined, and tyrants arose one after another. They pulled down houses in order to make ponds, and the people had no places to live. They turned fields into parks, and the people lost their means of livelihood. Then heresies spread and violence escalated. As more parks, ponds and lakes were built, wild beasts returned. By the time of King Zhou of Shang, the world was in chaos again. The Duke of Zhou helped King Wu to kill Zhou. He waged war against Yan for three years and punished its ruler. He drove Fei Lian to the seashore and killed him there. Altogether, he annexed fifty states. He drove tigers,

政治，打造烏托邦，古今中外都有。柏拉圖在敘拉古想建立理想國，海德格爾加入納粹為希特勒鼓吹，當代中國一些學者想當國師從而影響政治，都是例子。可惜，思想和政治各有各的遊戲規則，按某一種思想建立起來的烏托邦最後往往成了最糟糕的政治實驗品。現實的人性是複雜的，國家的維度很多，道德建國治國，會產生自身的問題。孟子如果成為聖王，一統天下，會不會打造出一個儒家道德烏托邦，令人做一些高不可攀的事？

三

公都子曰：「外人皆稱夫子好辯，敢問何也？」孟子曰：「予豈好辯哉？予不得已也。天下之生久矣，一治一亂。當堯之時，水逆行，氾濫於中國。蛇龍居之，民無所定。下者為巢，上者為營窟。《書》曰：『洚水警余。』洚水者，洪水也。使禹治之。禹掘地而注之海，驅蛇龍而放之菹，水由地中行，江、淮、河、漢是也。險阻既遠，鳥獸之害人者消，然後人得平土而居之。堯舜既沒，聖人之道衰。暴君代作，壞宮室以為污

leopards, rhinos and elephants to remote lands, and the whole world was filled with joy.The *Book of Documents* says:
'How splendid were King Wen's strategies!
How great were King Wu's achievement in inheritance!
Help and enlighten our descendants,
So they can keep doing right without shortcomings.'

"But the world declined and the Way waned. Heresies and violence recurred, and there were cases of murdering one's ruler as well as one's father. Confucius was alarmed and wrote the *Spring and Autumn Annals*, which should be the work of the kings. This is why Confucius said, 'Those who know me will do so through the *Spring and Autumn Annals*; those who condemn me will do so because of the *Spring and Autumn Annals*.'

"No sage kings have appeared since then. The vassal state rulers were reckless and unbridled and people who had no official capacity discussed the governance in an irresponsible way. The doctrines of Yang Zhu and Mozi had become so popular that any scholars one met would be either from the school of Yang Zhu or the school of Mozi.

"Yang advocates self-interest, thereby disregarding the ruler.

池，民無所安息；棄田以為園囿，使民不得衣食。邪說暴行又作。園囿污地沛澤多，而禽獸至。及紂之身，天下又大亂。周公相武王，誅紂、伐奄，三年討其君；驅飛廉於海隅而戮之；滅國者五十；驅虎豹犀象而遠之。天下大悅。《書》曰：『丕顯哉文王謨！丕承哉武王烈！佑啟我後人，咸以正無缺。』

「世衰道微，邪說暴行有作。臣弒其君者有之，子弒其父者有之。孔子懼，作《春秋》。《春秋》，天子之事也。是故孔子曰：『知我者，其惟《春秋》乎！罪我者，其惟《春秋》乎！』聖王不作，諸侯放恣，處士橫議。楊朱、墨翟之言盈天下。天下之言，不歸楊則歸墨。楊氏為我，是無君也。墨氏兼愛，是無父也。無父無君，是禽獸也。公明儀曰：『庖有肥肉，廄有肥馬，民有饑色，野有餓莩，此率獸而食人也。』楊墨之道不息，孔子之道不著，是邪說誣民、充塞仁義也。仁義充塞，則率獸食人，

Mo advocates universal love, thereby disregarding the father. To disregard the father and the ruler is to act like a beast. Gongming Yi said, 'There is fat meat in their kitchen and well-fed horses in their stables, yet the people look hungry and starved corpses are seen lying in the bush. This leads beasts to devour men.' If the ways of Yang and Mo don't stop and the way of Confucius is not known, people will be deceived by heretical views and the path to virtues will be blocked.

"By blocking the path to virtues one will encourage beasts to devour men, and men will in the end devour each other. This is why I was alarmed and I started to defend the way of the sages of the past and refute those extreme and erroneous views of Yang and Mo. If these thoughts get into a man's heart, they harm his deeds; if they capture his deeds, they harm his governance. Were a sage to rise again, he would surely not deny what I have said.

"In ancient times, Yu tamed the flood and the world was restored in peace. The Duke of Zhou annexed the Yi and Di tribes, drove the wild beasts away, and the people were at peace. When Confucius finished the *Spring and Autumn Annals*, rebellious subordinates and disloyal sons were terrified. The *Book of Poetry* says:

人將相食。吾為此懼，閑先聖之道，
距楊墨、放淫辭，邪說者不得作。作
於其心，害於其事；作於其事，害於
其政。聖人復起，不易吾言矣。

「昔者禹抑洪水而天下平，周
公兼夷狄、驅猛獸而百姓寧，孔子成
《春秋》而亂臣賊子懼。《詩》云：
『戎狄是膺，荊舒是懲；則莫我敢
承。』無父無君，是周公所膺也。我
亦欲正人心、息邪說、距詖行、放淫
辭，以承三聖者。豈好辯哉？予不
得已也。能言距楊墨者，聖人之徒
也。」（卷六　滕文公章句下‧九）

【今譯】

公都子說：「外面的人都說您老人家喜歡辯
論，請問是為甚麼呢？」孟子說：「難道我喜歡
辯論嗎？我是不能不這樣啊！人類社會產生很久
了，一時太平，一時動亂。堯的時候，大水橫流，
在中原一帶氾濫，地上龍蛇爬行，百姓無處安身。
低地的人在樹上搭巢，高地的人挖出窯洞。《尚
書》說：『洚水警示我們。』洚水是甚麼，就是

'It was the barbarians that he attacked,

It was Jing and Shu that he punished,

And no one dared to resist us.'

"The Duke of Zhou attacked those who acknowledged neither father nor ruler. I also want to rectify the men's hearts, refute heretical teachings, resist biased acts, and get rid of wanton speeches in order to inherit the cause of the three sages. How could it be that I am fond of argument? I simply have no choice. He whose arguments can refute Yang and Mo is a true disciple of the sages." (Chapter 6.9)

Contemporary interpretation:

Mencius was a fervent supporter of the "Repossession of the Way" tradition. In his view, order alternates with chaos in history, and whenever a chaotic situation persists long enough, a sage king (such as Yu the Great and the Duke of Zhou) emerges to restore peace and order and save people from their sufferings. Mencius lived in a world of chaos and he believed the spread of many heretical doctrines and fallacious arguments, of which those of Yang Chu and Mozi were prominent, caused the predicament. He considered his achievement of banishing the doctrines of Yang and Mo was tantamount to those of Yu, the Duke of Zhou and Confucius

洪水。命令禹來治水。禹挖地把水引到海裏，把
龍蛇趕到草澤裏。水順着河道走，長江、淮河、
黃河、漢水就是這樣。危險消失了，害人的鳥獸
也沒有了，人才能在平原上居住。堯舜逝世後，
聖人之道就衰落了。殘暴的君主一代代出現，他
們毀壞百姓的房屋來做深池，百姓沒有地方安
身。他們破壞農田來做園囿，百姓沒有吃的穿的。
荒謬的學說、殘暴的行徑隨之興起，園囿、深池、
草澤多了起來，禽獸又跑來了。到商紂的時候，
天下又大亂。周公輔佐武王，誅殺紂王，討伐奄
國，用三年的時間討伐它的君主；把飛廉趕到海
邊殺掉；一共滅掉了五十個國家；把老虎、豹子、
犀牛、大象趕得遠遠的，天下的百姓都興高采烈。
《尚書》說：『偉大而賢明啊，文王的謀略！偉
大的繼承啊，武王的功績！幫助、啟發我們後人，
使大家都正確而沒有缺失。』

　　「世道衰落，仁義之道又衰微了，荒謬的學
說、殘暴的行徑又出現了。臣子殺君主的有，兒
子殺父親的有。孔子懼怕這種局面，因此就編寫
了《春秋》一書。編寫《春秋》這樣的書，本來
是天子的事情。所以孔子說：『理解我的人，怕
只是因為《春秋》吧！譴責我的人，怕只是因為
《春秋》吧！』聖王再也沒有出現，諸侯肆無忌

because by doing so Confucian principles could be extended and the world could be put in order.

In retrospect, we can see that Mencius overstated the influence of Yang Zhu and Mozi and his attribution of the chaotic situation to their heretical doctrines was biased. The main cause of the political chaos during the Warring States period was the fact that the Zhou emperor was sidelined, creating a power vacuum that many vassal rulers relentlessly struggled to fill. The rulers competed against one another and waged war with each other. The world became split and the people were miserable. Numerous schools of thought put forward their own solutions for saving the world from chaos.

The fragmentation in effect created a censorship-free nursing ground for scholars to develop their ideas and contend against each other for political attention. It marks an exceptional period in ancient Chinese history in which freedom of thought was most honored and intellectual exchanges were most vigorous.

Yang Zhu and Mozi were two of the leading philosophers among the numerous schools of thought. Yang Zhu held a philosophy similar to individualism, prioritizing the rights of

憚，沒有官職的士人也胡亂議政。楊朱、墨翟的
學說彌漫天下。天下的主張，不歸楊朱，就歸墨
翟。楊朱主張一切為自己，這是目無君主。墨翟
主張人人平等地愛，這是目無父親。目無父親、
目無君主，這是禽獸啊！公明儀說：『廚房裏有
肥肉，馬廄裏有肥馬，百姓卻面有饑色，野外有
餓死的人，這是帶領野獸吃人啊！』楊朱、墨翟
的學說不停息，孔子的學說就不能昭著，這便造
成荒謬的學說欺騙百姓，而堵塞了仁義的道路。

「仁義的道路被堵塞，（諸侯）就會帶領着
野獸來吃人，人們就會彼此相殘。我懼怕這種局
面，才出來捍衛古代聖人的學說，反對楊朱、墨
翟的學說，摒棄荒謬的言論，使主張荒謬學說的
人不能抬頭。那種荒謬的學說，如果出現在心裏，
就會危害做事情；如果出現在事情上，就會危害
到政治。即使聖人復活，也不會否定我的這番話。

「從前禹治服了洪水，於是天下太平，周公
兼併了夷狄、趕走了猛獸，於是百姓安寧，孔子
編成了《春秋》，亂臣賊子怕得不行。《詩經》說：
『打擊西戎北狄，痛懲楚國舒國，就沒有人敢抵
禦我們了。』目無父親目無君主的人，是周公所
打擊的對象。我也想要端正人心，消滅歪理邪說，

the individual before anything else. Since he paid no attention to personal or social responsibilities, Mencius condemned his philosophy as "dishonoring the ruler." Mozi was a collectivist who advocated universal love and non-aggression and that one should love the fathers of others like one's own father. Mencius condemned his philosophy as "dishonoring the father."

In order to advocate Confucianism and convince the rulers to accept his governance measures, Mencius sought to refute the doctrines of the two leading philosophers and show how the Confucian principles of benevolence could help restore the world with a proper moral order that advocates differential benevolence, and respect for ruler and father. If we look at history, we can see that Mencius contributed greatly to Confucianism. During the reign of King Wu of the Han dynasty, a decision was taken to "renounce all schools of thought and revere Confucianism as the sole orthodoxy," making Confucianism the only officially endorsed philosophy of the state.

Looking into Chinese history, we see that the Spring and Autumn and Warring States periods really provided the opportunity for debates between contending doctrines,

反對不正確的行為，駁斥荒謬的言論，從而繼承禹、周公、孔子三位聖人的事業。我哪裏是喜歡辯論呀！我是不得不這樣做呀！能夠用言論來反對楊墨的，也就是聖人的門徒了。」

【時析】

　　孟子有很強的「道統感」。他的歷史觀，認為歷史一治一亂，亂久必有聖人出來治世，禹和周公就是這樣的聖人。孟子正當亂世，他認為原因在於歪理邪說太多，而這些歪理邪說主要是楊朱和墨翟的學說。他認為自己之辟楊、墨，功績跟大禹治水、周公兼夷狄、孔子編《春秋》差不多，因為辟了楊、墨，弘揚了儒家，就能使天下走上正道。孟子誇大了當時楊、墨的影響，將世亂歸於「邪說」，是有偏頗的。當時世亂的主要原因，是周天子大權旁落，諸侯蜂起，爭權奪利，互相兼併，暴力相向。當時天下分裂，民不聊生，各派思想家提出了各自的「救世學說」，分裂的現實也讓各種學說能夠不受審查地自由出現，可以說，當時華夏地區形成了各派思想家能夠出售自己學說的「思想市場」，他們互相競爭，彼此辯論，形成了中國歷史上少有的思想自由的高峰。當時楊朱和墨子是兩大學派。楊朱的主張類似於個人主義，主張「為我」，維護個人存在和

simply because of the inability of the vassal states to enforce any censorship on dissenting ideas. What is more, in order to strengthen the political power of the states, many of the rulers were eager to listen to governance ideas offered by different scholars. This became the major motivation for the scholars to improve their arguments in their attempts to win the debate against other scholars and impress the rulers. We see a culture of rational debates and free exchange of ideas then when we read the dialogues of *Mozi*, *Zhuangzi* and *Mencius*.

The culture of debate did not just facilitate the development of logic and rhetoric, it also nurtured a democratic attitude in people, encouraging them to resolve conflicts through rational rather than forceful means. Such a vibrant intellectual scene, however, was short-lived. When Qin unified China, China entered a new chapter in its history in which a centralized government has become the norm of governance.

After that, the scholars had only one client — the emperor, who was always the final judge of what was to be endorsed. Gradually, the demand for new ideas shrank, the culture of debate declined (except the internal debates in the court), and finally the freedom of thought and publication was no longer cherished.

權益，但對責任強調不夠，因此不利於社會凝聚力，所以孟子認為這是「無君」。墨子講兼愛非攻，是一位集體主義者。兼愛無差等，愛他人之父跟愛自己之父一樣，所以孟子說他是「無父」。在當時激烈的「思想市場」競爭中，孟子為了讓儒家爭一席之地，贏得諸侯的支持，就必須駁斥楊墨兩派，挺立儒家的有差等之仁，有君有父的倫理秩序與政治立場。從後來的歷史發展來看，孟子對於儒家是很有功勞的。在漢武帝時，「罷黜百家，獨尊儒術」，儒家取得了類似於國教的官方意識形態的地位。

說到辯論，縱觀中國歷史，只有在春秋戰國時期，各思想學派才真正有辯論的機會。當時國家眾多，各國政府不可能用審查制來限制思想自由（因為這國不能發表可以去那國），各家的救世主張都可能被某些國家實行，有潛在的「主顧」。學者之間的辯論，除了引經據典，還要根據邏輯、理性、經驗來戰勝對方，因此，當時有一股民主、理性的自由辯論的風氣，在《墨子》、《莊子》、《孟子》等書中都能看到這種辯論的景象。辯論帶來了邏輯學、修辭學的發展，還有助於養成一種民主的風氣（因為辯論不能用拳頭說話，要擺事實、講道理，用理性和經驗說話）。

Renowned Indian economist Amartya Sen in his book titled *The Argumentative Indian*, claims that India's long argumentative tradition since ancient times is important for the acceptance of the parliamentary system and democracy in the country. The reason for this is that the art of debating requires one to convince others with facts and rationale. The will to convince and to be convinced implies a democratic attitude that prefers dialogue over force as the way to resolve differences.

For most of the time in its history, India was divided into many states, which is conducive to perpetuating an argumentative culture. As with India, Europe also was made up of many small states, a situation which is conducive to contention between different schools of ideas.

The United Kingdom, which is one of the oldest democratic countries, has long had its laws for freedom of publication and a long tradition of public debate in parliament. Its freedom of thought and its democratic system have developed almost at the same pace. Since the grand unification under the Qin and Han dynasties, China has developed a tradition different from those of India and Europe — a fact that we have to take into account when discussing the related issues.

不過，隨着秦朝統一中國，中國歷史進入以「大一統」為主流的階段，天下才智之士的智慧只有一個買家——皇帝——因此，思想市場萎縮、消失，辯論也就逐漸消亡（除了朝廷的內部辯論），真正的思想自由、出版自由就沒有了。最終的拍板權都到了皇帝那裏，在許多重要的事情上辯論根本派不上用場。印度裔經濟學家薩馬亞森寫過一本書《慣於爭鳴的印度人》，認為印度自古以來就有辯論的傳統，因此接受議會制和民主制也就容易。這是有一定道理的。因為辯論就是要以事實和理性說服對方，而不是憑武力和權力，這就是一種民主的作風。印度歷史上以「分裂」的時間為長，小國林立，這也有助於其辯論傳統的延續。歐洲跟印度歷史上類似，也是小國林立，這有助於其百家爭鳴，百花齊放。最早實行民主制度國家之一的英國同時擁有出版自由的法律，以及議會制的辯論傳統，其思想自由與民主制度的發展幾乎是同步的。中國自秦漢大一統以後的發展形成了與印度、歐洲的不同傳統，我們討論問題時也不能不加以注意。

四

　　孟子曰：「盡信書，則不如無書。

Four

Translation:

Mencius said, "If one believes everything in the *Book of Documents*, it would be better for him not to have it.

In the chapter "Wu Cheng" I accept only two or three passages as true. The benevolent man has no match in the world. How, then, could it be the case that, when the most benevolent person [King Wu of Zhou] sent an expedition against the most cruel person [King Zhou of Shang], there was so much outflowing of blood that the battle sticks were seen floating on it?" (Chapter 14.3)

Contemporary interpretation:

The "book" mentioned in this passage refers in particular to the *Book of Documents*. Nowadays, people often use this quotation out of context and mistake it as referring to any book. During Mencius's time, the *Book of Documents* was one of the most widely acclaimed classics and seen by most people as representing the unquestionable truth. In doubting the reliability of it, Mencius demonstrated a discreet and reasonable attitude towards the classics. Such an attitude differs significantly from some of the religious traditions, for example Christianity, which sees its classics, such as the Bible,

吾於《武成》，取二三策而已矣。仁人無敵於天下。以至仁伐至不仁，而何其血之流杵也？」（卷十四　盡心章句下·三）

【今譯】

孟子說：「如果完全相信《尚書》的記載，那還不如沒有《尚書》。我對於《武成》，只認可兩三頁。仁人天下無敵，憑着周武王這樣最仁義的人去討伐商紂王這樣最不仁義的人，怎麼會流了那麼多血，以至於木杵都漂了起來呢？」

【時析】

這裏的書特指《尚書》。今天人們引用此句時斷章取義，把書泛化了，指一切的書，其實是不準確的。《尚書》在孟子的時候，相當於經書，人們對於經書是抱着信仰的態度的。因此，孟子對《尚書》提出質疑，堅持一種審慎的態度，就體現出一種理性地對待經典的態度。這和別的宗教傳統對待經書經常抱持「聖經無誤論」（如基督教認為《聖經》無任何錯誤）的態度是不同的。這也顯示出，孟子有一種經驗主義和理性主義的態度，並不迷信經書，並且反對本本主義。雖然孟子對經書有這種懷疑主義和理性主義的態度，

as totally free from errors. Mencius refused to adopt such an uncritical attitude towards the Chinese classics and was opposed to book worship. Instead, he took it as obligatory to examine the truth of any claims through experience and logic.

While appreciating Mencius's skepticism and rationalism towards orthodox beliefs, we may want to challenge the reasons for his doubt in the particular case of the Battle of Mu Ye — the war waged against Shang by King Wu of Zhou. Mencius, based on his moralist preconception, suggested that the *Book of Documents* might not be as accurate as it should be. Resting on the idealized image of King Wu as the most benevolent man, Mencius dismissed right away the possibility of heavy casualties being caused by a war under his leadership. It is clear that Mencius's claims about this period in history are perhaps even naïve.

The Battle of Mu Ye was a major war recorded in ancient Chinese history, and over half a million troops were involved in it. It is simply inconceivable for a war of such scale to be able to end without shedding blood, though some of King Zhou's troops did surrender. Hence, it could not be a historical truth that only with benevolence as imaged by Mencius the enemy would yield to King Wu.

但具體說來，他在這裏懷疑《尚書》的理由卻是可以討論的。孟子是從其道德哲學的「先入之見」來懷疑《尚書》關於武王伐紂的戰爭（牧野之戰）記載的。孟子認為，周武王是道德聖人，而「仁者無敵」，因此，他打仗時不可能殺那麼多人，以至血流漂杵。這無疑是把聖人理想化，也把歷史天真化。武王伐紂，是雙方出動幾十萬人的大戰，雖然當時有歸附的派別，但仍然打過仗，不流血是不可能的。光靠孟子所想象的「仁心」就讓敵人投降停戰，恐怕並非歷史的事實。

五

孟子曰：「說大人，則藐之，勿視其巍巍然。堂高數仞，榱題數尺，我得志弗為也。食前方丈，侍妾數百人，我得志弗為也。般樂飲酒，驅騁田獵，後車千乘，我得志弗為也。在彼者，皆我所不為也；在我者，皆古之制也，吾何畏彼哉？」（卷十四　盡心章句下‧三十四）

【今譯】

孟子說：「游說諸侯，就得輕視他們，別把

Five

Translation:

Mencius said, "When one talks to vassal state rulers, one has to belittle them and disregard their imperious manners. The base of their hall is several *ren* high, the eaves are several *chi* wide. If I were to become successful one day, I would not indulge in these things. There is a full one-*zhang* table of food laid before them, and hundreds of female attendants to serve them. If I were to become successful one day, I would not indulge in these things. They take pleasure in drinking and are thrilled at riding horses and hunting with a thousand chariots trailing behind. If I were to become successful one day, I would not indulge in these things. All the things they do I would not do; I would rather act according to the ancient system of the sages. Why should I be intimidated by them?" (Chapter 14.34)

Contemporary interpretation:

Mencius saw vassal state rulers and people in power or with professed famous lineage for what they were. He saw nothing in their inherited superiority that was worthy of his awe. If their glamor brought about by power was stripped away, these men would be no different from an average person. On the face of it, their inherited riches and prosperity might look intimidating and enviable, yet on taking a closer look, we will

他們高高在上的樣子放在眼裏。宮殿的台基兩三丈高，屋檐幾尺寬，我如果得志了，是不會這麼幹的。吃飯時菜肴擺滿一丈見方的桌子，侍奉的女子有幾百人，我如果得志了，是不會這麼幹的。飲酒享樂，趕着馬車打獵，後面跟着的車有上千輛，我如果得志了，是不會這麼幹的。他們所幹的，都是我不會幹的；我所想幹的，都是古代聖王的制度，我怎麼會怕他們呢？」

【時析】

　　孟子算是把諸侯、權勢、權力及其擺譜看透了，那不過是繼承下來的虛榮和傲慢。把權勢帶來的光環剝掉之後，那些所謂的「大人」不過是常人而已。諸侯享受着投胎繼承下來的榮華富貴，表面上可以震懾別人，令人豔羨，實際上這些東西都是不勞而獲，無功受祿，不過是寄生蟲罷了。他們魚肉百姓，高人一等，樹立起社會的等級制度，建立起意識形態，認為人生的目的就是一級一級往上爬，直到達到諸侯那樣的生活。孟子對權力的解構、批判和蔑視還是很有力的，這跟他的民本主義有關。民為貴，社稷次之，君為輕。如果君不能為民服務，改善人民生活，就沒有存在的價值和根據，人民可以革掉他們的命，換一任新的。要問儒家思想中有沒有左派，有沒有革命派，那是有的，孟子肯定可以算一個。

find that they were undeserving of their privileges and were parasites seeking their own happiness at the expense of the common people. These people set up the class system and propagated an ideology that justified the goal of climbing up the social ladder to live like vassal state rulers.

Mencius's disdain for the hollowness of power is grounded in his people-centric political philosophy: the people are the most important; the gods of the earth and grain come next; the ruler is the last of all. If it happened that the ruler was no longer able to serve the best interests of the people and improve their livelihood, Mencius took it as justified for the people to revolt against him and have a new leader.

Mencius deserves to be called the leftist or revolutionary in the Confucian tradition.

孟子今譯時析
Mencius — A Modern Translation and Contemporary Interpretation

編撰 Authors
呂子德 Troy Lui　　　周偉馳 Zhou Weichi　　　鄭偉鳴 Terry Cheng
英文翻譯 English Translation　　　伍美蓮 Ng Mei-lin

中文責任編輯 Chinese Editor　　　黃為國 Wong Wai-kwok
英文責任編輯 English Editor　　　鄭偉鳴 Terry Cheng

中文校對 Chinese Proofreading　　　苗淑敏 Miao Shumin
英文審校 English Copyediting　　　Carol Dyer

裝幀設計 Graphic Designer　　　方子聰 Paul Fong

策劃 Planning	保華生活教育集團文化委員會 Culture Committee, B & P Group
顧問 Advisor	葉國華教授，保華生活教育集團主席 Prof. Paul Yip, Chairman, B & P Group
督印人 Supervisor	陳保琼博士，保華生活教育集團行政總裁 Dr Betty Chan, Chief Executive Officer, B & P Group
出版 Publishing	耀中出版社 Yew Chung Publishing House
地址 Address	香港九龍新蒲崗大有街一號勤達中心１６樓 16/F, Midas Plaza, No.1 Tai Yau Street, San Po Kong, Kowloon, Hong Kong
電話 Tel	852-39239711
傳真 Fax	852-26351607
網址 Website	www.llce.com.hk
電郵 Email	contact@llce.com.hk
初版 First Edition	2020.10
承印 Printing	香港志忠彩印有限公司 HK Zhizhong Colour Printing Co., Limited
書號 ISBN	978-988-78352-6-4